Reasonable Faith for a Post-Secular Age

Reasonable Faith for a Post-Secular Age

Open Christian Spirituality and Ethics

Essays on Davidson, Hauerwas, Levinas, Rawls, Rivera, Rorty, Spivak, Stout, Taylor, Williams, and others

WILLIAM GREENWAY

CASCADE *Books* · Eugene, Oregon

REASONABLE FAITH FOR A POST-SECULAR AGE
Open Christian Spirituality and Ethics: Essays on Davidson, Hauerwas, Levinas, Rawls, Rivera, Rorty, Spivak, Stout, Taylor, Williams, and others

Cascade Books
An Imprint of Wipf and Stock Publishers
199 W. 8th Ave., Suite 3
Eugene, OR 97401

www.wipfandstock.com

PAPERBACK ISBN: 978-1-7252-7044-2
HARDCOVER ISBN: 978-1-7252-7045-9
EBOOK ISBN: 978-1-7252-7046-6

Cataloguing-in-Publication data:

Names: Greenway, William, 1963–author.

Title: Reasonable faith for a post-secular age : open Christian spirituality and ethics: essays on Davidson, Hauerwas, Levinas, Rawls, Rivera, Rorty, Spivak, Stout, Taylor, Williams, and others / William Greenway.

Description: Eugene, OR: Cascade Books, 2020 | Includes bibliographical references and index.

Identifiers: ISBN 978-1-7252-7044-2 (paperback) | ISBN 978-1-7252-7045-9 (hardcover) | ISBN 978-1-7252-7046-6 (ebook)

Subjects: LCSH: Faith and reason—Christianity. | Christian ethics. | Post-Secularism.

Classification: BT50 .G65 2020 (paperback) |BT50 (ebook)

12/14/20

For Ethel Mae Goddard Rigby,
and in loving memory of Charles Sheldon Rigby

Contents

Permissions

Acknowledgments

These essays were collected and revised over the course of a sabbatical year. I would like to thank the board of trustees of Austin Presbyterian Theological Seminary for their resolute support of sabbaticals—a singular time for research, reflection, and creative productivity.

I would also like to thank the board, all my colleagues (faculty, staff, administrators), and the students at Austin Seminary for their support and encouragement for my teaching, research, and writing, and for providing so stimulating a learning and research environment. I also want to offer my sincere thanks to Rodney Clapp, an excellent editor and advisor who has also become a friend and conversation partner. Finally, thanks to Jesselyn Clapp for her careful copyediting, and to Savanah N. Landerholm for a beautiful cover.

Many of these chapters originally appeared in scholarly journals, and I owe thanks to the anonymous readers and editors whose careful work helped to refine my thinking and writing. Namely, chapter 1, "Charles Taylor on Affirmation, Mutilation, and Theism: A Retrospective Reading of *Sources of the Self,*" was originally published in *Journal of Religion* (2000). Chapter 2, "Modern Metaphysics, Dangerous Truth, Post-Moral Ethics: The Revealing Vision of Bernard Williams," was originally published in *Philosophy Today* (2007). Chapter 3, "Chalcedonian Reason and the Demon of Closure," was originally published in *Scottish Journal of Theology* (2004). Chapter 4, "Cosmodicy: On Evil and the Problem with Theodicy," was originally published in *Insights: the Faculty Journal of Austin Seminary* (2006).

I wrote Chapter 5, "The Reasonableness of Affirming Free Will: On Kane, Taylor, Dennett, and Honderich" in 2007, but plans to pursue publication were disrupted when I received a cancer diagnosis (all good now); the essay is lightly revised and published here for the first time. Chapter 6, "On Ted Honderich's *Actual Consciousness*," was originally published as a book review in *Scottish Journal of Theology* (2017).

Chapter 7, "Christian Ethics in a Postmodern World? Hauerwas, Stout, and Christian Moral Bricolage" originally published in *Koinonia* (1994), won a national graduate student essay contest. The prize was the paper becoming the centerpiece essay of an issue of *Koinonia*, with a lecture version of the essay being made the keynote address of a conference at Princeton Theological Seminary, with the proceedings published in *Koinonia*. The conference and that issue of *Koinonia* featured responses by fellow doctoral candidates from across the country—Lois Malcolm (Theology, University of Chicago), J. Francis Watson, (Practical Theology, Drew University), Morag Logan (Old Testament, Princeton Theological Seminary), Willette A. Burgie-Gipson (Religion and Society, Princeton Theological Seminary), and Gavin Ferriby (History, Drew University). I also owe thanks to Professor Stanley Hauerwas (Ethics, Duke University) for contributing a response to the journal. Chapter 8, "Irreducible Tensions: Private Convictions in Public Space," published in the same issue of *Koinonia*, was my response to these respondents.

In my *Koinonia* essays I responded to Jeffrey Stout's first two books, *The Flight from Authority* (1987) and *Ethics After Babel* (1988). Chapter 9, "Jeffrey Stout, Original Sin, and the Significance of Christian Faith," is an essay I wrote in response to Stout's next two books, *Democracy and Tradition* (2004) and *Blessed are the Organized* (2012), and was originally published in *Always Being Reformed: Challenge and Prospects for Reformed Theology*, edited by David Jensen (2016).

The final two chapters, chapter 10, "On Paul's Philosophical Spirituality," and chapter 11, "A Time for Prophets? Non-Sectarian Affirmation of Particularities and Universal Morality," were originally written as sermons and preached at the Robert M. Shelton Chapel at Austin Presbyterian Theological Seminary in October 2015 and 2016, respectively; they have been significantly revised for this publication (2019).

This book is dedicated to Ethel Mae Goddard Rigby and in loving memory of Charles Sheldon Rigby. Both Chuck and Ethel, my parents-in-law, dedicated their lives to what is loving, good, and just—Ethel to scores of elementary school children, their parents, and elementary school teachers; Chuck to the lonely, needy, homeless and the well-to-do throughout New York City and, with his sonorous, comforting baritone, to congregations throughout New York and Florida.

Introduction

Toward an Age of Reasonable Faith

BEYOND SECTARIANISM: UNVEILING THE REALITY OF A GLOBAL SPIRITUAL CONSENSUS

Across the world we face extreme and growing economic inequalities, the capture of nations and transnational institutions by economic elites, a rise in religious fundamentalisms and secular extremisms, conflict-driven mass migrations, the spread of nuclear and chemical weapons, epoch-level species and habitat loss, over-population of eco-systems, and climate change as a multiplier on virtually all fronts. Like challenges have been familiar for millennia at regional levels, where they have consistently destroyed civilizations. For the first time in history, these challenges are rising on a global scale.

Good people from diverse secular and religious institutions fight these challenges to creaturely flourishing in a multitude of concrete ways. They are Hindu, Jewish, Sikh, Christian, Navajo, humanist, and Muslim. They work in governments, religious organizations, non-governmental organizations (NGOs), and advocacy groups. The vast majority share a common understanding of what is reasonable and respond to essentially the same love. But the reality of this common spiritual ground is largely invisible. The transition to a global village sharing a common language has been achieved in the natural and social sciences. Astronomers, chemists, physicists, psychiatrists, and economists from every faith and nation share a substantially common understanding of reality *qua* material.[1] But not even within the

---

1. "Material" here is a technical philosophical term and, since it brings an entire metaphysical scheme into play, is impossible to define in brief. Suffice to say by "material" I mean to refer a) to the world insofar as it is seen and described by the modern

1

West, let alone globally, do we generally recognize a shared understanding of reality *qua* spiritual.[2]

I believe, however, that in fact a common understanding of a spiritual dimension of reality is shared by multitudes across faith traditions and cultures. I argue that this spiritual dimension of reality can be just as evidently and reasonably affirmed as the understanding of a material dimension of reality common to astronomers, chemists, physicists, psychiatrists, and economists. And I argue that naming this shared spiritual reality is vital for the flourishing of life on earth, because overt affirmation of substantial cross-cultural and cross-faith spiritual consensus, including ethical consensus, would enhance spiritual reality's redemptive influence in our personal and political lives.[3]

In the wake of postmodern deconstruction of modern Western pretensions to objective and universal reason, it has become commonsense understanding that in matters of faith and ethics we live in a relativistic world. Faith and ethics are now commonly thought to be products of contingent, socio-cultural conditioning while, in stark contrast, the natural sciences are commonly thought to be objectively grounded in extra-linguistic reality. This ethos of ethical relativism feeds a sectarian spirit among culturally, ethnically, and religiously diverse, good people who share considerable common spiritual ground—and that includes considerable ethical common ground.

There is one group especially influential among Western cultural and intellectual elites who think, even as they typically accept postmodern deconstruction of modern pretensions to objective rationality, that vis-à-vis faith and ethics they do inhabit neutral, public ground. I refer to those who identify as secular—where "secular" designates those who claim they are in

---

natural and social sciences; and b) to that which is part of the causal flux in the modern Western determinate/indeterminate sense.

2. "Spiritual" in this context is as technical a philosophical term as "material," and is perhaps more difficult to define, because it not only brings a distinctive metaphysical scheme into play, but also because of the modern Western eliding of dimensions of reality best represented by vocabularies of the spiritual. In a detailed argument in *A Reasonable Belief*, I delineate two spheres of the spiritual (this in addition to the sphere of nature, which is the sphere of the material). The first of the two spiritual spheres is the existential sphere of poetic I's. The second, which is "spiritual" in the traditional moral and religious sense, is the spiritual sphere of agape, which includes faiths and ethics. These terms, in particular the reality, contour, and significance of the existential sphere of poetic I's and of the spiritual sphere of agape, are at the heart of the explorations in this book.

3. As this book goes to press, we are entering the first stages of a global pandemic that is already making, and I suspect will increasingly make, evident the vital need for "overt affirmation of substantial cross-cultural and cross-faith spiritual consensus, including ethical consensus."

no way religious. Before delineating their confusion, let me specify that as a Christian I share many secular ideals, just as I share many Buddhist, Jewish, and Muslim ideals, and even as I do not wholly accept or find spiritually sufficient the various metaphysics and ethics found among the wide array of modern Western secular thinkers—Nietzsche, Marx, Mao, Jean Paul Sartre, Hannah Arendt, Iris Murdoch, Jürgen Habermas, Arne Naess, Val Plumwood, John Rawls, Richard Rorty, Judith Butler, Gayatri Chakravorty Spivak, to name a few. Philosophical and practical problems arise when secular thinkers do not realize their positions are not objective and neutral but depend upon particular metaphysical commitments and rationalities that privilege certain ideas and realities.

In the ordinary sense that I use the term, those who self-identify as secular claim their ideals are not dependent upon any appeal to religion. This is socially and historically true insofar as, say, secular humanists or deep ecologists do not appeal to any historic faith tradition. But it is not true insofar as "religion," understood philosophically, names one's understanding of the ultimate character of reality, one's metaphysic. In this philosophical sense, everyone has some religion, some metaphysic, and for anyone to deny they have any notion of the ultimate character of reality manifests confusion and, witting or not, a protective strategy, for they are cloaking and thereby shielding their own metaphysic from criticism.

At the heart of modern Western philosophy lay Rene Descartes's appeal to the natural light of reason (adapted by John Locke for the empiricist tradition), which was believed to allow us to discern objective, certain, universal truths, including ethical truths. Appeal to the natural light of reason allowed for the modern distinction between public, secular understanding, which supposedly utilizes only the natural light of reason, and private, religious understanding, which is inherently traditioned and subjective. Today, the idea of appealing to the natural light of reason in order to ground knowledge and a neutral public sphere of reflection and debate is thoroughly debunked. All human reflection is subjective and traditioned.

Moreover, philosophers engaged in "critical theory" have shown how modern Western claims to objective, certain, and universal truth masked the privileging and perpetuation of elite, European, male, colonial interests. This is well-established. The way the modern idea of objective reason functioned as a self-serving self-deception that facilitated the rationalizing and violent imposition of self-interested, oppressive agendas (e.g., anti-Semitic, classist, colonial, heterosexist, racist, sexist, speciest) has been manifest at least since Horkeimer and Adorno's 1930s classic, *The Dialectic of Enlightenment*.

Despite these developments, many contemporary intellectual and cultural elites who embrace postmodern critiques of modern reason remain blithely confident we live in a secular age and can distinguish between biased religious reasoning and objective, value-neutral secular reasoning. Of course, this supports secular elites' claim to epistemic and cultural preeminence.

For instance, of all people the late Richard Rorty, an analytic philosopher rightly celebrated for acute analyses that played a major role in deconstructing empiricist pretentions to objective knowledge, entitled a 1997 essay, "Religion as Conversation-Stopper"—as if his own understanding of contingency, irony, and solidarity, his own neo-liberal revised pragmatism, his own "final vocabulary" was not itself part of a particular, contingent tradition of understanding; that is, as if his own final vocabulary was not a competing religious/metaphysical perspective, and also as if "Religion as Conversation-Stopper" is not itself a conversation-stopper vis-à-vis Buddhists, Christians, Jains, Muslims, and Wiccans.[4]

Unfortunately, Rorty is typical of modern Western intellectuals who fully affirm deconstruction of modern pretensions to value-neutral rationality while continuing to understand themselves as secular. This forgets that "secular," insofar as it purports to designate a neutral, a-religious, public sphere of rationality, has been debunked. On the basis of this philosophically inconsistent self-identification, all variety of self-identified secular thinkers dismiss all religious reflection as irrational and backward and strive to exclude theologians and other religious intellectuals from public scholarly forums (talk about conversation stoppers!).[5]

When those who self-identify as secular pit themselves against peoples of all faiths, they exacerbate sectarian tensions and model the very intolerant attitudes they often and rightly condemn in others. To be sure, such

4. Rorty, "Religion as Conversation Stopper." Rorty slightly revises his position in "Cultural Politics and the Question of the Existence of God."

5. The preeminent philosopher of religion Jeffrey Stout, an atheist and humanist whose work I engage in depth in three chapters of this book, defends a different, and in my view far superior definition of "secular." For Stout, "secular" merely designates an epoch when no one gets to presume the sole truth of their system of beliefs. So "secular" simply means that whether one is humanist, Christian, Marxist, or Hindu, one must be prepared to acknowledge the legitimate existence of other systems of belief. Because of his understanding, Stout engages in respectful disagreement with Christians and others. Again, this is a good definition of secular, but Stout has faced strong resistance to this definition even within the American Academy of Religion, and the problematic idea that "secular" designates "neutral"/"non-religious" (my operative definition here) remains predominant. On the other hand, even Stout still claims, in contrast to people of faith, to be doing "ethics without metaphysics," at which point the depth of his affirmation of his alternative definition of secular comes into question.

intolerance is also on display within every religious tradition. Wherever sectarian intolerance appears it should be decisively critiqued. Recognition on all sides of significant common spiritual and ethical ground could help to ameliorate tendencies toward sectarian intolerance.

In sum, secular, in the sense of non-religious, objective, and public, is endemic to a modern understanding of reason that is discredited. It disguises its own dominant interests and agendas behind purportedly disinterested claims to objectivity and neutrality, and in its haughty dismissal of all other metaphysics it engages in and fosters sectarianism. It also cuts us off from considerable subtle understanding within faith traditions that anyone interested in cultivating a good and spiritually rich global community would be wise to contemplate.

In practical terms, given billions of committed adherents to diverse faith traditions across the world, secular refusal to engage faith communities with respect for our self-understandings is politically disastrous. For instance, the United Nations' mission is compromised insofar as it cannot acknowledge diverse faith traditions and give reasons recognizable on grounds internal to each tradition for support of UN efforts. Unfortunately, if anthropologists from the Gemini star cluster were to gauge the character of life on earth based solely on a tour of United Nations headquarters, they would have little idea earth even had faith traditions. This stunning disconnect between the UN's secular vision and the real world is politically disastrous.

In a society in which intellectual and cultural elites disproportionately identify as secular, the modern idea that we live in a secular age is culturally predominant. But by this point there should be no question we live in a post-secular age, for the category of the secular is conceptually dependent upon affirmation of debunked modern Western philosophical pretensions. The philosophical distinction between secular metaphysics and the metaphysics of the world's great faith traditions has collapsed. New systems of understanding became going concerns in the modern period (e.g., Marxism, Humanism, Deep Ecology, Jungianism, Mindfulness), but all such streams of understanding represent traditioned, subjective spiritualities and presume some metaphysic just as much as do Hinduism, Buddhism, Judaism, Christianity, and Islam.

Unfortunately, many adherents among all these traditions manifest sectarian tendencies. Aside from the obvious threat of sectarian violence, this splintered state of affairs poses a subtle threat to a good and equitable global future. As Oxford geographer David Harvey presciently cautioned in the late 1980s in *The Condition of Postmodernity: An Enquiry into the Origins of Cultural Change*, vis-à-vis central philosophical questions concerning metaphysics, religion, ethics, and identity we live with uncertain, open, fragmented understanding. With regard to economic realities that exert tremendous influence over all our lives, by contrast, we are increasingly in the grip of tightly integrated globalized systems not indexed to ideals of justice and benevolence. At worst, these economic systems function in alignment with brutal, Darwinian, "survival of the fittest" dynamics. The potential for ethical shaping of this singular global reality is enfeebled by religious and socio-cultural fragmentation.[6] So the real-world stakes of sectarian fragmentation—including the arrogant dismissal of all peoples of faith by secular elites, and also including the arrogant dismissal of all peoples of different faiths by adherents of any one faith—the real stakes of sectarian fragmentation are directly related to global flourishing and suffering, benevolence and brutality, justice and exploitation.

Attending to theoretical dimensions of current global understanding is vital, then, because of a real danger the wonderful and locally effective efforts of those who understand themselves to inhabit one of various, mutually incompatible systems of understanding (e.g., humanist, Marxist, Hindu, Muslim, Maoist, Christian) will ultimately remain piecemeal, rear-guard actions destined to be overwhelmed by the singular logic of the global economic system. It is vital we foster recognition of the extant but largely unrecognized common core of global spiritual understanding, for it is sufficient to fund significant concerted global ethical judgment and political action.

To be clear, this common spiritual understanding must not be tyrannical or reductionistic. It must allow Jews to be Jews, Christians to be Christians, humanists to be humanists, Hindus to be Hindus, and Marxists to be Marxists. It must also meet general public standards of rationality and in no way compromise modern science.

The ambition of identifying a common core of spirituality and ethics across faith traditions and cultures that meets all these criteria may appear wildly optimistic, but I am not talking about creating anything new, I am talking about clarifying and so making manifest and effective an unrecognized but extant reality. Moreover, when it comes to current mainstream conceptual frameworks, the good news is that we are in the middle of a conceptual revolution, so there should be openness to the unveiling of the reality of substantial, cross-cultural, cross-faith, global ethical and spiritual consensus.

Certainly, there will be significant areas of enduring dispute. That has always been the case even within every major scientific and faith tradition. It has not prevented adherents within traditions from recognizing a core set of beliefs that unite them despite acute differences. It may be the case,

6. Harvey, *Condition of Postmodernity*, 113–18.

unfortunately, that the majority in every faith tradition (including secular traditions) are sectarian, understanding themselves in wholesale opposition to other faith traditions. But this harmful sectarianism need not endure. For, while every major faith tradition has been understood within zero-sum, there-can-only-be-one parameters, and while every major faith tradition has been misappropriated to justify injustice, violence, and oppression—major examples vis-à-vis Hinduism, Christianity, Islam, Maoism, and Marxism, among others, are familiar—calls to love, justice, hospitality, and welcome for the stranger are pivotal teachings in every major faith.

In the modern era there are emergent traditions that are overtly opposed to these classic spiritual ideals, for instance, social Darwinism or lifeboat ethics.[7] Few people openly affirm social Darwinism or lifeboat ethics, and social Darwinism and lifeboat ethics are incompatible with every historic faith tradition. However, anthropologists from the Gemini star cluster tracking global political and economic developments on earth would be justified in concluding that developments on earth are best understood and predicted if one presumes global commitment is precisely to social Darwinism and lifeboat ethics. The devastating, de facto global social Darwinism of our day urgently calls for cross-cultural and cross-faith spiritual awakening to an age of reasonable faith. My hope lies in an educated judgment that an overwhelming majority of the faithful across traditions share essential affirmations—regarding universal hospitality, justice, and love—that run contrary to a sectarian, selfish spirit.

In contrast to the closely argued chapters to come, I have here been painting with a very broad brush in an attempt to relate some major concerns and ambitions that motivate and direct my work as a Christian scholar. Continuing to paint with a broad brush, let me now set the book in its intellectual context along a complementary tack.

EYES TO SEE, WORDS TO SAY, AGAPE

By the middle of the twentieth century the horrors of World War I, the Holocaust, nuclear weapons, and the heating up of the Cold War had chastened late nineteenth-century optimism about human progress, but most Westerners still rightly considered themselves fortunate to live in the wake

7. I take "social Darwinism" to be a familiar category. "Lifeboat ethics," most prominently championed by celebrated social scientist Garrett Hardin (who is famous for his work on the "tragedy of the commons"), contends that since the human population far exceeds the carrying capacity of earth, the most advanced civilizations should not make the mistake of trying to save everyone and swamping the boat, but should prioritize the survival of communities that represent the most advanced forms of human civilization.

of the scientific revolution and the Enlightenment or, as the transition was often labeled, to live after an Age of Reason triumphed over an Age of Faith. In fact, the vast majority of Westerners remained moral realists and people of faith. Among many intellectual and cultural elites, however, the victory of reason over faith was increasingly interpreted in a wooden, totalizing fashion, and theology and people of faith were dismissed as irrational, even caricatured and scapegoated for a multitude of societal ills.

By the late twentieth century, predominant mainstream Western philosophical consensus (especially among so-called "analytic," mostly anglophone philosophers) affirmed metaphysical naturalism (the idea that, ultimately, everything was the product of mindless, material processes), mocked all versions of Cartesian dualism, idealism, and moral realism, and rejected (in the ordinary senses) free will and moral responsibility. Vis-à-vis the topic of faith, it was common to hear Western intellectuals speak confidently about humans moving out of adolescence by stepping beyond all religion. By the early twenty-first century, mainstream popular elites knowingly celebrated what they understood to be our secular age, and pop-intellectual books like Richard Dawkins's *The God Delusion* (2006), Daniel Dennett's *Breaking the Spell: Religion as a Natural Phenomenon* (2007), Christopher Hitchens's *God is not Great: How Religion Poisons Everything* (2007), and Sam Harris's *The End of Faith* (2004), populated bestseller lists.

In an avant-garde corner of the rarified world of professional philosophy, however, a small cadre of philosophers, many from France and Germany, were unraveling claims to objectivity and universality that anchored the Age of Reason, and were making distressingly clear modern rationality's inability to establish any foundations for ethics (even as their own work manifested clear ethical ambitions). This work, vaguely labeled "postmodern," was widely disparaged in the anglophone philosophical world in the 1970s and early 1980s. By the late 1980s, however, "postmodern" signaled an emerging consensus over the impossibility of delineating an objective, neutral public sphere wherein universally valid appeals to reason could be used to adjudicate ethical disputes and justify public policy.

In the immediate wake of these revolutionary conceptual developments in the 1980s, what would soon be described, often with astonishment and dismay, as a "theological turn" or "turn to religion" in philosophy, largely originating among Francophone philosophers, was gaining trans-Atlantic momentum.[8] By the second decade of the new millennium the spiritual poverty of modern Western rationality was widely recognized even by many of

8. See Janicaud, *Phenomenology and the Theological Turn*; de Vries, *Philosophy and the Turn to Religion*; the essays collected in de Vries, *Religion: Beyond a Concept*; and Benson and Wirzba, *Words of Life*.

its secular champions, who began writing books questing after spirituality, such as Simon Critchley's *The Faith of the Faithless: Experiments in Political Theology* (2012), Ronald Dworkin's *Religion Without God* (2013), and Sam Harris's *Waking Up: A Guide to Spirituality without Religion* (2014). Unfortunately, as these titles indicate—" . . . *of the Faithless*," " . . . *Without God*," " . . . *without Religion*"—renewed openness to spirituality was paired with enduring prejudice against classic faith traditions, so we see attempts to affirm modern Western secular identity while also laying claim to "*Faith*," "*Religion*," and "*Spirituality*."

As noted, secular rationality is problematic because it illicitly masks its particular interests behind discredited claims to neutrality and objectivity, and because it typically engages in sectarian rejection of all other faith traditions. As the theological turn and the pop-intellectual attempts of secular intellectuals to recover faith, religion, and spirituality suggest, another significant shortcoming of modern Western secular rationality is the degree to which it is spiritually impoverished. This is simultaneously the most poignant challenge for secular thinkers and the juncture where a positive way forward in communion with adherents of other faiths is most clearly manifest. Consistent with all I have been urging, I believe Critchley, Dennett, Dworkin, Harris, and Christians like me are not opponents living in conceptually siloed systems of understanding. I believe we actually share substantial spiritual and ethical common ground, and I am interested in finding a positive way forward.

Let me briefly illustrate potential for finding a positive way forward in conversation with Christian theologian Mayra Rivera's philosophical encounter with the renowned mother of post-colonial theory, Gayatri Chakravorty Spivak. In *The Touch of Transcendence: A Postcolonial Theology of God*, Rivera shows us how ethically passionate secular thinkers like Spivak find themselves compelled to turn toward traditional religious forms of thought to account for realities for which they lack language.[9] Spivak, Rivera notes, explicitly disavows any connection between her work and theology. Yet Rivera makes clear that when Spivak and other theorists want to move to the "affirmative mode of deconstruction,"[10] that is, when they move beyond strictly descriptive social, cultural, political and historical analyses and make ethical affirmations, they begin using religious language of "a call to the wholly other," "haunting," "ghosts," "prayer," "love," and the "sacred."[11]

---

9. Rivera, *Touch of Transcendence*.

10. Rivera, *Touch of Transcendence*, 111.

11. Rivera, *Touch of Transcendence*, 112–13, 120–23.

Spivak's language at these junctures, Rivera concludes, "tends to convey the very idea [of transcendence] that her work so forcefully rejects."[12]

Spivak's fundamental ethical affirmation, Rivera notes, is that "to be born human" is to be "born angled toward an other and others."[13] A representative paragraph on the "aporia of the ethical" in her essay, "The Moral Dilemma," makes painfully clear how Spivak is afflicted by the spiritual poverty of modern Western secular rationality. Spivak does not justify her ethical conviction but instead explains why it cannot be justified and calls this impossibility the "aporia of the ethical."[14] At the same time, she asserts a definitive ethical position, which turns out to be the motivating passion at the heart of her work.

At the start of the "The Moral Dilemma," Spivak simply asserts her convictions about ethical reality as "presuppositions" in a paragraph set apart from the balance of her essay, even though it becomes clear that her ethical presuppositions are the *raison d'etre* of her entire project:

> To begin with, some presuppositions.
> Radical alterity—the wholly other—must be thought and must be thought through imaging. *To be born human is to be born angled toward an other and others. To account for this, the human being presupposes the quite-other.* This is the bottom line of being-human as being-in-the-ethical-relation. By definition, we cannot—no self can—reach the quite other. Thus the ethical situation can only be figured in the ethical experience of the impossible. This is the founding gap in all act or talk, most especially in acts or talk that we understand to be closest to the ethical—the historical and the political. We will not leave the historical and political behind.[15]

"The Moral Dilemma" focuses upon Spivak's "reconciliation" of the two parts of her essay: "I. What I Learn in the Field: Other Women" and "II. What I Teach for a Living: Literary Criticism." Spivak says, with revealing incoherence, that "the reconciliation is fractured," and she ends the essay with a poignant gesture toward some vaguely sensed other-than-academic that might heal the fracture:

> A word in conclusion, a reminder of the fracture or incoherence in this essay in another way. What I describe in Part II is

12. Rivera, *Touch of Transcendence*, 113.

13. Rivera, *Touch of Transcendence*, 122.

14. Spivak, "A Moral Dilemma," 221.

15. Spivak, "A Moral Dilemma," 215 (emphasis mine). Note her stunning failure to name religion, more specifically the world's faith traditions, as closest to the ethical.

an obstinate attempt at a formal training of the imagination in the classroom. Filling it with substance would take us back to Part I. The obvious gap between the two cannot be filled by only academic labor, not to mention an academic lecture.[16]

Spivak's "academic," namely, her affirmation of the metaphysical bounds of modern Western secular rationality, is the unrecognized source of the fracture. Note the absence of any reference to the ethical in this set-apart, concluding paragraph. Spivak's "training of the imagination" is not merely "formal," to the contrary, it is straightaway moral, an attempt to use literature to awaken her students at Columbia University to concern for distant others, that is, to awaken them to spiritual reality. That spiritual reality, agape (I define agape presently), is the reality she herself is awakened to in her field work, the reality she is counting on when she portrays for readers and students the abuse and injustice she sees in the field, the reality that generates passionate affirmation of her postcolonial theory.

It is *revealing* that Spivak quite rightly neither anticipates nor reports indifference to her accounts of oppression and of abuse of women. However, because Spivak remains obedient to the "academic," to the metaphysics of modern Western secular rationality, she cannot name or affirm the violation of secular rationality she performs in her *de facto* invocation of spiritual reality, agape, in her writing and teaching. As a result, her efforts feel "obstinate," and she is left—just where we should encounter decisive and stirring ethical condemnation and exhortation—she is left gesturing vaguely to something beyond "only academic labor."

In reality, the reconciliation between Spivak's field work and her teaching is not fractured. The reconciliation is powerfully realized through agape, the essential reality to which Spivak is awakened in her field work, the reality that directly inspires her pedagogical theory and goals, the reality to which she has awakened so many students and readers. The "fracture" actually lies between Spivak's spiritual convictions and the spiritually impoverished bounds of the modern Western secular rationality by which she remains captivated.

For secular rationality the love that cannot speak its name, the love so thoroughly rejected that its reality is literally unthinkable even for secular theorists like Spivak, who live impassioned fidelity to it, is agape. So, when a modern theorist like Spivak is profoundly seized by and faithful to agape, she is dumbfounded. This is not only a personal loss, it impedes the real-world influence of agape. The spiritual poverty of modern Western secular rationality is not innocent, then, for insofar as it renders the reality of agape

16. Spivak, "A Moral Dilemma," 234.

literally unspeakable it subverts moral self-understanding and exhortation and becomes the unwitting accomplice of oppression.

Elsewhere, Rivera notes, Spivak affirms the ethical as "sacred," an "animating gift" of mysterious origin that, across cultures and history, has been assigned many names. Spivak suggests we assign this reality the name "planet" and think of our planet as the "sacred" origin of this "animating gift."[17] In the light of this way of understanding ourselves in the world, Rivera continues, Spivak urges that we can see ourselves as "planetary subjects rather than global agents, planetary *creatures* rather than global entities."[18]

Spivak is not engaging in ordinary secular modern scientific or existential reflection. No one looking at the indifferent geological processes that result in nutritious soil and fresh water but also deadly earthquakes, tsunamis, and hurricanes, or looking at the blind workings of nature that result in the evolution of marvelously complex organisms through the torturous processes that so haunted Darwin, would conclude the planet itself is "sacred" (at best "indifferent" might be reasonable). Humans clearly engage in both parasitic and symbiotic relationships. And we also, along with some other mammals, engage in reciprocal, kinship, and perhaps even group altruism (all in the biological senses). But none of the pertinent dynamics—all of which are understood in accord with a modern scientific notion of cause; that is, all of which are understood to be "blind," a function of the evolutionary mechanical or organic processes of nature and nurture, genes and memes—none of these dynamics can fund Spivak's conviction that we are "born angled toward an other and others."

Curiously, when Spivak does expand slightly (if vaguely) upon her understanding of the ethical in the body of "A Moral Dilemma," she shifts her appeal from the innate—"To be born human is to be born angled toward an other and others"—to the intentional, to human decision, to an "imaging that is the figuration of the ethical as the impossible," a "launching" that is "produced by imagination" in order to fill a gap that emerges when one "decides to speak of aporias":

> When one decides to speak of aporias, one is haunted by the ghost of the undecidable in every decision. One cannot be mindful of a haunting, even if it fills the mind. . . . In the aporia, to decide is the burden of responsibility. The typecase of the ethical sentiment is regret, not self-congratulation. In the aporia, *to decide* is the burden of responsibility.[19]

17. Rivera, *Touch of Transcendence*, 123.
18. Rivera, *Touch of Transcendence*, 123.
19. Spivak, "A Moral Dilemma," 221–22. She is on a stronger path when she suggests

Spivak's appeal to sheer decision anchors the ethical in each individual's choice. But this appeal to free decision is as ethically bankrupt as her appeal to nature, for free decision is as devoid of substantive moral content as the aporia, so appeal to raw decision reduces the ethical to the poetic (i.e., to fidelity to authentic, poetic self-determination). This is a bankrupt but familiar move in modern Western thought (see, *inter alia*, Nietzsche, Sartre, and Rorty). Attempts to ground the ethical in either nature or in free decision fail to capture the ethical dynamic clearly at play in the moments when we are most powerfully seized by moral conviction, that is, by agape—and this clearly includes the most decisive moments in Spivak's field work and classroom.

Though her secular metaphysics keep her from speaking with insight about the "impossible" reality by which she is "haunted," and which "discloses itself in being crossed," Spivak is engaging in precisely the sort of reflections upon reality that give rise to all the world's major faith traditions, all of which through complex engagement in this vale of tears discern the reality of agape. The most influential faith traditions even develop a conviction that agape is somehow ultimate (as expressed in beliefs in heaven, nirvana, or the Pure Land). Evidently Spivak senses the religious inflection of her reflections for, Rivera says, Spivak stresses her views are "alien" to theology and should not be understood to be offering any "religious sanction."[20]

Rivera gently criticizes Spivak for her knee-jerk rejection of theology (an all-too-common occurrence in the Western academy). And Rivera makes clear that a number of other contemporary philosophers with strong concerns about justice (including Jacques Derrida) also, like Spivak, find themselves appealing to a reality which is in essential respects identical to what Jews and Christians have long identified as the Spirit of God or the Holy Ghost. Unfortunately, Rivera observes, these secular theorists not only resist any attempt to articulate common ground with the spiritualities of the world's historic faith traditions, they all "rely . . . upon an unstated metaphysics—a ground they tend to foreclose" (where "foreclose" means "render theoretically invisible").[21]

Spivak's rejection of theology unnecessarily alienates her from billions of adherents of diverse faith traditions who in the terms of their respective traditions could all agree we find ourselves in the presence of an "animating

---

that the ethical "discloses itself in being crossed," which happens *in the wake of* a decision, but she does not develop this line of thought; instead she immediately turns her focus not to the decision in the context of awakening to agape, but in the context of the *aporia* (221–22).

20. Rivera, *Touch of Transcendence*, 123–25.
21. Rivera, *Touch of Transcendence*, 125.

gift" from a "sacred" dimension of reality and are "inclined toward an other and others." Spivak's secular identity also cuts her off from classic conceptual resources, namely, the age-old, historically refined, philosophically subtle ways the world's faith traditions have come to discuss these realities. Three philosophers whom Spivak celebrates, Immanuel Levinas, Luce Irigaray, and eventually even Derrida (thanks to Levinas), all understood this. As Rivera suggests, "Theology may offer us a language to say what Spivak seems to desire, but cannot quite say."[22] Though she writes as a Christian, I expect Rivera includes under "theology" the belief systems of all the world's historic faith traditions.

It should be no surprise the world's historic faith traditions provide invaluable resources for interpreting the sacred, for they are all focused upon mediating the sacred, and their texts, rituals, and practices, while by no means perfect, have been sifted in accord with their wisdom and honed over millennia by diverse peoples living in varied contexts of power, joy, defeat, and horror—so they should be respected at least as much as other literary or philosophical classics. Moreover, given that indifference, competition, violence, and injustice are ineradicable aspects of the way our planet works, it is impossible not to be skeptical of Spivak's rhetorical suggestion that we abandon all traditional ways of naming the sacred in favor of "planet."

On the other hand, Spivak may note all the ways the world's faith traditions have been misappropriated to justify prejudice and oppression and conclude it impossible not to be skeptical of my suggestion that we affirm theological language of "Holy Spirit" and "God." To a degree, touché. But are we in a mortal fight? Must this be a zero-sum game? Can we not all acknowledge that other faith traditions make good points? Affirm and build upon our considerable spiritual and ethical common ground? Appreciate one another's diverse ways of understanding and then, where there is substantial disagreement, enter into constructive debate, all as we proceed

---

22. Rivera, *Touch of Transcendence*, 125. Rivera's later work, *Poetics of the Flesh* (2015), appears to reject appeals to transcendence in favor of a revised materialism: "As models based on postmodern physics replace Newtonian mechanics in science, theoretical discussions in the humanities and other fields are also transformed. Instead of passive matter characterized by inertia, materiality is described in terms of forces and energies in complex networks of relations. We are interested in *processes* of materialization—not just in *matter*" (Rivera, *Poetics of the Flesh*, 9). But this is to describe a distinction without a difference, for what we might call materialism 2.0 has no more space for freely self-creating poetic I's or agape (and ethical realities) than did materialism 1.0. At the same time, ethical passions (most all of which I would affirm) remain pervasive in *Poetics of the Flesh*, but they can no more be grounded in postmodern physics' "processes of materialization" than they can be grounded in modern physics' "matter." That is, Rivera falls into the same confusion she discerns in Spivak, conveying in her work an idea of transcendence she can no longer adequately theorize.

along our respective and overlapping paths, duly cautioned by the other's critiques? More than that, might we not recognize that we are attempting to understand and mediate essentially the same aspect of ultimate reality?

Before addressing these questions, let me digress momentarily and note that, in addition to the unravelling of the modern Western notion of objective reason, developments in science and philosophy over the last few decades have shaken confidence in the idea of the materiality of that primordial reality (everything is ultimately atoms, strings, etc.) that anchors the materialist (metaphysical naturalist) standard for secular modern rationality in the twentieth century. Thus, for instance, we find renowned secular philosopher Thomas Nagel writing *Mind and Cosmos: Why the Materialist Neo-Darwinian Conception of Nature is Almost Certainly False* (2012).[23] Not only does the so-called problem of consciousness/mind remain stubbornly untamed by modern materialist reflection, the idea of causality in modern understanding has opened up in surprising ways. Many self-identified secular philosophers and scientists find themselves compelled to play with what are by modern Western standards bizarre ideas of causation being rooted in the future (some sort of inherent drive towards complexity or life), or of causation involving the perception of a perceiver (i.e., involving mind—this is sparking renewed interest in idealism).[24]

The birth of modern philosophy and the seventeenth-century scientific revolution is arguably best understood in terms of a momentous transition from medieval neo-Aristotelian fourfold causation (material, efficient, formal, and final causation) to modern causation. Speaking roughly, for here we are on the far side of a Gestalt shift in understanding, for mainstream modern Western thought ultimately there is only "efficient" (roughly, billiard ball) causation—it is distinguished even in its more recent, organic, neo-Aristotelian forms by a sense of closure or necessary connection. However, insofar as philosophers of science and scientists engaging in philosophy are beginning to wonder what precisely the "material" in materialism signifies, and are once again beginning to appeal to something akin to "formal" and "final" causation (i.e., causation in a sense coming from an intrinsic drive to some specified complexity in some entities, or dependent upon mind—though the idea of causal closure and necessary connection remains in play), we are in the middle of a conceptual revolution precisely on par with the epochal metaphysical/scientific revolution of the seventeenth century. At the same time, the burning need to redress the spiritual poverty of

---

23. Nagel, *Mind and Cosmos*.
24. E.g., see Parts I and II of Ward, *The Christian Idea of God*.

modern Western rationality is increasingly palpable. In sum, we stand on a momentous and potentially fruitful philosophical precipice.

Spiritual Consensus and Plurality

Let me now return to the issue of common spiritual ground and plurality. John Rawls published his acclaimed *A Theory of Justice* in 1971.[25] Over the subsequent two decades, however, Rawls came to be largely convinced by postmodern philosophers' unraveling of the modern understanding of objective reason that permeates *A Theory of Justice*. In his 1993 work, *Political Liberalism*, Rawls suggests we reconstitute a public sphere among incommensurable but internally coherent systems of understanding by reference to a sphere of overlapping consensus.[26] In Rawls, this overlapping consensus is fortuitous. I think, however, that even in the wake of postmodernism our situation can be understood in a less contingent fashion, that our understanding of global consensus in the realms of ethics and faith and its relation to reality can be understood in a fashion analogous to our understanding of the relation among various scientific theories and reality.

Consider, for instance, the ways in which Aristotle, Newton, and Hawking, each of whom saw the world through the lenses of radically different and incommensurable systems of understanding, all lived in an overwhelmingly common conceptual world. All three, when they saw the stem break, expected the apple to fall. All three knew where the goalie should move to catch the bouncing ball, all three expected rocks to sink to the bottom of the pond, expected to walk or wheel across the street without fear of suddenly floating away into space, and so forth a millionfold. Their understanding in each of these instances vis-à-vis physics and metaphysics differed radically. But those theoretical differences were built upon massively common experience of a world that, once beings like humans doing science exist, constrains the parameters of the incommensurable theories advanced about it (all this is consistent with Donald Davidson's "radical interpretation" and "principle of charity").[27]

Just as there is a dimension of reality amenable to empirical description that, given the existence of beings like us, can be distinguished and interpreted under many names (e.g., Aristotle's natural motion, Newton's gravity, Einstein's curvature in spacetime), there is ample reason to conclude that there is a dimension of reality amenable to spiritual description that,

25. Rawls, *A Theory of Justice*.
26. Rawls, *Political Liberalism*.
27. Davidson, *Inquiries into Truth and Interpretation*.

given the existence of beings like us, can be distinguished and interpreted under many names. In this sense, as I argue in detail in *A Reasonable Belief: Why God and Faith Make Sense*, the essence of what we might designate with "God," "the divine," or "agape" is as evident and real as the essence of what we might designate with the word "gravity."[28]

My theology is profoundly influenced by twentieth-century Jewish philosopher, Emmanuel Levinas. Levinas is also a major inspiration for Critchley, Derrida, Rivera, and Spivak, among others. I have defended Levinas's subtle philosophy and my distinctive, Christian appropriation of it at length in *A Reasonable Belief*. Here I will simply specify that on my reading, Levinas, Spivak, Jesus, Paul, and the originators and saints of every historic faith tradition on earth, along with me and I expect most every reader of these words, without any real doubt passionately concur about how we are seized by concern and moved to respond when we see the innocent girl run through with the bayonet, the boy sobbing over sexual abuse, or impoverished workers laboring dawn to dusk in sweatshops. We also concur about how we are seized by concern and moved to celebrate when we see dogs bounding and playing happily in the field, the beaming little birthday boy, the elderly couple quietly holding hands as they stroll through the park.

While our reactions vary according to context, in both horrific and joyful contexts we are seized by the same reality, by the same passionate concern for others. This is a passion, a love, a concern that is not from us, not a product of any decision on our part (though we might harden our hearts), not a product of our desires. It is most fully and accurately described as a passion not from us that seizes us for others. This is what Christians call agape: a passionate concern not from us that seizes us for others.

Agape should not be confused or conflated with eros. There is nothing wrong with eros. In romantic relationships, for instance, eros and agape should simultaneously be in play. But eros is distinct from agape.

As Levinas argues, our impassioned response is only partly explicable in secular, materialist terms. As a result, as we saw above, when attempting to name this reality even secular thinkers find themselves compelled to use non-empirical language of "ghosts" and "the other." Levinas speaks of being taken hostage by the face of the other and argues this is the way God "comes to mind." Spivak is leery of God-talk, but still refers to the "quite-other" and speaks of the sacred, animating gift of the planet. Derrida too is leery of God-talk but, as Rivera makes clear, begins talking at precisely such conceptual junctures about ghosts (just where Christians would refer to the Holy Ghost).

28. Greenway, *A Reasonable Belief.*

I, adapting Levinas, call this reality agape, the reality of having been seized in and by love for others and, indirectly but just as powerfully, since this love seizes *us*, the reality of having been seized in and by love for ourselves. In a fashion similar to Levinas I understand this to be God insofar as God *is* love. God may be more than agape (e.g., may be personal/agentival, may be triune, as Christians like myself confess), but insofar as we find ourselves seized by love for others and by non-selfish love for ourselves—not selfish self-love, but love for one's self received as a gift—God is primordially manifest as agape. It is critical not to import additional content into "God" at this most basic level of reflection. Notably, at this basic level of reflection God *as* agape is congruent with affirmation of the divine within all the world's major monistic and monotheistic faith traditions.

Whether in contexts of joy or horror, God *qua* agape is directly manifest. This claim is in accord with continual and passionate spiritual witness throughout history and across cultures. More poetically but no less literally, God in this exact sense is as real as our horror over trafficked children and as real as our joy over the delight of the awe-struck child playing in soft-falling snow. In this precise sense, to repeat, "God" or "agape" is just as historically, cross-culturally and surely experienced and attested, is just as evidently real as "gravity."

I define faith in relation to God *qua* passion of agape. To be a person of faith is to live surrender to having been seized by love for every Face, including one's own. Insofar as God *is* agape, faith is living surrender to having been seized by God for every Face, including one's own. This is faith in accord with Jesus's teachings in the Gospels. For example, note what distinguishes the sheep from the goats in Jesus's parable of the Sheep and the Goats (Matt 25:31–46). According to Jesus, it is not any belief or doctrine that distinguishes the sheep from the goats. The distinction is clear and repeated in the parable: who fed, clothed, visited, and comforted those in desperate need? Atheist, Hindu, Wiccan, Muslim, Christian, Samaritan, Jew, or anthropologist from the Gemini star cluster? It does not matter. The only question is, did you feed, clothe, visit, comfort? Accordingly, the Good Samaritan (Luke 10:25–37) and other sheep are all faithful because they actively live surrender to having been seized by love for every Face, and so they aid, feed, clothe, visit, and comfort.

Take care to distinguish between "faith" and "belief" in relation to the transcending reality Christians and Jews, among others, call "agape." "Faith" names our surrender/openness to the agapic dimension of the ultimate character of reality that seizes us in revelatory moments of having been seized by agape and that people give diverse names like "God," "Light," "Other," and even "planet." "Beliefs" are diverse ways we name and integrate this primordial unveiling of divine reality into the diverse systems of understanding that are Hinduism, Jainism, Judaism, Christianity, Latter Day Saints, Marxism, and Humanism.

"Faith," then, is understood in two related senses. Primordially, "faith" designates raw, living surrender to having been seized by agape. But insofar as faith in this raw sense is *understood*, reflected and expanded upon and formed into diverse *systems of understanding*, primordial faith *qua* surrender to agape gives birth to the diverse systems of understanding that are the world's faith traditions. Primordial faith yields diverse faiths. Without reduction of religious plurality, we can say the world's faiths spring forth from the same essential faith. This gives us non-sectarian pluralism, a wholly reasonable way—each from within the parameters of our own respective, discrete systems of belief—of being passionately humanist, Christian, or Muslim without being exclusively or intolerantly humanist, Christian, or Muslim.

This is congruent with massive historic, cross-cultural, and inter-faith concurrence about the character of the reality that Christians, Jews, and other faiths talk about using "agape" or "God," and that Spivak refers to in terms of the sacred, animating gift of the planet. This is also congruent with the loving concern peoples of diverse faiths (including Spivak) expect agape to generate. Given this global, cross-cultural, cross-faith, and historic witness under many names to what is recognizably the reality Christians refer to as agape, it is wholly reasonable, and consistent with overwhelming historical and cross-cultural evidential support, to conclude we are all responding to *the same reality*, even though we all immediately name it in terms of incommensurable systems of understanding.

Let me also specify something typically not noted but significant: no historic faith tradition says despise your neighbor, kick the downtrodden, exploit the weak, think and act only for you and yours, abuse creation. With just a few exceptions, most prominently social Darwinism, lifeboat ethics, and some infamous misappropriations of Adam Smith and of Nietzsche, such disturbing imperatives and hardheartedness towards others finds no place in major, emergent, modern Western faith traditions (e.g., social Darwinism and lifeboat ethics are anathema from humanist or Deep Ecology perspectives).

We tend to think of competing religious and ethical systems of understanding as closed wholes, incommensurable and incompatible, existing in zero-sum, there-can-only-be-one competition. Thereby we obscure the reasonableness and considerable historical and cross-cultural evidential basis for concluding we all respond to the same spiritual reality. Failure of recognition fuels sectarian tendencies and compromises potential for concerted global, ethical judgment, and action. Meanwhile, anthropologists from the Gemini star cluster tracking global political and economic developments on earth could quite reasonably conclude that social Darwinism and lifeboat ethics best describe a unified, global system of understanding dictating economic and geo-political developments. *This* is the devastating fracture that moral awakening and cross-cultural, cross-faith ethical consensus can heal: the fracture between the predominant social and political forces shaping global civilization, on the one hand, and globally shared affirmation of what is good and loving, on the other.

Another major reason the common spiritual passion at the heart of the world's diverse historic faiths has been obscured is, as Rivera suggests and as we saw in Spivak, because Western modernity's materialist and secular existential metaphysics foreclose upon its possible existence. Fortunately, though realization is only slowly dawning, the status of modernity's metaphysics is now far more uncertain than the status of the non-material, cross-cultural, cross-faith, millennia-old passion I am calling "agape." There is no warrant for materialist foreclosure upon agape.

Foreclosure upon spiritual reality no longer represents reasonable, strong-minded thinking, but secular dogmatism. This metaphysical dogmatism is especially prominent among cultural and intellectual elites, many of whom are fond of the philosophically inane claim that they have no metaphysics. As any critical theorist should be quick to point out, that not-so-subtle power-play illicitly shields their metaphysics from criticism, thereby protecting the privileged cultural status their materialist or secular existentialist metaphysic provides them.

In sum, insofar as I do not harden my heart I am continually seized by agape, a love not from me that seizes me for others and for myself. Insofar as God *is* love, this describes how, insofar as I do not harden my heart, I am continually seized by God. Me not hardening my heart to agape, me actively living surrender to agape, is "faith." That is, insofar as God *is* agape, living surrender to having been seized by agape for every Face, including my own, names the essence of wholly reasonable faith in God. This essence of Christian faith is continuous with the essence of Levinas's Jewish witness to the God who comes to mind in my having been taken hostage to concern for others. It is continuous with the essence of what Spivak awkwardly gestures toward with "to be born human is to be inclined toward an other and others." And it is continuous with the faith manifest by the Good Samaritan, the faith of the sheep in Jesus's parable, and the faith of Buddhism's Bodhisattvas. Examples could be multiplied from all the world's major faith traditions.

The relationship of various religious systems of understanding and global, historic, and cross-cultural manifestation of divine reality can be paralleled to various scientific systems of understanding in relation to global, historic, and cross-cultural manifestation of material reality. Just as Aristotle, Newton, and Hawking use diverse systems of understanding to signify reality *qua* material, so Siddhartha Gautama, Jesus, Levinas, and Spivak use diverse systems of understanding to interpret reality *qua* spiritual. In the more esoteric particulars of their understanding, Aristotle, Newton, and Hawking's physics and their metaphysics differed radically. But by far they lived in the same conceptual world. The same is true vis-à-vis primordial faith (surrender to having been seized by agape) and diverse faiths (understandings of the essence of faith in Christianity, Deep Ecology, Hinduism, Humanism, Jainism, Judaism).

The analogy fails insofar as Hawking's physics (not his metaphysics) is clearly superior to Aristotle and Newton's, whereas no faith tradition is, wholesale, superior to all others. Differences among faith traditions are significant. Aesthetic differences can be celebrated—why not celebrate diverse poetry about that which all faiths say transcends human understanding? With ethical differences there are no shortcuts. We can only debate and hope that clarity will eventually emerge.

Our focus, however, should not be on differences. Debate over ethical differences should occur with awareness of massive ethical consensus among all the world's historic faiths (including most secular faiths). For the overwhelming consensus about the reality and call of agape is massively significant for valuing and organizing our lives for the sake of the love of all Faces, including our own.[29]

Western societies are coasting on the fading momentum of a spiritually impoverished "age of reason" metaphysic. Meanwhile the *de facto* global dominance of social Darwinism is creating stark inequities, injustices, hardships, and fomenting socio-cultural dog-eat-dog dynamics, thereby amplifying tendencies towards sectarianism and violence. Democratic nation-states are being subverted by transnational economic elites, who tend to live cloistered lives and to see the world through Pollyannaish lenses. Unfortunately, in the context of *de facto* social Darwinism, the hard-hearted play with an advantage. All of this as we face epochal challenges of over-population, environmental degradation, and climate change as a threat multiplier. Our situation is potentially dire.

I am arguing, however, that our global spiritual resources are in fact incredibly well-developed and powerful, if only we can wake up to agape. If we can awaken to agape we can step beyond the narrow-mindedness and sectarian violence of the all too irrational "age of faith," and beyond the narrow-mindedness and *de facto* social Darwinism of a spiritually

---

29. For a specific treatment of the sort of socio-political and economic implications I have in mind, see Pope Francis's encyclical *Laudato Si*.

impoverished "age of reason." We can move into an age of faith *and* reason, a post-secular age of reasonable faith. We can affirm modern science and we can, each faithful to our distinct religious identities, affirm diverse faiths while together affirming at the heart of all our faiths surrender to having been seized by agape for every creature, including ourselves.

This "we" must include awakened global intellectual, political, and economic elites, whose role is essential if we are to navigate our challenges successfully. There is no hope on the whole of success through revolutionary violence (though this is not a call for wholesale pacifism in the face of oppression). In understandable frustration, some advocate just mucking things up, but the position of the vulnerable deteriorates frightfully amidst societal chaos, and oppressive possibilities for the empowered and ruthless are enhanced, so general advocacy of violence or anarchy is positively harmful. We need spiritual awakening and political reformation.

I concur when Spivak says you "cannot be against globalization; you can only work collectively and persistently to turn it into strategy-driven rather than crisis-driven globalization."[30] The term *strategy* manifests the vagueness that afflicts Spivak's prose whenever she means to invoke moral reality. "Strategy-driven" should be read as "ethically-driven." That is, globalization should in part be driven by what is in fact global consensus over a host of ethical convictions inspired by agape.

Ultimately, because of the technologically advanced and deeply complex and interconnected global dynamics of contemporary society—to provide just one example, think of the hundreds of nuclear power plants scattered across the globe that must be maintained without interruption by sophisticated systems dependent upon regional infrastructures (or else global catastrophe!)—our only hope finally lies not in violence but in global awakening and bottom-up plus top-down reform.

To be sure, it is no accident that struggles against oppression and inequity have historically come not from elites but from the oppressed. And there is truth to the ditty "power is never given, it must be taken." In our new day, however, civilization is global. We possess weaponry powerful enough to decimate life on earth, and we are quite likely taking more insidious paths to overwhelming planetary life support systems. The violent, revolutionary disruption that history suggests familiar societal dynamics are slowly but surely driving us towards, with quite possibly apocalyptic consequences, must be avoided through spiritual renewal and political reformation.

The good news is that people of diverse faiths, awakened to agape and sharing vast ethical consensus, populate all segments of all societies,

30. Spivak, "A Moral Dilemma," 222.

including corridors of wealth, influence, and power. In addition, unlike Spivak's moral heroes—Coleridge, Wordsworth, and Shelley, who she says failed because they had "no real involvement with infrastructure"[31]—the ashrams, churches, mosques, sweat-lodges, synagogues, and temples of the world have developed powerful infrastructures (taken together, one of the most powerful collections of infrastructures in existence) and among their members are many with significant political, economic, and socio-cultural power.

People of faith and the infrastructures of the world's major faiths are not going to disappear. The question is, to what degree will they be co-opted for evil, or have their prophetic witness marginalized, and to what degree will they mediate justice and the love idealized by the saints and prophets of every historic faith tradition? When Spivak marginalizes billions of adherents of historic faith traditions, along with all their prophetic traditions, she unintentionally abets co-optation and oppression. Unfortunately, such stereotyping and scapegoating of people of faith and faiths is standard fare among many secular elites, who thereby abet a global social Darwinism which, I like to think, most of them upon reflection would oppose. Despite her self-befuddling, conceptual alienation from faith, Spivak's fidelity in her life and work to being "angled toward an other and others" describes true faith in God. In the terms of Jesus's parable, Spivak is among the surprised, faithful sheep.

The struggle for peace on earth will never end. The world's faith traditions all wisely portray heaven, nirvana, and like utopias as eschatological realities, impossible for us to attain, but nonetheless guiding visions. Hope for relative success in the ongoing struggle lies in the concerted global efforts of people awakened and faithful to agape. People of faith permeate every segment of every society—"salt of the earth," one might say—and the potential combined influence of the people and institutions of the world's faiths is global and powerful. People of faith, people of all faiths, unite!

Secular philosophy's postmodern unraveling of the modern ideal of objective, universal reason threatens to usher us into a politically dangerous age of enthusiasm and violence among competing religious and secular players (individuals as well as nation-states, corporations, special interest and identity groups) who all think that realistically, self-interest and power are the bottom-line court of appeal (unmitigated *realpolitik*). We should tolerate no naivety with regard to bad actors and the forces that *realpolitik* quite rightly alerts us to. But the ultimate court of appeal in both science and spirituality should be to *reality*. After abandoning hope for objective, certain truth, we do not tumble willy-nilly into relativism. Vis-aà-vis science and spirituality (faiths, ethics) we can reasonably discern the far more from the

31. Spivak, "A Moral Dilemma," 230.

far less sure. In science *and* spirituality, the ultimate court of appeal is to extra-human reality which, given the existence of beings such as us, has palpable material or spiritual contour. Not only vis-à-vis the material (including nature and nurture, genes and memes), but also vis-à-vis the spiritual, that is, vis-à-vis what is just and loving, there is—unsurprisingly, given the power of material, poetic, and *agapic* reality—there is massive overlapping cross-cultural and cross-faith, scientific, and ethical consensus.

I personally understand God and faith in relation to a complex set of Christian beliefs (e.g., concerning incarnation, Trinity, forgiveness, atonement, *koinonia*, creation, eschatology) that add considerable particular nuance beyond the "living surrender to agape" essence of Christian faith. But a neo-Levinasian understanding of the "surrender to agape" essence of faith lies at the heart of my open Christian philosophical spirituality. My educated hope is that analogous open spiritualities, manifestly rooted in common standards of reason in response to essentially the same passion of agape, can be affirmed at the heart of the Hindu, Buddhist, Jewish, Muslim, humanist, Deep Ecological, and other traditions.

We are in the midst of an epochal conceptual revolution with massively significant real-world stakes. Basic questions about materiality, causation, and moral reality, however inchoate, abound—along with sophomoric dismissal of historic faith traditions and hubristic attempts to simply construct new spiritualities *de novo*. On the whole, given the spiritual poverty of the modern Western secular rationality predominant among global social, academic, and economic elites, this conceptual revolution is good news, for it marks an opening for awakening to reasonable faith in a post-secular age.

The select essays collected below develop my position in detailed conversation with influential, modern Western philosophers. They clarify the revolutionary conceptual character of our current moment and open space for faith and for all the world's faiths in direct dialogue with the spiritual and ethical insufficiencies of modern rationality and the concrete socio-political challenges of our day. They aim to clarify key conceptual contours of this revolutionary philosophical period, to clarify how classic existential and spiritual questions are being reframed, and to explore some of the considerable spiritual resources of Christian faith (my own faith tradition and area of expertise) for a post-secular age of reasonable faiths, all rooted in agape, and hence all sharing hugely significant spiritual and ethical common ground.

WILLIAM GREENWAY
Austin, TX
January 2020

Chapter 1

Charles Taylor on Affirmation, Mutilation, and Theism

A *Retrospective Reading of* Sources of the Self

> Do we have to choose between various kinds of spiritual loboto-
> my and self-inflicted wounds? Perhaps . . . But . . . I don't accept
> this as our inevitable lot. The dilemma of mutilation is in a sense
> our greatest spiritual challenge, not an iron fate. How can one
> demonstrate this? I can't do it here. . . . There is a large element of
> hope. It is a hope that I see implicit in Judaeo-Christian theism
> (however terrible the record of its adherents in history), and in
> its central promise of a divine affirmation of the human, more
> total than humans can ever attain unaided.[1]

FIREWORKS

"Important if true," grants Cambridge historian Quentin Skinner of Charles
Taylor's *Sources of the Self.*[2] But, Skinner continues, since Taylor's "final
message" is that "we cannot hope to realize our fullest human potentialities

---

1. Taylor, *Sources of the Self*, 521.
2. Skinner, "Who Are 'We'?" 133.

in the absence of God," all sane thinkers must conclude, *not true*.[3] Invoking intellectuals from Hume to Russell, Skinner insists that theistic belief is "obviously self-deceiving and erroneous."[4] In fact, Skinner asserts bluntly, we may now conclude "not merely that theism must certainly be false . . . [but] that it must be grossly irrational to believe otherwise," and thus that "anyone who continues to affirm it must be suffering from some serious form of psychological blockage or self-deceit."[5]

Skinner's blazing attack irked Taylor. In an uncompromising response, Taylor declares his intent to take "sharp issue" with Skinner's "mounting rhetoric." He denies linking necessarily our craving for meaning to an embrace of God, defiantly asserts that he is indeed "a believer . . . a Christian," and suggests Skinner's stance may betoken "an astonishing selective narrowness of spirit in an otherwise educated and open person."[6] It is paradoxical, Taylor laments pointedly, that vis-à-vis religion, elite academics often "have all the breadth of comprehension and sympathy of a Jerry Falwell, and significantly less even than Cardinal Ratzinger."[7] "The really astonishing thing," finishes Taylor, "is that they even seem proud of it."[8]

Skinner and Taylor later reengage their debate in a Festschrift for Taylor. Despite more decorous tones, their differences remain acute.[9] Skinner ends contending that, in contrast to the "dangerously irrational creed" of theism, the death of God leaves us the "opportunity . . . to affirm the value of our humanity more fully than before."[10] "Great," Taylor retorts, but then he simply reaffirms his "hunch that there is a scale of affirmation of humanity by God which cannot be matched by humans rejecting God."[11] A desire to affirm humanity clearly fuels both Skinner and Taylor's passion for this issue. But Skinner thinks theism obstructs this affirmation, while Taylor suspects that theism alone may enable full affirmation. Taylor admits he is "far from having proof" for his hunch but, eager to spark debate, invites readers to experiment with the idea that God may facilitate fuller affirmation of

3. Skinner, "Who are 'We'?" 133.

4. Skinner, "Who are 'We'?" 148.

5. Skinner, "Who are 'We'?" 148.

6. Taylor, "Comments and Replies," 240–41.

7. Taylor, "Comments," 242.

8. Taylor, "Comments," 242.

9. Skinner, "Modernity and Disenchantment"; Taylor, "Reply and Re-articulation" 222–26.

10. Skinner, "Modernity and Disenchantment," 47.

11. Taylor, "Reply and Re-articulation," 226.

humanity.[12] It is unfortunate that incredulity and misunderstanding shortly smothered the discussion Taylor hoped to initiate.

It must be said that Taylor is partly responsible for all the confusion. Indeed, Taylor scatters provocative and vague appeals to God throughout *Sources*.[13] It is not surprising, then, that Quentin Skinner is only one among a host of critics who authored essays accusing Taylor of searching for moral foundations, of attempting to prove the existence of God, or of asserting that God alone is an adequate moral source.[14] In response, Taylor authored a series of replies in which he vigorously denied ever entertaining such aims.[15] And with the opposing sides' claims thus firmly staked, the debate has stalled.

But misunderstandings, not irreconcilable differences, have stalled this debate, and precluded recognition of some of Taylor's most suggestive insights. In order to surmount this impasse, I use Taylor's replies to illuminate a retrospective reading of *Sources*. In particular, the replies alert one to Taylor's failure clearly to distinguish two distinct trajectories in his argument, for while *Sources* is manifestly dedicated to attacking disengaged reason and naturalistic reduction, the complex contours of Taylor's talk of affirmation, mutilation, and theistic hope emerge in proper relief only *after* this initial engagement is won. One must think in terms of a second, masked trajectory, a trajectory that inquires into existential tensions that become visible only *after* the hypergoods are fully articulated. Only then can one comprehend fully Taylor's re-articulation of a modern Western spiritual dilemma more commonly (and misleadingly) called a "quest for meaning."

Prima facie, then, Taylor's critics are right to take him to task. In the light of Taylor's responses, however, I will attempt first to clarify the import of several critical but often misconstrued concepts in *Sources*: inescapable frameworks of meaning, life goods, hypergoods, constitutive goods, and moral sources. I will then detail the precise contours of Taylor's question of affirmation, his dilemma of mutilation, and his theistic hope. After performing these two tasks, I will be in a position to explain how Taylor's question of affirmation and dilemma of mutilation, along with his correlate openness to

12. Taylor, "Reply and Re-articulation," 226. The import of "affirmation" is delineated below.

13. See, for instance, *Sources of the Self*, 10–11, 74–76, 219, 270, 310–11, 317–19, 342, 516, 518, 521.

14. See, *inter alia*: Braybrooke, "Inward and Outward with the Modern Self"; Lane, "God or Orienteering?"; Low-Beer, "Living a Life"; Rosen, "Must We Return to Moral Realism?"

15. See all of the following from Taylor: "Reply to Braybrooke and de Sousa"; "Comments and Replies"; "Reply and Re-articulation"; and "Reply to Commentators."

theism, paints with unprecedented subtlety those spiritual longings Westerners commonly struggle to articulate in terms of a "quest for meaning." In the end, I will suggest why even those (like Quentin Skinner) who reject Taylor's appeal to theism should—on their own terms and without changing their convictions—unhesitatingly cede the perspicuity of Taylor's formulation of "our greatest spiritual challenge."

INESCAPABLE FRAMEWORKS OF MEANING, LIFE GOODS, AND HYPERGOODS

Since humans are both physically and linguistically constituted, argues Taylor, and since languages are historical and communal (not private), selves are inescapably embedded within culturally specific, evolved webs of interlocution. Such linguistic webs frame all self-interpretation, so we cannot but understand and value ourselves *vis-à-vis* some cluster of webs. Thus Taylor talks of "dialogical" selves and "inescapable frameworks of meaning." Some strive furiously to realize the Enlightenment ideal of radical autonomy by simply creating meanings and declaring significance. But attempts to extricate self-valuation from predetermined webs of interlocution are futile, for they are actually self-defeating attempts to abstract oneself from the very conditions necessary for attributing significance.

Consider Sartre's famous example of the young man who must choose between joining the French Resistance and caring for his ailing mother.[16] Sartre emphasizes that the young man (call him Jean) is faced with a radical choice. Jean must decide in utter freedom whether he will choose to value mother or homeland more. Thus, Sartre suggests, the decision itself bestows higher value on one or the other option. As a consequence, any desire to defer to some external authority demonstrates bad faith—denial of one's freedom authentically to create oneself.

Taylor too affirms Jean's freedom, but he rejects the coherence of his desire to escape all external authorities. Taylor directs our attention to Sartre's reliance on the context of the scenario. The example evokes a predictable empathetic response because we recognize both joining the Resistance and caring for one's mother to be virtuous. We readily imagine Jean agonizing over the decision because we can imagine how powerfully we would feel called by each of these competing demands. But while Jean is free, he is not

---

16. The Sartre illustration can be found in "Existentialism is a Humanism," 354–56. I am building upon Taylor's invocation of this illustration in *Human Agency and Language*, 29–31.

radically free, for his powerful senses of call to mother and country trade upon background frameworks of meaning.

For instance, imagine another young man, Michel, whose rare acumen with explosives is absolutely vital to the success of the Resistance, agonizing over whether he should join the Resistance or stay home to compose poetry. Michel feels vitally a call to help the Resistance, but more compelling still is a bursting drive continually to create himself through his poetry. Michel believes a decision to play a prescribed role within the Resistance would deny and deface his drive to poetic self-creation. It is a painful choice, but he is determined authentically to create his own identity. So Michel remains home and composes poems.

We may not agree with Michel's decision. Given the severity of the Nazi threat, we may even judge it naive and self-centered. But most Westerners would agree that Michel's struggle is serious, for it pits concern for others against another good embedded powerfully within Western culture: autonomy (i.e., the choice of authenticity over the evil of bad faith). Imagine a third version of Sartre's scenario. This time we find Jacques safely hidden away, reveling in strawberry ice cream while his town burns and his mother perishes. We find him intelligent, well spoken, and well aware of the events transpiring outside his hideaway. Jacques shows no remorse or concern about either his mother or his country, nor does he appeal to autonomy. Certainly, he admits, fidelity to homeland and parents is good, but so is enjoyment of strawberry ice cream, and on his estimate the delights of ice cream are simply more important than fidelity to either his mother or his country.

Do we believe Jacques can bestow value sheerly through choice in this instance? The die-hard Sartrean should respond, "Yes, that's his prerogative as long as it is his authentic choice; the key is to avoid bad faith." But here I hope even Sartre would pause, for we cannot but judge Jacques to be morally disoriented. If his insensitivity to others involved malicious actions, we would confine him (e.g., perhaps his pleasure is not ice cream but sex with children). Of course, the delights of strawberry ice cream are good, and investment in such goods is a relevant aspect of self-valuation. We each create our individual identities in relation to a wide range of life goods, but we do not value all goods equally. We do not equate the value of discerning the nuances of a fine wine with the value of resisting Nazis. We distinguish among life goods, and those goods that stand above others and adjudicate among them, Taylor labels "hypergoods."

In *Sources of the Self*, Taylor traces the emergence of three hypergoods with which he expects Westerners to resonate: first, *benevolence*, which calls upon us to care for justice and the well-being of others; second, *affirmation of ordinary life*, familiarly expressed in our sense that all humans are "created equal"—which means that benevolence extends to all, no matter their social status; and third, *autonomy*, the poetic concern that we transcend the confines of social conditioning and freely create unique selves. According to Taylor, we may not be taught these hypergoods (or other life goods) explicitly, but since they are embedded within our practices (laws, rituals, literature, turns of phrase) they constitute the background against which we live and evaluate our lives within Western societies. (Skinner criticizes Taylor's invocation of "we" here as leveling and hegemonic—I address this below.)

Each of these hypergoods was implicit in my play with Sartre's example. Consider the second scenario, where Michel struggles between a call to aid the Resistance and a call to poetry. I expect most readers find Michel's decision to be ill-advised, but even given the extremity of the scenario, I do not expect a rush to judgment. Why? Because Michel appeals to a hypergood—autonomy, the good of self-creation. Michel opposes autonomy to benevolence. So while we may question Michel's rationale, we cannot simply dismiss it, for he brings two hypergoods into opposition.

In the third scenario, where Jacques explains his decision to opt for ice cream over his mother and his country by appealing simply to the delights of ice cream, all sense of moral dilemma fades, for Jacques appeals not to a competing hypergood (autonomy) but to a lesser life good (the delights of strawberry ice cream). Thus the hypergood of benevolence is put into direct conflict with the lesser life good of enjoying ice cream. We cringe because we cannot but believe that Jacques's privileging of ice cream reflects a horrible moral disorientation, and if the hypergood of benevolence were not merely mocked by the choice of ice cream but violated by the brutalizing of children, then we would not hesitate to take forcible action.

The evocative power of Sartre's original example similarly trades on background frameworks of meaning. Its pathos depends on opposing mutually exclusive calls to benevolence (to one's nation or to one's mother). If Sartre had pitted a hypergood against a lesser life good, no sense for Jean's dilemma would have arisen—"*homeland* over ice cream, of course; what's wrong with you, anyway?" And if Sartre had expected that his readers would just as quickly have chosen ice cream just for the taste of it, then he could not have expected to evoke any pathos at all—"Country? Mother? Who cares? Just flip a coin, for Pete's sake." But Sartre clearly counted on evoking a sense of pathos with his either/or. Thus, Sartre, by taking his example seriously, implicitly acknowledges the acuity of Taylor's identification of the hypergood of benevolence and his delineation of the significance of inescapable frameworks of meaning.

Taylor agrees that Jean will have to choose for himself, but he emphasizes that the choice is between alternatives whose significance trades on background frameworks of meaning. Taylor rejects radical autonomy, not contextualized autonomy. Delineating the hypergoods, then, does not lessen our chance of facing tragic decisions; like Jean, for instance, we may face situations where we will violate our sense of benevolence whichever direction we turn. Taylor, moreover, discerns an ineluctable tension among the three hypergoods. For the affirmation of ordinary life and the ethic of benevolence combine to call us to actions and evaluations that are not functions of individual and radically free choice. This puts these two hypergoods in tension with the hypergood of autonomy, which values our ability to escape social conditioning and create ourselves according to individual and radically free choice. Taylor states the relevant tension succinctly in *Hegel and Modern Society*, where he identifies a basic tension between an "aspiration to radical autonomy on one hand, and to expressive unity with nature and within society on the other."[17]

Might we someday transcend the trajectories sustaining this tension? "Who knows?" Taylor replies. But he does consider it de facto impossible for those embedded within the mainstream of the Western tradition to disavow any of the three extant hypergoods. We have no choice, he argues, but to keep tensions in play as we struggle in various concrete instances to decide how to create ourselves in the face of diverse and conflicting life goods and hypergoods.

Contra numerous critics, then, Taylor does not specify a single, incomparable hypergood; nor does his delineation of the hypergoods provide a hegemonic formula for moral decision making. On the contrary, his analysis identifies the formal contours of a tension afflicting our most powerful moral convictions (one manifest, for example, in debates pitting aesthetics against ethics relative to artists' rights and responsibilities—consider recent debate over artists' decisions to photograph nude children in suggestive poses or to place a cross in a vat of urine). I will not explore further the permutations of this critical tension, however, for I want to pursue the contours of a deeper tension, one that leads to Taylor's question of affirmation, his dilemma of mutilation, and his theistic hope. But before I can bring that tension into proper focus, I must also clarify Taylor's subtle distinction between "constitutive goods" and "moral sources."

CONSTITUTIVE GOODS AND MORAL SOURCES

Insofar as they describe the dominant frameworks against which we evaluate ourselves, our hypergoods will be significant constitutive goods. But it

17. Taylor, *Hegel and Modern Society*, 69.

is critical to distinguish between a hypergood and a constitutive good, for with "constitutive good" Taylor invokes a dimension of moral intuition experienced as an external calling. Taylor introduces the notion of constitutive goods because he finds his historical account of the evolution of hypergoods insufficient to account for our lived experience of the good.

Consider the following example: I am driving down a lonely road in the Kentucky countryside when, rounding a bend, I see that two cars have collided and crashed into a stand of trees. The drivers are unconscious and bleeding. No one else is about. In one sense, one might say that I desire to help. But this is not like the "desire" I might have for a fine wine. In that sense, I may not feel any desire to get involved with this bloody scene. Yet I feel called upon to help. This call, this sense that "benevolence" requires me to lend assistance, is clearly not a function of my ordinary desires. Is an appeal to hypergoods sufficient to explain this sense of call?

Yes, one might reply. On Taylor's own account hypergoods are precisely those values so deeply embedded in our socialization that, despite their contingency, we experience them as inviolate. Only the strongest Sartrean poet could even begin to respond *authentically* to persons unconscious and bleeding (i.e., understand her response exclusively in terms of her autonomous choice to bestow value). Because of the power of socialization, most of us will feel an irresistible call to render aid. This sense of external call, however, points only to the power of utterly contingent social conditioning, not to any call from some extra-human moral order. Confusion on this point, the Sartrean might argue, tempts us to abandon responsibility for authentic self-creation, tempts us to seek metaphysical comfort in the belief that some external realm of values commands our obedience.

This response sounds plausible. Taylor, however, believes that it fails to capture an important aspect of our moral experience. I admit that one of my hypergoods is benevolence, and without a certain history of socialization and access to specific moral vocabularies, I certainly could not recognize this hypergood. Yet I do not react in this situation to the hypergood as to a rule. That is, the historical and linguistic explanation of hypergoods is necessary but not sufficient to explain my moral experience. What the account fails to address and explain is the focus of my attention. For that which moves me—and which I must fight to forget if I am to decide to ignore the accident, drive on, and resume my enjoyment of the beautiful Kentucky countryside—is not only my awareness of some hypergood but also the injured drivers. That is, our sense of call is not merely abstract, is not only a response to a hypergood *qua* hypergood; it is always a response to some concrete particular, to those people hurt in those cars, to that child being abused, to that person unjustly imprisoned.

Life goods (including the hypergoods) name the semantic background against and within which we interpret our actions, but we respond to concrete particulars that we experience as commanding "our moral awe or allegiance."[18] An anthropologist from Neptune who is expert in Earth cultures may be familiar enough with Western hypergoods to predict my reaction to the accident scene, but the Neptunite may know all this without understanding the hypergood *qua* constitutive good. Explanation of the hypergood "benevolence" allows us to predict and partly to understand the person who stops to help the injured drivers. But the spirit of the response—the sense of person-to-person encounter that constitutes the most powerful dimension of our moral experiences—is ignored in such a third-person account. Thus, Taylor concludes that while his account of hypergoods truly depicts sources of the modern identity, it fails to account fully for our lived moral experience. So Taylor attempts to account for that dimension of our experience missing from his tale of life goods with the notion of "constitutive goods."

Only when we recapture our ability to articulate this dimension of our experience does the question of moral sources arise, for constitutive goods turn on acknowledging an external call.[19] The language of "call" is critical, for Taylor does not interpret our moral sense as merely a valuative reaction to a neutral universe, the call truly comes from without.[20] But Taylor is no crass realist, for he does not maintain that we simply discover goods "out there." There would be no such thing as good or evil, agrees Taylor, "unless human beings existed."[21] And if that is "all that is meant by non-realism," continues Taylor, "then I am a non-realist after all."[22]

Taylor is a moral realist, however, insofar as he contends that constitutive goods describe a source of moral motivation which is a function of more than personal desire or the power of contingent socialization. For with constitutive goods Taylor invokes:

18. Taylor, "Comments and Replies," 243.

19. Taylor distinguishes four forms of call to which we might open ourselves: "certain ways of being are higher than others in virtue of the way we are (the 'Aristotelian' component); certain demands are made on us by other human beings in virtue of the way both we and they are (the 'moral' component). I would want to add: certain demands are made on us by our world in virtue of what we are and how we fit into it (the 'ecological' component). And further, I believe that certain goods arise out of our relation to God (the 'theological' component)." Taylor, "Comments and Replies," 245–46.

20. Taylor, "Comments and Replies," 245–46.

21. Taylor, "Comments and Replies," 245–46.

22. Taylor, "Comments and Replies," 245–46; Rosen, "Must We Return to Moral Realism?" 189–90.

features of the universe, or God, or human beings, (i) on which the life goods depend, (ii) which command our moral awe or allegiance, and (iii) the contemplation of or contact with which empowers us to be good.[23]

On the one hand, then, the valuative sphere would not exist without sentient beings. On the other hand, we do not simply create this sphere; there is a sense in which moral demands are "something we discover."[24]

Taylor is skating on preciously thin ice, but he is emboldened by an unwavering commitment to articulate fully our concrete moral experiences. In accord with this commitment, Taylor's "appeal is to the language that we can't help using to deliberate and think out our lives and those of others."[25] Given this inescapable usage, Taylor concludes that we have "no good grounds to question the [realist] ontology implicit in the terms which allow us our best account of ourselves."[26] Thus Taylor claims the mantle of the moral realist, but, he insists, not in the sense of "the old Platonic model."[27] In fact, Taylor confesses that he is left occupying an uncertain middle ground between projectivism and Platonism, and the question of the ontological status of the semantic sphere races front and center.[28]

One can understand Taylor's calm over adopting this precarious philosophical stance only if one grasps the paramount significance of his ordering of questions. For by building his argument out of an articulation of our moral experience, Taylor disallows all foundational theology and ontotheology. That is, realist speculation over God, Ideas, or Reason comes only in *response* to prior recognition of constitutive goods. Taylor takes care to make the flow of argument clear: "In virtue of (iii) [see previous offset quote], such constitutive goods function as what I call 'moral sources'. Examples of candidates for constitutive goods available in the tradition are: God, Plato's Idea of the Good, Kant's power of rational agency, which commands the awe of the agent him/herself."[29] Taylor can remain calm regarding questions over the precise contours of his moral realism because they arise at the end of the discussion. This is the absolutely critical philosophical realignment missed by incredulous critics: *the theological or onto-theological realism question*

23. Taylor, "Comments and Replies," 243.

24. Taylor, "Comments and Replies," 245–46.

25. Taylor, "Reply to Commentators," 208.

26. Taylor, "Reply to Commentators," 208.

27. Taylor, "Comments and Replies," 245–46.

28. Taylor, "Comments and Replies," 245–46. On Taylor's neo-Hegelian, historicist realism see Descombes, "Is There an Objective Spirit?"

29. Taylor, "Comments and Replies," 243.

is consequent, not antecedent, to concrete ethical intuitions and debate. This is not to say, of course, that the love of God *qua* creator, for instance, is not the ultimate source of the love we share for one another (indeed, this may be Taylor's conviction). But this understanding is consonant with the contention that our love for others is a reaction *to* the other, and not the consequence of some internalized prior theory regarding the nature and will of God or the categorical imperatives of reason.

The existence of God, then, is consonant with but not necessary to Taylor's account of constitutive goods. So Taylor disavows any argument from a sense of constitutive goods to the existence of a particular moral source like God. Indeed, Taylor is careful to note that one need not appeal to anything like God or Platonic Ideas to acknowledge constitutive goods: "Contemporary unbelieving and 'post-metaphysical' naturalists also recognize constitutive goods. Only now they are features of the human predicament and human potentialities."[30] There is, insists Taylor, "no a priori truth here."[31] A sense of constitutive goods could arise "precisely in facing a disenchanted universe with courage and lucidity"; the constitutive reality could be simply "humans as beings capable of this courageous disengagement."[32]

The key lies in acknowledging our intuition that we recognize significance. If this significance is thought to be arbitrarily bestowed, and thus equally susceptible to withdrawal, it would not be consistent with the intuition that life presents us with this significance. And this is an intuition Taylor finds in practice undeniable. He would expect us, for instance, to consider ill, not merely different, anyone who confessed their delight in torturing people for pleasure—and he would expect us to be equally ill at ease with anyone who commented that while torturing people for pleasure was certainly not their preference, they nonetheless felt no right to judge other people's preferences. But Taylor wants to make this assertion without requiring us to be either Platonists or theists. He confesses that he stands on uncertain ontological ground, but he expects his audience to share his basic intuitions, even if he cannot yet fully account for them. Taylor will not allow his inability conclusively to settle the realist question to prevent him from articulating and acknowledging his sense of the call of constitutive goods. And it is his post-foundationalist ordering of the realism question that allows him to assume this philosophical stance on constitutive goods, a stance that appears hopelessly confused from classic ontotheological or modern epistemological philosophical perspectives.

30. Taylor, "Reply to Commentators," 210–11, see also 212.

31. Taylor, *Sources of the Self*, 342.

32. Taylor, *Sources of the Self*, 342, 94.

Given his postfoundationalism, Taylor never argues from the existence of a particular moral source like God to the validity of a particular constitutive good. On the contrary, according to Taylor, the experience of constitutive goods comes first, and any reversal of the order of explanation—that is, from some preconceived notion of the will of God or the contours of some ontic logos to the validity of a particular moral position—reveals that "something rather sick and oppressive is going on."[33] Moreover, and absolutely critical to our exploration, once the subtle order of explanation among hypergoods, constitutive goods, and moral sources is clarified, it becomes clear that whether or not there is a God *behind* creation, "the world's being good" cannot remain "entirely independent of our seeing it and showing it as good."[34] That is, even if there is a God, we can designate the good only via appeal to its resonance with our sense of external call. Because epistemically, though perhaps not ontologically, constitutive goods precede moral sources, being able to affirm the world as good requires our being able to see it as good. With this realization explicated, I am poised finally to articulate Taylor's question of affirmation and his dilemma of mutilation.

AFFIRMATION AND MUTILATION

Taylor's postfoundational moral realism proves to be a double-edged sword, for the moral intuitions it preserves inform ideals that contrast markedly with the harsh realities of existence. This tension—between utopian expectations and extant reality—turns our desire for affirmation into a dilemma of mutilation. For while Taylor frees us to affirm our deepest moral intuitions, these very intuitions, in our hands, and in the face of our own and our world's imperfection and cruelty, preclude us from affirming ourselves. It would seem that we can either acknowledge our deepest moral intuitions and sit in judgment on ourselves and our world, or we can extirpate these intuitions, and thereby cut ourselves off from our deepest moral intuitions. To judge ourselves negatively or mutilate ourselves spiritually—this either/or constitutes Taylor's "dilemma of mutilation," the West's "greatest spiritual challenge."[35]

Taylor illustrates the dilemma in conversation with Dostoyevsky and Nietzsche. For instance, Taylor suggests, consider Dostoyevsky's Ivan Karamazov, who "wants to give God back 'his ticket' to this world of unacceptable suffering . . . because he has the moral sensitivity to feel that the ultimate happiness of the whole of humanity isn't worth the tears of

33. Taylor, "Reply and Re-articulation," 219.
34. Taylor, *Sources of the Self*, 448.
35. Taylor, *Sources of the Self*, 521.

an innocent child."[36] In fact, the cosmos appears to be disproportionately suffused with suffering. What sensitive soul can consider the unremitting suffering that has afflicted untold multitudes and not feel a loathing? The cosmos is at worst cruel and at best indifferent. The natural reaction for the morally sensitive will be a loathing, and self-loathing will follow loathing of the universe, for even if one has led a perfectly innocent life, one's own existence and happiness have been purchased through the existence of this irredeemable cosmos.[37] Indeed, the higher one's moral sensitivity, the more likely one is to reject the world.[38] How, then, can any affirm cosmos or self?

Nietzsche, contends Taylor, answers that the moral person simply cannot affirm cosmos or self. The possibility of affirmation arises only when one "overcomes" one's moral consciousness.[39] Taylor believes the highest moral sensitivity lies behind Nietzsche's antimoral imperative. Nietzsche's acute moral sensitivity leads to his realization that the moral demand cannot be met and drives him to conclude it must be overcome. Moreover, because he realizes that the moral demand is embodied within our deepest moral intuitions, Nietzsche speaks of a self-overcoming.[40] On Taylor's reading, Nietzsche believes that:

> Morality brought us to the notion of something pure and great and infinitely worth affirmation and love—only it wasn't us as we are, but the negation of our essential being, the denial of the will to power. What we have to do . . . is overcome the force of morality and find the strength to rise above its demands, which sap our strength and fill us with the poison of self-hatred. . . .This power to affirm does indeed repose in us. . . .what really commands affirmation is this very power itself. . . . We can say "yes" to all that is.[41]

Only those who overcome the moral can affirm world and self, but now what is affirmed is a sort of beauty that arises not in the world itself but in our willing ourselves to see the world as beautiful, in our adoption of a "stance of unflinching acceptance."[42]

Nietzsche, then, suggests that we jettison our moral intuitions and rid ourselves of feelings of guilt and loathing. Such affirmation sounds

36. Taylor, *Sources of the Self*, 451.
37. Taylor, *Sources of the Self*, 451.
38. Taylor, *Sources of the Self*, 451.
39. Taylor, *Sources of the Self*, 453.
40. Taylor, *Sources of the Self*, 453.
41. Taylor, *Sources of the Self*, 453.
42. Taylor, *Sources of the Self*, 454.

liberating, but, Taylor warns, we sacrifice mightily for this "liberation," for Nietzschean self-overcoming involves eliding some of our most powerful spiritual aspirations.[43] This form of spiritual mutilation, Taylor emphasizes, is "a heavy price to pay."[44] "Is this the last word?" asks Taylor, "Do we have to choose between various kinds of spiritual lobotomy and self-inflicted wounds?"[45] "Perhaps," Taylor concedes, but it is at this point that Taylor confesses his investment in a hope he finds in Judaeo-Christian theism. Before discussing Taylor's theistic hope, however, we should return to Quentin Skinner. For I can now suggest why even Skinner (and other nontheists) should appropriate, not attack, Taylor.

SKINNER'S QUEST FOR MEANING

At the close of his critique, Skinner inadvertently testifies to the acuity of Taylor's delineation of the dilemma of mutilation. Note the pathos that attends Skinner's description of existence without God:

> many of us have . . . come to realize that, since there is no God, we shall somehow have to manage on our own. It is strange that Taylor has so little to say about this familiar but tragic element in modern consciousness. . . . While Taylor continues to insist that the only ultimate way to satisfy our craving for meaning must be to embrace God, many of "us" have come to recognize that such cravings will somehow *have* to be satisfied by whatever meanings we can find in everyday life. It is true . . . that these may not amount to much; but there are no other meanings to be had.[46]

We cannot return to theism, continues Skinner, for "too many of us have come to the painful conclusion that, even though it would be a fine thing to converse with angels, there are in truth no angels with whom to converse."[47]

Skinner clearly (and correctly) expects widespread resonance with his sentiment that the realization that there is no God is a tragic and painful element in modern consciousness and with his contention that it would be a fine thing to converse with angels. But he does not reflect upon this expectation. Why do we want to talk to angels? And how exactly could God satisfy our craving for meaning? Nothing suddenly becomes more meaningful

43. Taylor, *Sources of the Self*, 520.
44. Taylor, *Sources of the Self*, 520.
45. Taylor, *Sources of the Self*, 520.
46. Skinner, "Who Are 'We'?" 149.
47. Skinner, "Who Are 'We'?" 149–50.

simply because there is an angel or supreme being around. We already have all the meaning we need. God or angels are not necessary for suffering, injustice, horror, love, justice, or beauty to have meaning. On the contrary, it is precisely the profundity of the meaning of such as these that sends many questing for God.

But Skinner is voicing an oft-heard sentiment. What could be so significant about God? Could it be a belief that God may grant life after death? Well, how does that help us reconcile ourselves to the suffering that surrounds us? Even if one believes in an afterlife, or in contemporary equivalents like a future social utopia or the taking up of the whole into the eternal memory of God, how, Taylor would ask *à la* Ivan Karamazov, does that help us affirm the world? Can the torturing of the child be undone tit for tat, future good for present evil? Taylor, I think, would judge not. On the contrary, I suspect he would think that all such turns to imagined future utopias function as opiates, deadening sensitivity to the present. At any rate, Taylor pursues none of these options.

So what relevant difference could the existence of angels or God make? Well, it would make a difference if the angels or God indicated that a sphere of love, beauty, and goodness somehow transcends, subverts, or reframes the apparent ultimacy of the world's suffering and injustice (i.e., facilitates full affirmation). That is, Skinner's sentiments about meaning make better sense if recast ethically and aesthetically in Taylor's terms. What we crave is not meaning but affirmation. We crave the ability fully to affirm cosmos, other, and self, and it is this craving, this desire that our irredeemable cosmos might be redeemed, that our intimate acquaintance with evil apparently precludes (whether there be heaven or no).

Upon reflection, then, one realizes Taylor's "affirmation" is what Skinner is really talking about with his invocation of "meaning." Thus Skinner himself testifies to Taylor's discernment, for the dynamics of his "painful conclusion" and crisis of meaning are better expressed in terms of Taylor's dilemma of mutilation and crisis of affirmation. And, because of Taylor's ordering of the relation between moral sources and constitutive goods, convinced non-theists like Skinner can appropriate Taylor's subtle delineation of the extant dynamics of this tension without affirming his appeal to theism.

THEISTIC HOPE?

But what are we to make of Taylor's cryptic appeal to theistic hope? We return to Taylor's deadly serious question, "Do we have to choose between various kinds of spiritual lobotomy and self-inflicted wounds?" In terms of extant possibilities, Taylor believes the answer is clearly yes. We must either suppress our deepest moral intuitions or rage against existence, for extant evil precludes affirmation; we simply cannot see the universe as good. Typically, of course, we live somewhat erratically in the middle, moderating our sensitivities and hopes, suppressing and raging by turns. Yet within the Christian and Jewish traditions there is testimony to those who remain morally sensitive to the nth degree and yet somehow do win through to full affirmation (think of the "twice born" in William James's *Varieties of Religious Experience*).[48] This somehow happens in the dynamic Christians describe via notions of agape and grace (i.e., of a love that empowers one to love). While his own testimony remains oblique, Taylor is clearly moved by the love others have mediated to him, finding such love provides "an ability to love the world and ourselves, to see it as good in spite of the wrong."[49] "Loving the world and ourselves is in a sense a miracle," contends Taylor, "in the face of all the evil and degradation that it and we contain."[50] But this miracle becomes possible precisely as we find ourselves loved by others, for through this love we find ourselves able to affirm ourselves and others. Taylor sees here "a central idea of the Christian tradition . . . that people are transformed through being loved by God, a love that they mediate to each other . . ."[51]

All this clarifies the contours of Taylor's theistic hope. Taylor is not confessing belief in the Christian God (though such is not excluded). Rather, his is the confession of one so sensitive to evil that he cannot affirm himself or the cosmos without some form of spiritual mutilation. Taylor finds himself unable to escape this dilemma of mutilation. Is this dilemma, then, our iron fate? Not according to Taylor, who is unwilling to settle for that conclusion, for he hears testimony to, and evidently has some intimations of, a love that allows some fully to affirm themselves, others, and cosmos without succumbing to spiritual mutilation. But Taylor's modern, Western consciousness is such that he is unwilling to proclaim the reality of this affirmation, for he is unwilling in any way to deny the reality of evil. Thus, Taylor throws his emphasis onto the open-ended character of hope. "Hope" expresses Taylor's poetic openness to the possibility of full affirmation in the face of suffering. The dilemma of mutilation is an iron fate only for those who take the modern mentality (i.e., the standard modern array of vocabularies), which ineluctably presents us with the dilemma of mutilation, as final. Taylor considers the dilemma extant and unavoidable, but

48. See James, *Varieties of Religious Experience*, 166–88.
49. Taylor, *Sources of the Self*, 452.
50. Taylor, *Sources of the Self*, 452.
51. Taylor, *Sources of the Self*, 452.

the testimony of extraordinary individuals and the openness of the future combine to fuel his hope that the dilemma is not necessarily final.

Taylor suspects, moreover, that this level of affirmation is not within the purview of humans alone; he suspects his hope for full affirmation involves the divine. In fact, he believes he is investing in the form of hope he sees implicit in Judaeo-Christian theism. While Taylor's notion of God remains vague, then, the nature of his hope in God is clear: Taylor hopes for a participation with the divine that returns us to this world in such a way that we are able fully to embrace our deepest spiritual aspirations and fully to affirm the world, others, and ourselves without spiritual mutilation and without simply denying the reality of suffering and evil—a miraculous transformation indeed.

"WE" WESTERNERS

Given the formative influence of the Jewish and Christian traditions on Western consciousness, Taylor's account of our dilemma and of his theistic hope is clearly circular. But the circle is not vicious; it simply alerts us to the fact that we are not offering foundational arguments. We find ourselves thrown into particular existences, and we struggle to live authentic, creative, meaningful, good, and beautiful lives. Taylor strives to increase our understanding and ability to flourish by clarifying the shape of the crisis of affirmation as experienced by the average Westerner.

This brings us to Skinner's contention that Taylor's "we" is leveling and hegemonic. This is an important objection. Skinner goes too far when he suggests Sources of the Self is ultimately "a vindication of modern bourgeois life," but it certainly is not a history of or from the margins.[52] Sources of the Self is a history of ideas that have profoundly shaped elite classes and institutions in the West, and thereby exercised a disproportionate influence on Western culture. Thus Taylor quite reasonably expects twentieth-century Westerners, socialized in cultures that are steeped in a fairly standard set of literary, philosophical, artistic, religious, and scientific traditions, to resonate with, or at least to recognize, his account of the hypergoods and the crisis of affirmation.

As a thinker situated within the mainstream of Western culture, moreover, Taylor's proposed path to resolution of the crisis of affirmation involves appeals to God, grace, and agape—and there is no a priori reason to judge these appeals false or misleading. But if the shoe does not fit—as it certainly will not for those raised within different cultures or subcultures—then,

52. Skinner, "Who Are 'We'?" 142.

Taylor would maintain, none should be forced to wear it. In fact, remembering the contingency of their conditioning, mainstream Westerners should be especially curious to converse with those for whom the shoe does not fit. Who knows, for instance, how conversation with persons representing diverse cultures, subcultures, and religious traditions might change even the most fundamental Western conceptions of self, good, and evil? Though Taylor does not engage these diverse communities in *Sources of the Self*, he should readily accede to Skinner's urging that he enter into cross-cultural dialogue, for such conversations may greatly enrich our understanding.[53]

Rich conversation, however, requires frank confession of one's own spiritual aspirations. The key is not to deny or suppress our most profound spiritual convictions but to hold them as confessions about which we have no real doubts (but not as knowledge about which there can be no possible question). In the course of conversation with those who differ, new and real doubts may arise, but it is pointless to try to feign post-epistemological quasi-objectivity with the unbelievable (and literally unlivable) claim that, *qua* ironist, one holds all one's convictions equally in doubt. It is far better honestly to acknowledge and specify our deepest convictions. For if we forthrightly express our convictions, we can better discern the shape of the spiritual challenges confronting us—and better expose our convictions to the rigors of open debate with those who differ.

Skinner reflects widespread Western intuitions when he describes his craving for meaning and expresses a conviction that it would be wonderful to converse with angels or to be able to believe in a loving God. But the contours of these potent intuitions remain distressingly vague among Westerners. Taylor provides critical clarification by precisely delineating the tensions among life goods, hypergoods, constitutive goods, and moral sources, and by explicating the shape of the spiritual challenge posed by these tensions in terms of a dilemma of mutilation that afflicts many Westerners' cravings for affirmation. Thus, theist and nontheist alike should attend carefully to Taylor's spiritual reflections, for with unprecedented subtlety, he articulates the contours of a spiritual challenge commonly but confusedly discussed in terms of a quest for meaning.

53. Skinner, "Modernity and Disenchantment," 45.

Chapter 2

Modern Metaphysics, Dangerous Truth, Post-Moral Ethics

The Revealing Vision of Bernard Williams

So, what is the final word on the celebrated analytic philosopher Bernard William's final work, *Truth and Truthfulness*? Is it, as *The Economist* contended in an otherwise admiring obituary, so obviously the "swan-song of a sick man" that reviewers, "forbore to draw attention to its faults"?[1] Was Thomas Nagel right—despite his warm observation that a "virtuoso blend of analytic philosophy, classical scholarship, historical consciousness, and uninhibited curiosity marks *Truth and Truthfulness* unmistakably as a work by Bernard Williams"—that *Truth and Truthfulness* constitutes "a very strange project," for it attempts a bizarre, impossible twist on Nietzsche, trying to derive intrinsic moral values from a wholly materialist, wholly historicist genealogy of morals?[2]

Is it the case, as an *Ethics* review concluded, that *Truth and Truthfulness* is "disappointing in its treatment of truth as opposed to myth, or perhaps interpretation"?[3] And is this not tragic if it is true, as the review also contends, that for "ingenuity, provocativeness, breadth of knowledge, and sharp, elegant, highly memorable writing, there is no one to touch

1. *Economist*, June 28, 2003, 83.
2. Nagel, "Honesty and History," 26–28.
3. Fleischacker, "Review of *Truth and Truthfulness*," 381.

43

Williams"? And, given that the explicit ambition of *Truth and Truthfulness* was to defeat dangerous "deniers" like Richard Rorty—Williams's prime named nemesis—is it not tragic when Barry Allen, in an otherwise highly respectful essay in *History and Theory*, is nonetheless forced to a devastating conclusion:

> Williams seems to think that being serious about truthfulness requires being serious about truth, in a sense that goes beyond due concern for accuracy and sincerity, neither of which presuppose anything beyond contingent discursive practice. He seems to think that being serious about truth requires acknowledging a standard transcending the contingent consensus of cultural politics. That is why Rorty's pragmatism is so wickedly wrong. Yet there is no argument for either assumption in this book, which on this point must look to Rorty as fifty percent missing the point (no pragmatist denies the value of truthfulness), and fifty percent begging the question.[4]

Is it not tragic when Allen's conclusion is echoed in a *Theological Studies* review which, though it applauds Williams's "care and honesty," calls for "sharper positions" and takes Williams to task for a sophomoric oversight, namely, of attempting "to consider truth and truthfulness without ever entering the debates about the notion of truth itself"?[5] In sum, does, "swan-song of a sick man" constitute our most generous response to *Truth and Truthfulness*? Or, is something more subtle and far more significant going on?

This essay argues that *Truth and Truthfulness* makes clear that Williams, moving rigorously within analytic philosophical parameters, has long, though not without ambiguity, been traveling along a Nietzschean trajectory. The reading advanced here is slightly strong, insofar as it moves beyond any orienting framework ever explicitly and unambiguously suggested by Williams. But the extensive use of Williams's own words should make clear that the conclusions are not unduly forced—and in their light it becomes clear that Williams's final work is no faltering swan-song, but a brilliant strategic effort designed, for socio-political reasons, to confound straightforward reading. More significantly, this essay attempts to delineate a profound but largely unarticulated philosophical consensus among Western philosophers typically considered to be in almost wholesale opposition. For instance, it will become clear that the often fierce feud between Williams and Rorty is a spat between close philosophical siblings. Indeed, contrary to common misperception, it should become clear that the sole remaining

4. Allen, "Another New Nietzsche," 375.
5. Kerlin, "Review of *Truth and Truthfulness*," 221.

disagreement Williams has with Rorty concerns what Williams takes to be Rorty's naïve faith in truth.

WILLIAMS: ETHICAL REALIST

Williams is frequently read as an ethical realist. It is in this vein that Allen in *History and Theory* concluded that Williams "seems to think that being serious about truth requires acknowledging a standard transcending the contingent consensus of cultural politics." With the same realist expectation, the *Ethics* reviewer concluded that *Truth* is "disappointing in its treatment of truth as opposed to myth."[6] *The Economist* concluded that Williams, "never managed to work out the extent to which objective truths of the sort to be found in science (which he firmly believed in unlike some postmodern thinkers) could also be found outside it."[7] And *Theological Studies* lamented that, since it "is clear that he presupposes something like a correspondence notion [of truth]," it is a shame he did not defend it, for "defending the presupposition explicitly would have made for a more direct confrontation with thinkers like Rorty."[8]

Many passages can be cited that seem to indicate that Williams intended to argue for objectivity in ethics just as he famously argued for objectivity in science in *Descartes: The Project of Pure Inquiry* (1978). In 1981, in the preface introducing the essays collected in *Moral Luck*, Williams notes that there are analogous demands for "objectivity" in science and morality, and reminds readers that "to assess those claims and to compare them remains a central and pressing demand on philosophy."[9] In 1985, in *Ethics and the Limits of Philosophy*, Williams does caution that "we must reject the objectivist view of ethical life as in that way a pursuit of ethical truth," but immediately notes that this, "does not rule out all forms of objectivism. There is still the project of trying to give an objective grounding or foundation to ethical life."[10]

In the "Postcript" to *Ethics*, moreover, Williams says that the book rests on assumptions that "some people will think are optimistic. They can be compressed into a belief in three things: in truth, in truthfulness, and in the meaning of an individual life."[11] "Truth," Williams reminds us, and

6. Fleischacker, "Review of *Truth and Truthfulness*," 381.

7. *Economist*, June 28, 2003, 83.

8. Kerlin, "Review of *Truth and Truthfulness*," 221.

9. Williams, *Moral Luck*, xi.

10. Williams, *Ethics and the Limits of Philosophy*, 152.

11. Williams, *Ethics and the Limits of Philosophy*, 198.

in particular "objective truth," is something of which the natural sciences are capable.[12] Some, Williams continues, deny objectivity to natural science in a "misplaced rhetoric of comfort."[13] Admittedly, the "idea that modern science is what absolute knowledge should look like can be disquieting," but beyond futile attempts to shore up ethics by bringing down science, "What matters more, and may have something to do with comfort or with optimism, is how far notions of objective truth can be extended to social understanding."[14] In particular, Williams continues, if we are dealing with "thick ethical concepts," then we are justified in considering that "the judgments made with these concepts can straightforwardly be true."[15]

References to intrinsic value, the values of truth, ethical knowledge, and to ethical judgments that are straightforwardly true are sprinkled throughout Williams's writings, and *Truth*, which is dedicated to vindicating the "value of truth," the "virtues of truth," "plain truth," "truthfulness," and "realism," certainly seems to continue in this vein. In *Truth*, Williams inveighs bitterly against postmodern "deniers" like Rorty. "Deniers" are those who "cheerfully leave the values of truthfulness as instrumental and accept that there is no intrinsic value to these qualities at all."[16] For Williams, this is a momentous political issue. Deniers are a real danger to society, Williams maintains, for "no society can get by . . . with a purely instrumental conception of the values of truth."[17] Deniers remain oblivious, claiming:

> there is no value of truth: they think that the value of these states or activities, if they have any, is not to be explained in terms of truth, and it is this I reject. For instance, they may say that even if some people think it is very important in itself to find out the truth, there is not really any value in having true beliefs beyond the pragmatic value of having beliefs that lead one toward the helpful and away from the dangerous. Some who hold just this much may be very moderate deniers; so far as the everyday concept of truth is concerned, they may even belong to the common-sense party. But I shall claim that they as much as the more radical deniers need to take seriously the idea that to the extent that we lose a sense of the value of truth, we shall certainly lose something and may well lose everything.[18]

12. Williams, *Ethics and the Limits of Philosophy*, 198–99.
13. Williams, *Ethics and the Limits of Philosophy*, 198–99.
14. Williams, *Ethics and the Limits of Philosophy*, 198–99.
15. Williams, *Ethics and the Limits of Philosophy*, 200.
16. Williams, *Truth and Truthfulness*, 59.
17. Williams, *Truth and Truthfulness*, 59.
18. Williams, *Truth and Truthfulness*, 7.

Williams's unabashed "may well lose everything" makes explicit a fear that animates many of Rorty's most vociferous critics. By the end of *Truth* one realizes Williams is profoundly worried about the future of Western civilization. He fears that if we lose our sense for the intrinsic value of the virtues of truth, we will lose all ability to legitimate duly vested authorities, and "if no authority, then only power."[19]

In response, Williams defends the *intrinsic* value of truth and truthfulness. Thereby, Williams declares, he does not:

> have the problem that some deniers have of pecking into dust the only tree that will support them, because my genealogical story aims to give a decent pedigree to truth and truthfulness. Some of it aims to be, quite simply, true. As a whole, it hopes to make sense of our most basic commitments to truth and truthfulness.[20]

All this in marked contrast to the dangerous, "demure civic conversation of Richard Rorty's ironist," or the "smug nod that registers a deconstructive job neatly done."[21]

WILLIAMS: ETHICAL REALIST?

If Williams is an ethical realist in the straightforward sense suggested in the foregoing section, then critics are right to conclude that Williams's attempt in *Truth* to derive intrinsic moral values from a genealogy is "very strange" and confused (Nagel). In the balance of this essay, I argue that the truth is more subtle and revealing. I advance a reading of the Williams who is a convinced moral relativist, and so delineate the considerable common ground he shares with Rorty, seeking to clarify the parameters and implications of a pivotal but often unspecified consensus among contemporary intellectuals, namely, that the dangerous but undeniable truth is that, contrary to long-cherished but now vanquished hopes, modern metaphysics entails the abandonment of morality and ethics as understood and cherished by most everyone in the West for more than two millennia. In Williams's vocabulary, the dangerous truth, foreseen by Nietzsche, is that modern metaphysics requires post-moral ethics.

It is Williams's appreciation of the danger of this truth that makes his relationship to truth deceptively complex. It is why in *Truth* Williams insists

19. Williams, *Truth and Truthfulness*, 8.
20. Williams, *Truth and Truthfulness*, 19.
21. Williams, *Truth and Truthfulness*, 18.

that our "hope can no longer be that the truth, enough truth, the whole truth, will itself set us free."[22] It is why Williams thinks that contemporary Western civilization is in fact dependent upon denial of the truth, why he warns against making that fact transparent and why, in his closing sentence, he urges us to continue a delicate task barely begun in *Truth* in the hope that someday, "the ways in which future people will come to make sense of things will enable them to see the truth and not be broken by it."[23] Indeed, as I attempt to make clear, it is primarily his sense for the danger of the truth that separates Williams from Rorty.

METAPHYSICAL REALISM AND ETHICAL TRUTH

In his celebrated *Descartes: The Project of Pure Inquiry*, Williams defended the ability of science "to give absolute explanations of a determinate and realistically conceived world."[24] Williams's defense of modern scientific metaphysical realism in *Descartes* lies at the core of his thought. In particular, there is the fundamental ontological fact that ultimately the sphere of what *is* is wholly physical. This fact definitively distinguishes the physical sciences. The physical world exists in and of itself. This, Williams argues, is why it makes sense in science to talk about truth as a matter of correspondence between our ideas and the world, to see science as world-guided and thereby capable of objectivity, to see scientific claims as universally valid, and to talk about the ideal—functional if perhaps unattainable—of an "absolute conception" upon which scientific knowledge converges.

The same ontological fact means that the sorts of objective truths found in science can be found nowhere else. For while science is about an independent physical world, the social sciences, including ethics and philosophy (except where it serves as handmaiden to the natural sciences) are about a world that is wholly derivative, a world originated and sustained by social forces. This means that scientific realities (e.g., that which science names "electrons") have autonomous ontological status (i.e., they in-themselves

22. Williams, *Truth and Truthfulness*, 268.

23. Williams, *Truth and Truthfulness*, 269. Williams's complex relationship to truth will also explain the cryptic close to his opening chapter (cited in part above): "my genealogical story aims to give a decent pedigree to truth and truthfulness. Some of it aims to be, quite simply, true. As a whole, it hopes to make sense of our most basic commitments to truth and truthfulness. Whether, if it were to succeed in doing that, it could as a whole properly be called 'true' is doubtful but unimportant. It is certainly less important than that the story as a whole should be truthful" (Williams, *Truth and Truthfulness*, 19).

24. Williams, *Descartes*, 302.

exist), but ethical realities (e.g., justice, good, evil) do not (i.e., their existence is entirely derivative). Precisely Williams's uncompromising defense of modern scientific metaphysical realism, then, entails his rejection of metaphysical realism and objectivity in the humanities.

While Williams explicitly drew this conclusion at the close of *Descartes*, making clear the implications of modern scientific metaphysical realism for ethics and morality is the whole point of *Ethics and the Limits of Philosophy*.[25] In *Ethics*, Williams reiterates:

> If [ethical knowledge] is construed as convergence on a body of ethical truths which is brought about and explained by the fact that they are truths—this would be the strict analogy to scientific objectivity—then I see no hope for it.[26]

Even if there were to emerge global "convergence in ethical outlook," Williams makes clear, that will not have happened "because convergence has been guided by how things actually are, whereas convergence in the sciences might be explained in that way if it does happen."[27] This is so because making ethical judgments involves capacities "involved in finding our way around in a social world, not merely the physical world, and this, crucially, means *in some social world or other*," which will be the product of one of "many different cultures . . . differing in their local concepts."[28] Unlike scientific truths, ethical truths are relative to culture. *That*, argues Williams, is "the truth in relativism."[29] In short, Williams says bluntly, "science has some chance of being more or less what it seems, a systematized theoretical account of how the world really is, while ethical thought has no chance of being everything it seems."[30]

Williams is driven to these conclusions by "reflection." "Reflection" names the uncompromising, rigorous, objective ratiocination of modern analytic philosophy and science. "Reflection" produces "theory," which in

25. Williams, *Descartes*, 302. See also Williams, *Moral Luck*, ix–x.

26. Williams, *Ethics and the Limits of Philosophy*, 151–52.

27. Williams, *Ethics and the Limits of Philosophy*, 136. The future may well bring convergence, but that would be due only to factors such as "assimilation and a higher degree of interdependence," for there is no ethical truth "out there" guiding convergence. It is not relativism that limits philosophical ethics but ontology. Even if humanity developed a method agreed to be universally valid for ethics, the method would not be objective and its conclusions would not be truths in the scientific sense (Williams, *Making Sense of Humanity*, 178).

28. Williams, *Ethics and the Limits of Philosophy*, 150.

29. Williams, *Moral Luck*, 132, 141–43. Says Williams, "the only area in which I want to claim that there is truth in relativism is in the area of ethical relativism" (132).

30. Williams, *Ethics and the Limits of Philosophy*, 135.

the natural sciences is guided by the objective reality of the physical world. Insofar as there is no objective reality to guide ethics, there is in ethics no metaphysical realism, and no possibility of reflection, theory, correspondence truth, or objective knowledge. Varieties of ethical realism, however, are intrinsic to popular Western ethical understanding. Thus the popular understanding of Western ethics is in tension with the dominant trajectory of Western science and philosophy, for rigorous reflection entails rejecting as incomprehensible in ethics realist ideas of truth, knowledge, and objectivity that are valid in science. That is, contrary to modern hopes, modern metaphysics entails ethical relativity (again, to be clear, the salient point does not pivot upon ethical differences, this relativity would obtain even if there were global ethical consensus).

Reflection, then, poses a threat to Western civilization because it produces intolerable ethical "transparency." "Transparency" in Williams names recognition of the contingency (i.e., relative to culture, non-realist status) of ethical concepts that are traditionally entertained as objectively true. Reflection, then, yields knowledge that makes the derivative, contingent status of ethics intolerably transparent. In this way, "in ethics, *reflection can destroy knowledge*."[31] Indeed, as *Ethics and the Limits of Philosophy* is dedicated to making clear, reflection *will* destroy any classically realist version of ethical knowledge (e.g., Jewish, Christian, Platonic, Aristotelian, Kantian, Hegelian).

This makes evident a practical reality that gives Williams pause. Our most prized ethical values are sustained only by contingent social structures, traditions, and practices. Their status is precarious, for they exist by virtue of nothing other or deeper than "people's dispositions."[32] The "preservation of ethical value," then, "lies in the reproduction of ethical dispositions."[33] Williams, therefore, attends especially to how theory supports ethical dispositions, our seemingly innate and instinctual *felt* sense of ethical obligation.

For those interested, like Williams, in preserving the values of the Enlightenment, attention to the role of "people's dispositions" flashes a critical caution. For, consistent with Enlightenment expectations, people's ethical dispositions are overwhelmingly realist. Thus "transparency" poses

---

31. Williams, *Ethics and the Limits of Philosophy*, 148. Williams does speak loosely of "thick" ethical concepts that "survive reflection," but it turns out that he means by this only that these particular concepts reside so deep in our psyches that they in fact endure even after their contingency has been unmasked. As Williams clarifies: "The thick concepts under which we can have some pieces of ethical knowledge are not themselves sustained by knowledge, but by confidence" (Williams, *World, Mind, and Ethics*, 208).

32. Williams, *Ethics and the Limits of Philosophy*, 51.

33. Williams, *Ethics and the Limits of Philosophy*, 51.

a potent real-world threat, a threat that suggests one should not simply tell the truth and undercut the realist understandings supporting the vast majority's ethical dispositions. The threat is especially clear in light of two specific consequences of modern metaphysical realism: free will is fantasy and mainstream understanding of morality is incoherent.

MORALITY, THE "PECULIAR INSTITUTION"

Williams's fundamental ontology is not only wholly materialist, it is wholly mechanistic. Everything that happens—including our every thought and action—is a product of either determinate causal antecedents or (possibly) quantum indeterminacies.[34] This emphasis upon mechanism is obvious when Williams talks about "moral luck," though here *The Economist* manifests a popular misunderstanding:

> He coined the term "moral luck" to mark a fact that is incomprehensible to Kantians, but which—once he had highlighted it—came to seem undeniable: that whether or not a person's behaviour emerges as good or bad can sometimes depend on pure chance.[35]

The "moral luck" *The Economist* highlights has long been understood. What is incomprehensible to Kantians is conjoining "moral" and "luck" when *everything* is luck, which is Williams's position.[36] That is, what is incomprehensible is holding people morally responsible for actions they had no power to prevent. Kantians think it only makes sense to talk about moral responsibility where a person might have done otherwise—where there is freedom *and* free will.

Williams not only realizes but intends for "moral luck" to sound "radically incoherent."[37] For the phrase makes clear the implications of the fact that modern scientific metaphysical realism has no conceptual space for free will. For modern science, the murderer who smothers you no more exercises free will than the avalanche that smothers you.[38] Williams's interest in conjoining

---

34. See, for instance, the essays collected in the first section of Williams, *Making Sense of Humanity.*

35. *Economist*, June 28, 2003, 83.

36. Williams, *Moral Luck*, 21.

37. Williams, *Moral Luck*, 20–21.

38. Of course, the murderer will have intentions, desires, plans, and ideas that the avalanche does not have, but the critical point is that the murderer has no free will regarding the content of the intentions, desires, plans, and ideas, nor over the action to which they inexorably lead.

"moral" and "luck" is precisely about interrogating "moral" in an in/deterministic world where all actions and events are entirely a matter of luck.

The "bitter truth (I take it to be both)," Williams says, "is that morality is subject to luck."[39] It is a bitter truth, Williams concedes, because, first:

> skepticism about the freedom of morality from luck cannot leave the concept of morality where it was, any more than it can remain undisturbed by skepticism about the very closely related image we have of there being a moral order, within which our actions have a significance which may not be accorded to them by mere social recognition.[40]

More poignantly, it is a bitter truth because the pressure for "a voluntariness that will . . . cut through determination, and allocate blame and responsibility on the ultimately fair basis of the agent's own contribution," is itself the expression of an ideal presented in a "most moving" fashion by Kant: "the ideal that human existence can be ultimately just."[41]

Unfortunately, these hopes—for an autonomous moral order, for significance beyond social recognition, for free will, for fair blame and praise, for ultimate justice—are all utterly beyond reach.[42] Moreover, continues Williams, alluding to the ubiquity of the modern scientific rationality wherein two familiar deterministic trajectories of explanation, nature and nurture, exhaust science's explanatory repository for human action, this is, if not consciously acknowledged, "known to everyone, and it is hard to see a long future for a system committed to denying it."[43]

All of this, Williams knows, undercuts ideas of ethical truth, free will, and moral responsibility at the conceptual core of modern Western democracies. In particular, by debunking free will, reflection undercuts morality. Williams thinks morality is a "peculiar institution" not only because as almost universally understood it is conceptually incoherent (i.e., insofar as it traffics in "free will"), but because as long "as morality itself remains, there is danger in admitting the fact [of its incoherence], since the system

39. Williams, *Moral Luck*, 21.

40. Williams, *Moral Luck*, 39. Williams is not quite a compatibilist because he does not think morality is compatible with determinism (he calls it a "bitter" truth). Neither, however, does he quite fall into the category of hard determinist, insofar as it tends to remain fixed within extant options. He calls himself a "reconciler" because he wants to develop resources—many extant but poorly understood—that will allow us to embrace new understandings of freedom, character, and ethics within the bounds of modern scientific metaphysical realism.

41. Williams, *Ethics and the Limits of Philosophy*, 195.

42. Williams, *Ethics and the Limits of Philosophy*, 195.

43. Williams, *Ethics and the Limits of Philosophy*, 195.

itself leaves us, as the only contrast to rational blame, forms of persuasion it refuses to distinguish in spirit from force and constraint."[44] In short, "morality" has a built-in defense mechanism which threatens our society if we dare allow reflection to assail it:

> morality makes people think that, without its very special obligation, there is only inclination; without its utter voluntariness, there is only force; without its ultimately pure justice, there is no justice. Its philosophical errors are only the most abstract expressions of a deeply rooted and still powerful misconception of life.[45]

Morality is part of a "deeply rooted and still powerful misconception" which—*caution*—sustains our civil order. Undercut morality without developing—not only in theory, but in people's dispositions—an alternative, and the potentially ferocious contraries morality mitigates—inclination, force, injustice—will be unleashed. The reality, then, is that our society's ethical and civil order is primarily secured by an institution which, due to its irrationality, is increasingly unstable. That, thinks Williams, makes morality a peculiar, and a peculiarly dangerous, institution.

DANGEROUS TRUTH

Rigorous reflection in the light of modern scientific metaphysical realism and "an ideal of truthfulness," Williams explains matter-of-factly, leads inexorably to the "fact summarized in the slogan 'God is dead'—that the traditional metaphysical conceptions . . . have terminally broken down."[46] For Williams this is *the* truth: reality is only and wholly "extension" in the Cartesian sense (e.g., wholly physical, wholly bodily, wholly material, wholly mechanical). Typically, when Williams speaks of the truth, not "truth," "simple truth," "the virtues of truth," "truthfulness," or "the values of truth," but *the* truth, he has this sober, rigorous vision in mind.

This is the truth Williams admires Nietzsche for facing squarely. This is the truth which may not be bearable, which threatens civilization. This is the truth that, if immediately it became generally and transparently known, most probably would *not* set us free. For this truth entails first, that no good, evil, justice, or injustice is part of the ultimate fabric of the world (i.e., the dream that the world might ultimately be just is not just wrong but empty),

44. Williams, *Ethics and the Limits of Philosophy*, 195.
45. Williams, *Ethics and the Limits of Philosophy*, 196.
46. Williams, *Truth and Truthfulness*, 13.

and second, that there is no free will (thus no moral responsibility in the everyday sense, no ultimately fair basis for allocating praise or blame). Thus the truth poses at least two ethical challenges, one existential, one political. First, how, in full knowledge of the truth, will one value and understand oneself? Second, how will society effectively preserve civil and moral order? The challenge lies in negotiating an epochal shift, for the truth warns us that people's ethical dispositions must come to be sustained in a world "irreversibly different . . . from any world in which human beings have tried to live."[47]

At root, both existentially and politically, Williams contends, the basic challenge stems from the fact that our recognition of the contingency of our ethical ideals, given current Western understanding, will "be in tension with something that our ethical ideas themselves demand, a recognition of their authority."[48] A sense for the authority of our ethical ideals must be maintained. We must find a new way of affirming their intrinsic value. Given the truth, no objective, extra-cultural, ethical realist appeal is possible, so, following Nietzsche, Williams delivers a genealogy, *Truth and Truthfulness: An Essay in Genealogy*. In contrast to Nietzsche, however, Williams means for his genealogy to be "vindicatory," to "make sense of our most basic commitments to truth and truthfulness,"[49] to "show why truthfulness has an intrinsic value; why it can be seen as such with a good conscience; why a good conscience is a good thing with which to see it."[50]

WILLIAMS'S REVISED CARTESIANISM: THE TWO SPHERES

How does Williams establish the intrinsic worth of contingent values? He knows the task is impossible by definition. So he changes the definitions. Arguably, he follows his own suggestion in *Ethics* and goes "in a direction opposite to that encouraged by ethical theory" by allowing "reflection" itself to carve out a logically distinct sphere of "reflective criticism."[51] That

47. Williams, *Ethics and the Limits of Philosophy*, 197. Later, in *Shame and Necessity*, Williams turns hopefully to the pre-Socratic Greek society of Homer to see what lessons might be learned from a society that did live innocent of any of the traditional metaphysical conceptions (see below).

48. Williams, *Truth and Truthfulness*, 20–21.

49. Williams, *Truth and Truthfulness*, 19.

50. Williams, *Truth and Truthfulness*, 263. Williams wants not a Nietzschean "transvaluation of all values," but new and coherent support for modern Western civilization's highest values. Notably, Williams's humanitarian and democratic values appear to be virtually indistinguishable from Rorty's.

51. Williams, *Ethics and the Limits of Philosophy*, 117.

is, though he nowhere articulates this division himself (i.e., this is where this reading becomes particularly strong), Williams basically delineates two distinct spheres of discourse, one pertinent to the physical world (i.e., reflection), one pertinent to social worlds (i.e., reflective criticism), each with a logic appropriate to the distinct ontological status of its own sphere.[52]

The sphere of *reflection* is the sphere of modern science. It concerns the physical world. It takes an "external" perspective and involves modern realism about the world, objectivity, truth as correspondence, world-guidedness, universality, and knowledge as a function of certainty. It is the sphere within which ethical values are recognized as culturally relative and contingent (in this sphere, reflection destroys ethical knowledge).

The sphere of *reflective criticism* is the sphere of ethics. It addresses social worlds and operates wholly within some social world or another. It applies where concepts "express knowledge about the world to which they apply"—those worlds that are, ontologically, wholly dependent upon the discourse of some community.[53] So reflective criticism takes an "internal" (to culture) perspective.[54] Accordingly, knowledge in this sphere is local, subjective, and absent any extra-communal ontological support. In this sphere, one abandons "the error of thinking that what conviction in ethical life has to be is knowledge, that it must be a mode of certainty."[55] Knowledge in ethics is a function of confidence.[56] Of course, Williams cautions, "we do not want the confidence of bigotry—if there is to be confidence, it should be reasonable confidence," but this should satisfy our ethical needs, for, "reasonable confidence in what is indeed true is knowledge."[57]

"Reasonable" and "true" here must be understood and affirmed in relation to the logic of reflective criticism (not of reflection), that is, as indexed to the perspectives and considered opinions of one's own culture. There is no appeal to reason or truth that will allow us to draw an objective line between "reasonable confidence" and "bigotry." Nonetheless, Williams thinks we gain enough traction from this shift to facilitate talk of ethical knowledge. If

52. Williams never explicitly divides his work in terms of these two spheres, but I am contending that, as I will illustrate, they helpfully describe a *de facto* division within his thought. Barry Allen names roughly the same divide I am invoking when he speaks of "Williams' Nietzschean transposition of philosophy's concept of truth from the metaphysics of realism to the genealogy of values" (Allen, "Another New Nietzsche," 367).

53. Williams, *Ethics and the Limits of Philosophy*, 147.

54. For the passage contrasting internal and external perspectives, see Williams, *Ethics and the Limits of Philosophy*, 51.

55. Williams, *Ethics and the Limits of Philosophy*, 168–69.

56. Williams, *Ethics and the Limits of Philosophy*, 170–71.

57. Williams, *Making Sense of Humanity*, 203.

one asks in the sphere of *reflection* if a society has ethical knowledge, then the answer is clearly "no." But if one asks in the sphere of *reflective criticism*, then the answer can be "yes." For the question is not asking for scientific certainty or objectivity, but about concepts that "express knowledge about the world to which they apply," and since, in the sphere of reflective criticism, this world is precisely the social world sustained and defined by that society, then, to the degree that society knows itself and has settled opinions (e.g., "thick" ethical concepts), that society has ethical knowledge.[58]

Within the sphere of reflective criticism, which dominates the conceptual space of *Truth*, Williams speaks freely of such things as ethical knowledge, ethical truth, realism, the virtues of truth ("Accuracy" and "Sincerity"), plain truths, everyday truths, and facts. These terms must be understood intra-culturally. "Plain truths," for instance, are not certainly, objectively, or absolutely true.[59] "Plain truth" designates a claim that would gain spontaneous agreement from all local observers. A "fact" that is "an everyday truth" or "plainly true" for us may, for another culture, equally be "plainly false."[60] When it comes to ethical disputes *between* cultures there is no higher court of appeal—again, that is Williams's "truth in relativism."

Likewise, for the "virtues" or "value" of truth. Williams begins *Truth* admitting that in the "strict sense" such talk is a category mistake and explaining vaguely that he means these phrases as "short-hand for the value of various states and activities associated with the truth."[61] Williams's extended discussions of his two virtues of truth, "Sincerity" and "Accuracy," are very insightful. But despite the capital letters, they boil down to perceptive descriptions of extant Western values. Sincerity is about representing oneself honestly. Accuracy is about taking care with one's reflections (e.g., avoiding wishful thinking or intellectual laziness). Realism, notably, is defined as

---

58. Williams, *Ethics and the Limits of Philosophy*, 147. The passage is worth quoting in full: "It is important to be quite clear what ethical knowledge is in question. It is knowledge involved in their making judgments in which they use their thick concepts. We are not considering whether they display knowledge *in using those concepts rather than some others*: this would be an issue at the reflective level. The question 'does the society possess ethical knowledge?' is seriously ambiguous in that way. The collective reference to the society invites us to take the perspective in which its ethical representations are compared with other societies' ethical representations, and this is the reflective level, at which they certainly do not possess knowledge. There is another sense of the question in which it asks whether members of the society could, in exercising their concepts, express knowledge about the world to which they apply them, and the answer to that might be yes" (147).

59. Williams, *Truth and Truthfulness*, 49.

60. Williams, *Truth and Truthfulness*, 51, 10.

61. Williams, *Truth and Truthfulness*, 7.

an aspect of Accuracy, where it boils down to the everyday idea of "being realistic" or "getting real."[62] Williams does spend several pages declaring Accuracy's demand that science use "truth-acquiring methods." But, as Barry Allen notes, Williams never manages to give criteria for "truth-acquiring" and finally just abandons the effort.[63]

Williams, then, revises the Cartesian dualism by ordering the spheres ontologically. Descartes considered the spheres of mind and of matter to be equally ultimate. For Williams, in accord with modern scientific metaphysical realism, only the sphere of the physical is ontologically ultimate. The sphere of mind is real for us, but is wholly derivative. The distinct logics of reflection and reflective criticism follow. The threat, again, stems from the fact that contemporary "morality" turns upon confused varieties (Platonic, Christian, Cartesian, Kantian) of ontological dualism. Our challenge is successfully to negotiate a transition to a civil society in which the truth (i.e., that only the sphere of the physical is ontologically ultimate) is generally and transparently known.

WILLIAMS'S NEWLY AUSTERE
METAPHYSICAL REALISM

In *Truth*, Williams retreats significantly from the full-bodied modern scientific metaphysical realism he had affirmed in *Descartes*. Following Donald Davidson, Williams now affirms the scientific realist idea of "an independent order of things to which our thought is answerable" only in the severely curtailed sense that objects mentioned in empirical statements "play a causal role in the formation of our true beliefs, while, conversely, our thoughts about them and, specifically, our wishes do not affect the objects' existence unless those thoughts are mediated by causally effective interventions."[64] There is nothing in this bare affirmation of realism that even Rorty does not affirm. Williams admits, furthermore (again, explicitly following Davidson), that, given his newly austere realism, there is "no useful content to the idea that a given fact makes a given sentence true," and thus that, "there can be no interesting correspondence theory [of truth]."[65] Williams does not explicitly abjure his hallmark notion of the "absolute conception,"

62. Williams, *Truth and Truthfulness*, 127.
63. Williams, *Truth and Truthfulness*, 133; Allen, "Another New Nietzsche," 371.
64. Williams, *Truth and Truthfulness*, 136.
65. Williams, *Truth and Truthfulness*, 64–65.

but, as Allen notes, it appears in *Truth* precisely once, in a footnote, without defense, characterized as "controversial."[66]

Notably, Williams minimizes his "absolute conception" as early as *Ethics*, where, with a positive reference to Rorty, he agrees that, "there is an insoluble difficulty with the notion of 'the world' as something that can determine belief."[67] As Allen realizes, Williams's appropriation of Davidson now mirrors Rorty's. Allen interprets all this as a move away from metaphysical realism, exclaiming, "with metaphysical realism set aside, Williams and Rorty disagree less than ever."[68] *This is importantly incorrect. To the contrary, what becomes visible is a highly austere yet highly significant version of metaphysical realism affirmed both by Williams and Rorty (de facto), along with by far the mainstream of analytic philosophy and science and, indeed, by Western intellectuals across disciplines.*

This austere version of modern scientific metaphysical realism is consistent with Rorty's own Davidsonian anti-representationalism. It is the realism Rorty affirms in his understanding of "world" even as he urges us to "distinguish between the claim that the world is out there and the claim that the truth is out there."[69] It is the realism he affirms in the "physicalism" of Davidson's non-reductive physicalism and anomalous monism.[70] It is the realism behind the physicalism, determinism, and compatibilism he praises in Daniel Dennett's *Darwin's Dangerous Idea* and *Freedom Evolves*.[71] It is why he says in *Philosophy and the Mirror of Nature* that, "physicalism is probably right in saying that we shall someday be able, 'in principle,' to predict every movement of a person's body (including those of his larynx and his writing hand)."[72] It is why in *Contingency, Irony, and Solidarity* he equates human creativity with physical novelty, why he urges us to learn to "treat chance as worthy of determining our fate," and why he suggests we "attempt to see a blind impress as not unworthy of programming our lives or our poems."[73] I cannot here detail the point, but elsewhere I argue that this austere metaphysical realism is a fourth dogma of empiricism from which

---

66. Allen, "Another New Nietzsche," 370; Williams, *Truth and Truthfulness*, 295n19.

67. Williams, *Ethics and the Limits of Philosophy*, 138. Along this trajectory, even in the midst of a severe review of *Contingency, Irony, and Solidarity*, Williams affirms Rorty's work in *Philosophy and the Mirror of Nature* (Williams, "Getting it Right," 3–5).

68. Allen, "Another New Nietzsche," 373.

69. Rorty, *Contingency, Irony, and Solidarity*, 4–5.

70. Rorty, *Objectivity, Relativism, and Truth*, 113–25.

71. Rorty quotes on book jackets of Dennett's *Darwin's Dangerous Idea* and *Freedom Evolves*, and also in "Cranes and Skyhooks," 62–66.

72. Rorty, *Philosophy and the Mirror of Nature*, 354.

73. Rorty, *Contingency, Irony, and Solidarity*, 6–20, 22, and 35.

Rorty has yet to extricate himself, the penalty being a severe short-circuiting of his vaunted celebration of poetic self-creation.

This version of metaphysical realism is such a deep background premise of modern thought that Allen unwittingly but precisely identifies it when discussing intrinsic value.[74] Intrinsic value, notes Allen, is a new idea in Williams. This is surprising, he explains matter of factly, because it:

> is also a notion philosophers tend to be wary of, much as they are wary of teleological ideas. An "intrinsic" value, it seems, would have to be valuable all on its own, valuable by its "essence," its "intrinsic" nature. But like perception or perspective, value is relative to us. Nature has no values, as it has no purposes. *It is primary qualities, physical mechanism, cause and effect.*[75]

Williams has indeed reduced his claims even in science to this austere metaphysical realism: the world in-itself is primary qualities, physical mechanism, cause and effect (i.e., Descartes's sphere of extension). This austere realism is retained while the ideas of facts making theories true, of truth as correspondence, and the intelligibility or functionality of an absolute conception are all abandoned. More on this presently.

INTRINSIC VALUE AND THE METAPHYSICALLY AMBITIOUS

We can now understand how Williams derives truth and intrinsic value from genealogy:

> I suggest that it is in fact a sufficient condition for something (for instance, trustworthiness) to have an intrinsic value that, first, it is necessary (or nearly necessary) for basic human purposes and needs that human beings should treat it as an intrinsic good; and second, they can coherently treat it as an intrinsic good.[76]

Williams explains that for people coherently to keep hold on the intrinsic value of a good even as they see its instrumental origins (i.e., its tie to basic purposes and needs), it is required only that they be able to relate the good "to other things that they value, and to their ethical emotions."[77] With regard to the virtue of "Sincerity," for instance, "the motivations of honour and

---

74. Allen, "Another New Nietzsche," 365.

75. Allen, "Another New Nietzsche," 366 (emphasis mine).

76. Williams, *Truth and Truthfulness*, 92.

77. Williams, *Truth and Truthfulness*, 91–92.

shame play an important part."[78] The "intrinsic value that Sincerity bears makes it an unlovely idea to turn into a liar."[79] It is not only the unattractiveness of being viewed negatively by others, Williams explains, but also the way in which one's status as a liar "involves a sense of oneself and of the respect one might have or lose from people one can oneself respect."[80] It is precisely this interlaced set of virtues and desires—nothing other, above, or prior to them—which gives Sincerity intrinsic value. Likewise with all other intrinsic values.[81]

Williams's argument is not existentially weak. The social-psychic forces that circumscribe certain goods as, for us, "intrinsic" are nicely described by Charles Taylor in *Sources of the Self* in terms of "constitutive goods" and "inescapable frameworks of meaning."[82] Given our socio-cultural conditioning, there are a variety of goods over and against which we cannot help but judge ourselves. For instance, given who we are, and assuming (or, more precisely, defining) mental health, it would be literally and absolutely impossible for any of us even to torture a small child for days, then slaughter and consume her, let alone to do so while seeing ourselves as good. This makes manifest what are for us a set of, in Williams's terms, "intrinsic" goods (and evils).

If one understands "basic human purposes and needs" in this context (i.e., in terms of an existential need to see and value ourselves as good), then it is inconceivable that we would abandon these goods. Nonetheless, Taylor would make the obvious point that while Williams's account may explain why certain values are inescapable, it does not establish their intrinsicality. How can we coherently ascribe intrinsic value?[83] As Allen pointed out, Williams's ontology should disallow any such predication of "intrinsic."[84]

---

78. Williams, *Truth and Truthfulness*, 120.

79. Williams, *Truth and Truthfulness*, 120.

80. Williams, *Truth and Truthfulness*, 121.

81. This—not appeal to objective ethical truth—explains the "thickness" of thick ethical concepts (see notes 16 and 44, above).

82. Taylor, *Sources of the Self*, Part 1. Williams approvingly references Taylor's parallel work on "frameworks" in *Sources of the Self* in World, Mind, and Ethics. In *Sources of the Self*, Taylor credits Williams's early work in refutation of utilitarianism as a source of inspiration (53). In *Truth and Truthfulness*, Williams develops his point via a fascinating contrast between Rousseau and Diderot (chapter 8).

83. Williams, *Truth and Truthfulness*, 92.

84. As the scare quotes betray, Allen's own desperate attempt to make Williams make sense only highlights the problem: "Intrinsic value is not a value inhering in things 'intrinsically.' It is a matter of our *valuing* them 'intrinsically,' that is, non-instrumentally, as providing sufficient reasons for or against action (including speech)" ("Another New Nietzsche," 367).

Williams is impatient when pressed so, for he understands the challenge to traffic in an illicit metaphysic. His predication of "intrinsic" occurs within the sphere of reflective criticism. The challenge comes from the sphere of reflection. Taylor, of course, is well aware of the contingent character of our most basic ethical convictions. In *Sources*, Taylor, beginning from Plato and Augustine, traces the concrete, contingent, historical emergence of the goods that, to greater and lesser degrees, Westerners today experience as inescapable. But, despite his historicism, Taylor remains open to the classic realist (idealist) option, suggesting we might plausibly, "treat our deepest moral instincts, our ineradicable sense that human life is to be respected, as our mode of access to the world in which ontological claims are discernible and can be rationally argued about and sifted."[85] Thus he can raise the question over intrinsicality.

Despite his evident fondness for Taylor, on this point Williams is blunt and dismissive. For on the basis of modern scientific metaphysical realism—that is, on the basis of the truth—Williams *knows* Taylor is wrong. Taylor allows wishful thinking to compromise his naturalism, he has forsaken realism (in Williams's modern sense), he has fallen victim to "the 'siren songs of old metaphysical bird-catchers' . . . calling 'you are more, you are higher, you are of a different origin!'"[86] All such wistful understanding, Williams contends, confusedly takes ethical resonance for ethical reference.[87] Truthfulness should lead Taylor to accept the truth, no matter how bitter. Taylor should allow a thoroughgoing naturalism to cleanse him of irrational metaphysical dreams.

Similar metaphysical ambitions afflict moderns who still demand theory in ethics (the demand of "cognitivism"). The "demand for a cognitive genealogy of liberalism seems particularly pressing," Williams explains, "because our attachment to its principles is so often represented as a triumph of moral understanding."[88] But there is "no plausible cognitive account" of liberalism, nor could there be: "there is no true teleological history of liberalism, because (roughly speaking) there is no true teleological history of anything."[89] Williams judges cognitivism to be not only quixotic, but existentially confused. In *Ethics* (taking aim at Thomas Nagel's *View from Nowhere* and John Rawls's *Theory of Justice*), he urges us not even to desire

85. Taylor, *Sources of the Self*, 8.

86. Williams, *World, Mind, and Ethics*, 203, citing Nietzsche, *Beyond Good and Evil*, section 230.

87. Williams, "Ethics and the Fabric of the World," 177.

88. Williams, *Truth and Truthfulness*, 264.

89. Williams, *Truth and Truthfulness*, 264.

escape from the contingencies of our subjectivities and local judgments: "I must deliberate *from* what I am. Truthfulness requires trust in that as well, and not the obsessional and doomed drive to eliminate it."[90]

Similarly, with regard to justice, Williams urges us to adopt a naturalistic, Humean "common interest" account as opposed to "a Platonic idealization of that interest."[91] The only ones who will be "dissatisfied" with this, Williams chides, are those "who already have an ethically ambitious view of justice."[92] We must empty our minds, Williams warns, of the Kantian "obsession" with the notion of "a Moral Law that governs us all equally without recourse to power," for, "there is no Moral Law."[93] With regard to free will being fantasy, that will be worrisome "only for those who have metaphysical expectations . . . there is a problem of free will only for those who think that the notion of the voluntary can be metaphysically deepened."[94] In light of all of this, it should not be surprising that whenever "the concept of truth is itself inflated into providing some metaphysical teleology of human existence, of the kind [Nietzsche] rejected in Platonism," Williams explicitly *affirms* Rortian insouciance and smug deconstruction.[95]

Williams sees no philosophical problem in his inability to give metaphysical depth to truth, justice, good, evil, free will, or intrinsic value. The problem is his critics' illicit, classically realist, and so terminally confused, metaphysical ambitions. Williams is disappointed but not surprised to find even scholars confused, for the denial of the truth is at the core of the entire Western moral history Taylor traces. Contrary to standard understanding, the story of the development of modern conceptions of "freedom, autonomy, inner responsibility, moral obligation and so forth"—from Plato and Augustine to Kant and Hegel—is not, as "progressivists" would have it, a tale of emerging moral maturity, but of "the accretions of misleading philosophy."[96] Taylor's magisterial account of the sources of modern identity may be brilliant and even accurate, but it is a history of a massive confusion. It may explain why we find the truth bitter, even unbearable, but it cannot guide us into a truthful future, for it depends upon denial of the truth.

90. Williams, *Ethics and the Limits of Philosophy*, 200.

91. Williams, *Truth and Truthfulness*, 36.

92. Williams, *Truth and Truthfulness*, 36.

93. Williams, *Truth and Truthfulness*, 122.

94. Williams, *Shame and Necessity*, 68.

95. Williams, *Truth and Truthfulness*, 18. Williams also explicitly rejects the last-gasp Habermasian attempt to salvage Platonic-style realism by grounding it within the essential dynamics of communication (*Truth*, 225–32).

96. Williams, *Shame and Necessity*, 5, 21.

SHAME AND NECESSITY

Modern morality considers the Homeric Greeks "premoral." "The Greeks were indeed children," Williams says, "and young children, in a Piagetian tale of moral development."[97] But morality, the "peculiar institution," is precisely the problem. So for Williams access to a society like Homer's, which existed innocent of morality, is useful, for in truth we:

> are in an ethical condition that lies not only beyond Christianity, but beyond its Kantian and Hegelian legacies. . . . We know that the world was not made for us, or we for the world, that our history tells us no purposive story, and that there is no position outside the world or outside history from which we might hope to authenticate our activities . . . we are like those who, from the fifth century [BCE] and earlier, have left us traces of a consciousness that had not yet been touched by Plato's and Aristotle's attempts to make our ethical relations to the world fully intelligible.[98]

Williams has no ambition of simply reinstating Homeric ways, nonetheless, we may find "things of a special beauty and power in what has survived from that world."[99] We may learn, for instance, how to construct an ethic of shame and necessity, an ethic that can stand transparently before the truth. And we can work to substitute an ethic of shame and necessity for our morality of guilt and free will. Defending such an ethic and explaining how it might accommodate many of our most prized modern ethical affirmations is the task of *Shame and Necessity*, Williams's most straightforward attempt to suggest some beginning contours of a post-moral ethic. The degree to which *Truth and Truthfulness* is an accommodation to confused post-Socratic expectations is evident when one notes that in *Shame and Necessity* attention to realism, truth, truthfulness, and intrinsic value is *entirely* absent.

Of course, Williams realizes that we will find moral understanding more attractive than pre- or post-moral. Being ourselves products of a two-millennia plus confusion, we will naturally find the truth, which requires rejection of morality, to be bitter. For against all Christian, Platonic, Aristotelian, Kantian, and Hegelian dreams, the truth requires us to forsake the thought that "in this life or the next, morally if not materially, as individuals or as an historical collective, we shall be safe; or, if not safe, at least reassured that at some level of the world's constitution there is something to be

97. Williams, *Shame and Necessity*, 77.
98. Williams, *Shame and Necessity*, 166.
99. Williams, *Shame and Necessity*, 167.

discovered that makes ultimate sense of our concerns."[100] In truth—that is, as we know in light of modern metaphysics—no.

WILLIAMS AND THE DENIERS

One can understand why Rorty thinks that Williams has joined him on "the dark side" and expresses puzzlement over Williams's "hostility to pragmatism in the first half of [*Truth*]."[101] Ironically, Rorty is puzzled because he is thinking philosophically. Williams's disgust with the deniers is not philosophical but practical. Williams, in contrast to the deniers, appreciates the practical value of the bankrupt metaphysical conceptions the "deniers" are blithely "pecking to dust."[102] The deniers:

> want everyone to agree that the virtues of truth have a purely instrumental value. But what makes them think that if everyone agreed with this, the virtues of truth would still have the same instrumental value—indeed, that they would exist at all?[103]

The work of Rorty, Williams contends, "provides a striking example of what in this respect might be described as running on empty."[104] Rorty's "we pragmatists" encourage us to get over worries about truth and to focus our compliments upon "technical and social benefits, solidarity, democracy, the discouragement of cruelty, and other laudable ends."[105] What such deniers do not consider, Williams stresses, is that "even if the ideals of discovering and telling the truth were themselves illusions, [even] if the idea of 'the truth' were itself empty, *those illusions might well play a vital part in our identifying and pursuing those objections*."[106] In a revealing footnote to this passage Williams says that "Rorty's position is an illustration of a famous

---

100. Williams, *Shame and Necessity*, 164.

101. Rorty, "To the Sunlit Uplands," 13–15.

102. Williams, *Truth and Truthfulness*, 19.

103. Williams, *Truth and Truthfulness*, 59.

104. Williams, *Truth and Truthfulness*, 59.

105. Williams, *Truth and Truthfulness*, 59.

106. Williams, *Truth and Truthfulness*, 59 (emphasis mine). For instance, Saul Smilansky, in *Free Will and Illusion*, argues that though free will is an illusion, it should nonetheless be affirmed because it is a social necessity. Along these lines, in *Truth and Truthfulness* Williams grants that, "It is not foolish to believe that any social and political order which effectively uses power, and which sustains a culture which means something to the people who live in it, must involve opacity, mystification, and large-scale deception," but, he continues, we can still live "in the hope" that this is not true (232).

and deep joke ascribed to Sydney Morgenbesser: 'Of course pragmatism is true; the trouble is that it doesn't work.'"[107]

Williams is profoundly worried that the truth will undercut the only extant source of authority for the already fragile ethical ideals now preserving civility and justice (and, in particular, protecting the weak from the strong). A first casualty of the truth, Williams warns, is likely to be "the Kantian sense of presented duty."[108] One must also remember that for the vast majority the truth will be intolerably "bitter," so the response could well involve a vigorous, irrational, and violent reassertion of the old myths. Williams thinks our situation is perilous.

In this context, Williams thinks blithely "cheery souls" like Rorty demonstrate dangerous faith in the truth with reckless attempts to make it immediately transparent. Rejecting such naïve faith in truth, Williams pragmatically concludes that the "hope can no longer be that the truth, enough truth, the whole truth, will itself set us free."[109] Williams's publications reveal a multi-faceted strategy. Roughly, in *Descartes*, *Moral Luck*, *Ethics*, and *Making Sense of Humanity*, he explicates the truth and its existential, moral, and ethical implications. In *Shame and Necessity*, looking to the Homeric Greeks, he investigates resources for a post-moral ethic, thereby contributing to the long-term task of creating new institutions that will "support and express" prized liberal values and standards for existential valuation.[110] Such a wholesale transformation, however, will take generations. So, in *Truth and Truthfulness* Williams works practically to "broaden the we" that shares liberal values by shoring up support for the virtues of truth.[111] In particular, though Williams no less than Rorty thinks classically realist understandings of truth, truthfulness, Accuracy, Sincerity, and intrinsic value are incoherent, he considers such terms to be as yet too potent to abandon. Thus he works to revalue the terms, so that we (in particular, Western intellectuals) can continue to use them with a clear conscience.

The danger, of course, is that people might realize that Williams is retaining classic moral language but dropping classic moral realism. Many are likely to conclude that Williams too is running on empty and that Rorty, if equally problematic, is at least more straightforward. (Rorty, for his part, might wonder if after all Williams was right on this final, wholly political

---

107. Williams, *Truth and Truthfulness*, 285n14.
108. Williams, *Making Sense of Humanity*, 180.
109. Williams, *Truth and Truthfulness*, 59, 268.
110. Williams, *Truth and Truthfulness*, 268–69.
111. Williams, *Truth and Truthfulness*, 268.

and rhetorical point of disagreement.)[112] Williams certainly recognized the precariousness of his position. "But," one can imagine him quite reasonably retorting, "in the midst of this epochal shift in ethical understanding, that is, in light of the dangerous truth unveiled by modern metaphysics and the consequent need for post-moral ethics, what better alternative do we have?" At any rate, at this point we can more fully appreciate both the urgency and the dogged optimism of the final lines of *Truth*, his final book, where he calls on those with ears to hear to prepare for general apprehension of the dangerous truth via a transvaluing of our most prized ethical ideals, a transvaluing that builds conceptual and political institutions that will secure our ethical ideals upon post-moral ground:

> The hope can no longer be that the truth, enough truth, the whole truth, will itself set us free. But it is a lot more than the hope, merely, that the virtues of truth will keep going—in some form or other, they are bound to keep going as long as human beings communicate. The hope is that they will keep going in something like the more courageous, intransigent, and socially effective forms that they have acquired over their history; that some institutions can exist that will both support and express them; that the ways in which future people will come to make sense of things will enable them to see the truth and not be broken by it.[113]

Of course, the concerns of the many critics of Rorty who worry over nihilism, and who may have thought that in Williams they had an ally, will now be directed at Williams as well. But now there should be more clarity over where concern and arguments for moral realism must be focused. For Williams has rightly discerned the dangerous truth that modern metaphysics entails the rejection of the versions of morality and ethics cherished by the vast mainstreams of Western civilization for more than two millennia. That is, Williams has rigorously discerned the ethical and moral implications of a highly austere and significant version of metaphysical realism which is

---

112. In the final chapter of *Contingency, Irony, and Solidarity*, Rorty says, "The fundamental premise of the book is that a belief can still regulate action, can still be thought worth dying for, among people who are quite aware that this belief is caused by nothing deeper than contingent historical circumstances" (189). The widespread consternation with which Rorty's work was greeted even among intellectuals would seem to recommend Williams's more cautionary judgment regarding reaction to such a deflating premise. In fairness to Rorty, one should note the increasingly practical/political focus of his work over the last decade (e.g., *Achieving Our Country* and many of the essays collected in *Philosophy and Social Hope*).

113. Williams, *Truth and Truthfulness*, 268–69.

now affirmed by the mainstreams of philosophy and science and, indeed, by Western intellectuals across disciplines. Critics who want something stronger than a genealogy behind their ethical convictions need to do far more than critique messengers like Williams or Rorty, they need to take on that incredibly potent and broad modern metaphysical consensus. Those convinced any such quest would be Quixotic, on the other hand, should attend to Williams's pragmatic chastening of Rorty, and think carefully over how to proceed in light of the frightening socio-political dangers of the truth.

Chapter 3

Chalcedonian Reason and the Demon of Closure

My prey in this essay is elusive. It is not so much an articulated principle as a haunting of reason. It associates reason and closure. It portrays—*needs*—knowledge as something that we, after great effort, finally, clearly, *wholly* grasp, understand, comprehend. Emmanuel Levinas—describing it as a sort of "gripping"—traces its lineage to Aristotle's metaphysics.[1] Charles Taylor identifies it as reason's background urge to homogenize or converge. Within multiple areas of inquiry, but perhaps most devastatingly within theology, it makes chimeric concerns appear urgent, encourages false trajectories of inquiry, fosters unnecessary fears, propagates intolerance, and instigates violence—all without quite itself appearing. I call it the demon of closure.

The demon of closure instills in us the conviction that rationality entails extant conceptual coherence. It is, in fact, an irrational extension of an essential principle of reason, the principle of non-contradiction. By hugging tightly to non-contradiction, the demon of closure has long portrayed itself as an obvious aspect of Western rationality. "After all," it asks innocently, "I'm only asking that all your ideas be *coherent*. What in the world could be more reasonable than that?" In modernity, the demon of closure worked intimately with its less subtle sibling, the demon of certainty. The demon of

1. Levinas, *The Levinas Reader*, 76.

certainty is largely exorcized. But not—despite the efforts of Levinas and Taylor, among others—the demon of closure. In this essay, I strive clearly to unveil the demon of closure so that, finally, it too might be exorcized.

I begin with Charles Taylor's critical exposure of the demon of closure in the context of modern philosophy's free will/determinism debate. Second, I sketch the demon's haunting of the Patristic trinitarian and christological controversies, and its recent haunting of theology *vis-à-vis* the problem of evil. Third, I roughly delineate and champion what I call "Chalcedonian reason" (Taylor calls it "revised transcendental reasoning"), which emerges in the wake of the exorcism of the demons of certainty and closure.[2] Chalcedonian reason is as old as Job, emerges amazingly triumphant, if unrecognized, in the Patristic period, fosters humility and openness to the Spirit, and is wonderfully consonant with Christian theology and spirituality.

CHARLES TAYLOR'S EXORCISM OF THE DEMON OF CLOSURE

In his 1971 essay "How is Mechanism Conceivable?" Taylor illustrates the conceptual promise of overcoming the demon of closure's irrational demands when he tackles the "antinomy of mechanism," that is, the antinomy between actions and events (i.e., free will/determinism). The antinomy is familiar. The mechanistic causal explanations typical of modern science leave no conceptual space for agentival ascriptions. There are no freely chosen *actions*, only *events* happening along a causally deterministic/random continuum.[3] This is significant, for exclusive appeal to mechanism means that all our intentions and actions are necessary products of causal streams that antedate us. We do not originate or influence our own "actions." Thus is denied the reality of, among other things, free choice, creativity (in contrast to novelty), and moral responsibility. Given the success of mechanistic science, it can seem reasonable to expect the eventual triumph of mechanism. "After all," asks Taylor, "we have not privileged the ordinary teleological view of inanimate object behaviour which earlier attempts at physics enshrined. Why should we be more tender with animate behaviour?"[4]

2. Detailed defense of Chalcedonian reason is impossible here, but its broad outline and promise should emerge clearly.

3. Note that randomness no more funds free will than does determinism.

4. Taylor, *Human Agency and Language*, 169. Also critical to my argument is Taylor's work on the validity of revised transcendental argument (Taylor, *Philosophical Arguments*, 20–33).

Taylor's audacious and seemingly non-philosophical response is that the wholly mechanistic account is *"just too preposterous to be believed."*[5] But while Taylor adamantly refuses to accept the ultimate triumph of mechanism, neither will he baptize Cartesian dualism or any occasionalist doctrine to resolve the antinomy. Nor will he reject mechanism. Indeed, Taylor has no counter-suggestion regarding resolution of the antinomy. Nor does he legitimate or even acknowledge any urgent need to provide one. And with precisely that lack of concern, Taylor illustrates the overcoming of the homogenizing, converging spirit that has long haunted epistemology—he has exorcized the demon of closure.

Taylor points out that there is no *a priori* way to invalidate either mechanistic or agential understandings. Moreover, both vocabularies are *indispensable* to our richest and most complete articulations about ourselves and our world. At present, we can no more make sense of our lives if we reject the mechanistic vocabularies of the natural sciences than if we reject the agential vocabularies of the humanities. Both vocabularies are presently indispensable to understanding. So, where does Taylor stand? Well, since Taylor realizes we cannot dismiss either mechanistic or agential vocabularies, and since neither vocabulary can fulfill all the needs met by the other, he fully embraces *both* of these mutually exclusive (i.e., incommensurable) vocabularies.[6]

He cannot, of course, embrace either as a *final* or *absolute* vocabulary, and so he remains open to further developments, to creative modifications in our understanding that might mitigate the tensions. At this point, however, he has no such modifications to suggest, nor can he dismiss either vocabulary. So, adopting the most rational position imaginable, he retains both vocabularies, oscillating between them according to ordinary if *ad hoc* conventions—utilizing deterministic, event vocabularies when dealing with earthquakes or the cold in his chest, and free will, action vocabularies when evaluating a colleague's ethical culpability, or when with thanks he accepts credit for praiseworthy insights.

Standing thus, Taylor asks his title question, *"how* is mechanism conceivable?" And he speculates that it is conceivable that we will someday evolve an enriched mechanistic vocabulary that will *not* "show . . .

5. Taylor, *Human Agency and Language*, 169. It turns out that Taylor's position is more problematic than I indicate here; see further on this my later essay on free will, chapter 5 below.

6. Note that "incommensurable" simply means that no common coordinate system can currently be found in relation to which one might adjudicate among vocabularies. It does not follow that we are incapable of *understanding* more than one incommensurable vocabulary.

intentional concepts to be eliminable at a more basic level."[7] Some future vocabulary may save the all dominant phenomena—the major aspects of the
mechanistic causal phenomena to which modern scientific theory attests,
and the major aspects of the agentival purposeful phenomena to which several millenia of first-person experience attest. This new vocabulary will be
not quite mechanistic in the sense we understand today, and it will be not
quite agentival in the sense we understand today. Taylor is gesturing toward
the possibility of a genuinely new vocabulary. But we do not yet know this
vocabulary. So, for the present Taylor quite reasonably stands upon incommensurable vocabularies, frankly acknowledging the lacunae and tensions,
and remaining open to any promising developments.[8]

Note that Taylor is not *anti*-closure. A single vocabulary serving all
the indispensable purposes now served by event and action vocabularies
may emerge. On the other hand, such a vocabulary may simply lie beyond
our (or anyone's) conceptual ken. Perhaps the two causal streams are simply
and finally incommensurable. We must admit the possibility that our fullest understanding may involve the unending embrace of incommensurable
vocabularies that we appeal between on an *ad hoc* basis. This means that the
seemingly innocent demand that all our ideas be coherent (i.e., commensurable) is, in instances such as these, *unreasonable*.[9]

The demon of closure, however, hugging tightly to the principle of
non-contradiction to camouflage itself, demands total conceptual coherence *now*. This homogenizing drive for conceptual closure compels determinists to opt for the consistency of a full-blown mechanism. It is critical
to realize that *any such premature theoretical move, which seems obviously
rational to those possessed by the demon of closure, is motivated not by new
discovery, enhanced explanatory productivity, the clear conceptual dominance*

7. Taylor, *Human Agency and Language*, 179.

8. This is why Taylor labels this "revised transcendental reasoning." Kant famously
utilized transcendental reasoning in his critique of pure reason. Given that we can
make synthetic *a priori* judgments, he asked, what must be our epistemic capacities?
As is now commonly agreed, we cannot make synthetic *a priori* judgments, so Taylor
proffers *revised* transcendental reasoning. Here is his transcendental question: given
that a mechanistic vocabulary is indispensable and incommensurable with an agentival vocabulary, and given that the agentival vocabulary is also indispensable, *how* is
mechanism conceivable?

9. The overwhelming majority of the time, the demand for extant coherence is
perfectly reasonable. But if incommensurable vocabularies are internally coherent and
indispensable (as determined by a communally broad and historically deep consensus
of qualified evaluators), *then* the demand for extant conceptual coherence is unreasonable. I am here gesturing toward a looser form of indispensability than does Taylor, who
aims at a sort of revised apodicticity (Taylor, *Philosophical Arguments*, 20–33).

of any single vocabulary, or the promise of more enriching articulation, but only by the desire for closure itself.

On Taylor's account, the demon appealed to our intellectual hubris with an epistemological "temptation . . . to a . . . self-possessing clarity," a clarity mortally threatened if we understand ourselves according to two incommensurable vocabularies.[10] It is this temptation that leads the vast majority of today's philosophers and scientists to conclude, with determinism and in stark rejection of first-person experience, that popular notions of free will are chimeric. Even many determinists concede our experience of free choice and the attractiveness of the idea, but in the end they succumb to the epistemological temptation to preserve the clarity and finality of reason at all costs. Thus the totalizing impulse to conceptual closure. That is the hubris that, ironically, yields the dehumanizing, mechanistic view.

But Taylor shrugs his shoulders. Taylor's revised transcendental approach prevents any hubris regarding our current epistemic capacities from forcing us to dismiss indispensable aspects of self-understanding. We are to keep everything that's just too preposterous to throw out—which is simply a modest and utterly reasonable way of beginning with what we honestly and most confidently affirm, and of arguing realistically over the relative strength of various affirmations after the irrational demand for closure has been abandoned. We in fact daily use and presuppose the accuracy of incommensurable mechanistic (e.g., when we turn on our computer) and intentional (e.g., when we assign moral praise or blame) vocabularies. So Taylor accepts mechanistic *and* intentional vocabularies.

Taylor's post-closure temper keeps him from seeing the incommensurability itself as the problem. Taylor has exorcized the demon of closure. So he is not tempted to generate literally unbelievable and unlivable theories whose sole point is to ameliorate the incommensurability but which otherwise do nothing to resolve real doubts or real problems. Incommensurability surely points to conceptual rifts, attention to which may hold special promise for the creation of new vocabularies, but the incommensurability itself is not a problem upon which to focus, and resolving incommensurability should not in itself be a prime goal of inquiry. We rightly retain focus upon the real problems that challenge us. But we must shed the hubris inspired by the demon of closure, the hubris that demands, *now*, a single, coherent vision of the world. Someday we may attain unto a comprehensive "mechanistic" account, but for now we should continue fully to affirm and

10. Taylor, *Philosophical Arguments*, viii.

with rigor and enthusiasm continue to develop the currently incommensurable vocabularies of both the natural sciences and the humanities.[11]

THE PROMISE OF CHALCEDONIAN REASONING FOR CHRISTIANITY: CASE STUDIES

The promise of revised transcendental reasoning (henceforth, Chalcedonian reasoning) for Christianity can be illustrated in conversation with three representative loci: the trinitarian and christological controversies, and the problem of evil.[12]

The Trinitarian Controversy

Chalcedonian reasoning is not marginal in the Patristic period. To the contrary, it defines the spirit of the reasoning which, after tremendous struggle with the epistemological demon's drive toward closure, prevailed in the trinitarian and christological controversies (albeit surreptitiously). The Council of Nicea's (325) affirmation of the *homoousious* aggravated an already bitter fight over the relation of the Father and Son that was resolved only when the Council of Constantinople (381) specified that the Father, Son, and Spirit were three *hypostases* and one *ousia*. "A superficial glance at the polemical literature of the period," comments J. N. D. Kelly, "leaves the impression of a battle-royal between Sabellians and Arians."[13] These "epithets" were indeed front and center in the debate but, Kelly notes, with the exception of some

---

11. A recent example of revised transcendental reasoning was the incommensurability involved in understanding light simultaneously in terms of waves and particles. In the face of this incommensurability, and the powerful justification for each vocabulary, scientists had no choice but to oscillate on an *ad hoc* basis between wave and particle vocabularies. Much to the annoyance of many scientists, theologians quickly drew comparisons to Jesus Christ being fully human and fully divine. Scientists, however, saw the incommensurability as a tremendous problem, so the analogies drawn to Jesus Christ were hardly seen as appeals that lent either intelligibility or credibility to the christological affirmation. (I am told the incommensurability in understanding light has now been resolved mathematically.) My appropriation of Taylor will specify why the particle/wave incommensurability (resolved or no) very nicely illustrates the wisdom of revised transcendental reasoning, and why careful christological comparison is appropriate.

12. I analyze the controversies in conversation with J. N. D. Kelly's classic, *Early Christian Doctrines*. In the notes I argue that Kelly, though unawares, nonetheless delineates brilliantly the thwarting of the demon of closure.

13. Kelly, *Early Christian Doctrines*, 238–39.

highly visible extremists, *neither side was actually either Sabellian or Arian.* Kelly cites Socrates (*c.* 380–450), a contemporary historian:

> The situation was exactly like a battle by night, for both parties seemed to be in the dark about the grounds on which they were hurling abuse at each other. Those who objected to the word *homoousios* imagined that its adherents were bringing in the doctrine of Sabellius and Montanus. So they called them blasphemers on the ground that they were undermining the personal subsistence of the Son of God. On the other hand, the protagonists of *homoousios* concluded that their opponents were introducing polytheism, and steered clear of them as importers of paganism. . . . Thus, while both affirmed the personality and subsistence of the Son of God, and confessed that there was one God in three hypostases, they were somehow incapable of reaching agreement, and for this reason could not bear to lay down arms.[14]

The upshot of the contentious debate was the classic three *hypostases* and one *ousia* formula. The critical conceptual work that would thwart the demon of closure was done at the synod of Alexandria (362), which affirmed the "three *hypostases*" and the "one *ousia*" while disallowing anti-Sabellian and anti-Arians' reciprocal attacks upon *the logical entailments* of each other's positions.

Significantly, "*homoousious*" *does* logically entail some sort of Sabellianism. And "*homoiousious*" *does* logically entail some sort of Arianism. So the combatants' respective attacks were logically valid. But Alexandria directed focus upon and upheld the central positive affirmations: upholding the Arian metaphysical concern over the Oneness and holiness of God; and upholding the Athanasian soteriological concern over the full personality and subsistence of the Son.[15] And they thwarted the demon of closure by denying both sides full-fledged logical closure. The "three hypostases" was affirmed, but the polytheism it logically entails was rejected. The "one *ousia*" was affirmed, but the compromise of the discrete integrity of the subsistence, divinity, and personality of the Son that it logically entails was rejected. Father, Son, and Spirit were affirmed as three *hypostases*. The Godhead was affirmed as one *ousia*.

The formula, of course, is literally unthinkable. Not only were both sides in the debate required to abandon any claim to logical closure, but

---

14. Kelly, *Early Christian Doctrines*, 239–40.

15. See especially Kelly's description of this exact process in *Early Christian Doctrines*.

the affirmation itself requires abandonment of any claim to closure. At the beginning of the debate "ousia" and "hypostases" meant essentially the same thing. The resolution did not pivot on any magical redefinition of those terms such that the reality of "God, Father, Son, and Spirit, three *hypostases* and one *ousia*" could suddenly be grasped singly and whole. The confession is, in that sense, literally incoherent. It is very tempting but quite mistaken to appeal at precisely this juncture to "mystery."

"Mystery" is an important theological concept logically related to the claim that God is uniquely unique (*sui generis, totaliter aliter*). In the precise theological sense, however, it is critical to remember that to say, "God is love" is *just as mysterious* as saying "God is three *hypostases* and one *ousia*."[16] Theologically, "mystery" applies to anything predicated of God. The incoherence in the trinitarian formula, however, *afflicts the predicate itself.* To appeal to the mystery of God does not meet the objection—considered devastating by those haunted by the demon of closure—that the formula is literally incoherent (e.g., like confessing that God is a triangular round square—what could you possibly imagine you are confessing?). The objection pertains not to predication *vis-à-vis* God, but to the utter meaninglessness of babbling an unthinkable thought as a confession. The perceived potency of this objection results from the haunting of the demon of closure.

Chalcedonian reasoning (it could as easily be "Alexandrian reasoning"), without any philosophically objectionable special pleading, allows theologians to articulate a historically and theologically precise and utterly reasonable defense of the trinitarian formula. Recall the pattern of Taylor's revised transcendental reasoning. Incommensurable, extant intentional (action) and mechanistic (event) vocabularies are both indispensable. So it is completely unreasonable to allow a presumptuous and premature drive for closure to force the rejection of either. Analogously, early Christians found confession of God's Oneness and Holiness, and of the full divinity and discrete integrity of the personhood of the Father, of the Son, and of the Spirit to be indispensable to full articulation of their faith. So, utterly reasonably, Constantinople rebuffed premature drives for closure and affirmed confession of all these vocabularies.

Of course, we cannot think "one *ousia* and three *hypostases*" any more than we can think "triangular round square" or "event action."[17] But just as there are significant experiential and philosophical reasons to affirm both

16. [In light of my later work on general revelation, I would qualify this assertion about how mysterious it is to say "God is love."]

17. So, it is unsurprising, for instance, that when various Fathers in their individual writings attempted to grasp singly and whole the *hypostases/ousia* relationship they inevitably slid toward one "heresy" or another.

event and action vocabularies, so there are significant experiential, theological, and liturgical reasons to affirm the vocabularies of each of the three
hypostases and of the one *ousia*. This is not irrational, for we are not denying
the principle of non-contradiction, we are simply and quite reasonably denying the demon of closure's invidious demand for *extant* conceptual closure.[18]

We should take care to remember that, since the vocabularies are currently incommensurable, one should not attempt to speak more than one
at a time. To be very precise, when making the confession we should not
understand ourselves to be confessing, as if thought singly and whole, "three
hypostases and one *ousia*." That *is* literally impossible. We should understand ourselves to be confessing, *as discrete conceptual moments*, each of the
three *hypostases*, and also, *as a discrete conceptual moment*, the one *ousia*
(i.e., four vocabularies).[19] It is not "triangular circle" but, in discrete conceptual moments, "triangle" *and* "circle" (in a case where, though they cannot
be thought together, each is confessed with equal power). Just as we cannot
but oscillate on an *ad hoc* basis between event and action vocabularies, so
we cannot but oscillate on an *ad hoc* basis when talking about God in terms
of each of the three *hypostases*, or as one *ousia* (thus avoiding an otherwise
inevitable slide toward either modalism or tritheism).[20] Of course, none of
this means that the trinitarian confession may not be mistaken. But those
convicted of its truth need not worry that it is either incoherent or irrational.

18. Kelly affirms the formula's virtues but, subtly haunted by the demon, describes
Alexandria's distinctive approach in terms that are hopelessly vague: "[Alexandria]
formally recognized that what mattered was not the language used but the meaning
underlying it" (*Early Christian Doctrines*, 253). Nonetheless, Kelly's summary of Alexandria's accomplishment superbly if unwittingly illustrates the form and promise of
Chalcedonian reason (see especially *Early Christian Doctrines*, 253–54).

19. This clarifies the discrete theological vocabularies implicit in the formula. First,
the vocabularies of the Father, of the Son, and of the Spirit (i.e., *qua* three *hypostases*).
These vocabularies have two foci: a) the relation of each of the persons to us (economic
Trinity); b) the relation of the persons to one another (immanent Trinity). Note that
the immanent Trinity does not address God *in se*. We would not expect God *in se* to be
inconsistent with the immanent Trinity, but it should hardly be controversial to suggest
that God *in se* may far exceed the finite experience and understanding that has gener-
ated the trinitarian formula. Second (often confused with the vocabulary of the Father
or simply neglected), there is the vocabulary of God who is One (i.e., *qua* one *ousia*).
Each vocabulary deserves distinct and rigorous development.

20. Augustine wisely suggested this oscillating approach for discussion of the time/
eternity relation; namely, one cannot but speak either from the perspective of God's
temporality or of God's eternity (e.g., those who ask "what was God doing in eternity
before creating the world?" make a category mistake by mixing the two vocabularies,
for there literally is no time in eternity [no "before creating"]). See *Confessions*, Book
XI: 10 and 11. Revised transcendental reasoning is similarly applicable to discussion of
human freedom and providence or divine foreknowledge.

The Christological Controversy

Unfortunately, the revised transcendental reasoning utilized to resolve the trinitarian controversy was not explicitly identified and affirmed. Thus the bitter dynamics of the trinitarian controversy repeated themselves in the christological controversy, for the demon could still succeed in asking, "Precisely how are we to grasp the idea of a being which is human and divine?— I ask only that your theology be coherent."

Since only coherent christologies can meet the demon's demand, the Chalcedonian formula is excluded. Consider the "four adverbs" that summarize Chalcedon's affirmation that the divine and human natures are both found fully in Jesus Christ "without confusion, without change, without separation, without division." Two distinct substances simply cannot be united in such a fashion. *Necessarily* there is *either* confusion *or* division. The formula, for those demanding extant closure, is incoherent by definition (the affirmation, like "triangular circle," literally cannot be thought— here again, appeal to mystery is misplaced).

By contrast, Kelly notes that Apollinarius offered, "in fact the most subtle and thorough-going attempt to work out a theory of Christ's Person in the fourth century, and carried tendencies long accepted in the Alexandrian school to their logical limit."[21] Likewise, it is at junctures where Alexandrians like Athanasius, Gregory of Nazianzus, Gregory of Nyssa, or Cyril, or Antiochenes like Diodore of Tarsus, Theodore of Mopsuestia, or Nestorius, were most coherent and logical in describing the precise nature of the union of the two natures that their theologies came closest to coherence—and simultaneously veered towards troubled extremes such as "Apollonarianism" or "Nestorianism."[22]

---

21. Kelly, *Early Christian Doctrines*, 289. Likewise, Arius's theology was more coherent than the Nicene Creed's.

22. Notably, Kelly shows that Nestorius was "not a Nestorian," and that the "two sons" or adoptionistic doctrine his opponents detected "was a travesty of what Nestorius intended to teach" (Kelly, *Early Christian Doctrines*, 317). The root of Nestorius's troubles was his attempt to explain the human/divine relation precisely *via* a "common *prosopon*." This formulation *was* Nestorian and masked the saving inconsistences Kelly finds to be clear in his writings. Likewise, "nothing could have been more explicit" than that Eutyches, if "muddle-headed," was "no Docetist or Apollinarian." "The traditional picture of Eutyches, it is clear, has been formed by picking out certain of his statements and pressing them to their logical conclusion" (Kelly, *Early Christian Doctrines*, 331, 332–33). Cyril, like Nestorius, gets into trouble when he explains the human/divine relation precisely *via* "hypostatic union," but makes an enduring contribution when, eluding the demon's haunting, he accepts "two natures" and abandons "hypostatic union" (accepting a bare assertion of union) in the Symbol of Union because he is satisfied that affirming "two natures" would not be understood, "to lead logically

Chalcedonian christology represents a crisp conceptual pinnacle, if unrecognized, of reasoning free from the demon of closure. The dynamics are analogous to Alexandria and Constantinople. The problematic extremes of both the Alexandrian and Antiochene trajectories, Nestorianism and Apollinarianism, were rejected. At the same time, the central affirmations of the incommensurable Alexandrian and Antiochene trajectories, which had come to be indispensable for the richest Christian confession, practice, and liturgy, were all affirmed. The definitive brilliance of the negative formulation of the "four adverbs" lies precisely in the refusal to provide closure *via* "common *prosopon*," "hypostatic union," or any surrogates. Chalcedon even properly preserves incommensurable but indispensable affirmations by oscillating *ad hoc* among various vocabularies (e.g., " . . . as regards His Godhead . . . as regards His [humanness])."[23]

To those haunted by the demon, the formula looks utterly incoherent. In accord with Chalcedonian reasoning, however, the humble willingness to live upon multiple, strongly and reasonably attested incommensurable trajectories—affirming that which is indispensable and rejecting that which is most problematic (even if logically entailed by any single conceptual scheme)—it is utterly reasonable.[24] Though perhaps in contrast to any single

to a 'separation' of the natures"—where, logically, it certainly *does* lead (Kelly, *Early Christian Doctrines*, 323). If Kelly can see that it is obvious that the Sabellians were not Sabellian, the Arians were not Arian, Nestorius was not Nestorian, and Cyril and Eutyches were not Apollinarian, then such should have been obvious to all involved, and the self-righteous invective and violence that characterized the trinitarian and christological controversies and disgraced the gospel should have been entirely avoidable. But the spirit of the demon of closure (aligning itself with ambition for power?) prevailed among the major players, so the church was left with a shameful stain, a compromised witness, a distraction from mission, and many cautionary tales.

23. The Chalcedonian definition suggests development of four vocabularies: in regard to the humanity ("fully human"), in regard to the divinity ("fully divine"), in regard to the human who is God ("and"), in regard to the God who is human ("and"). Each vocabulary independently, though never in isolation, deserves rigorous development—the point of which is *never* closure for closure's sake (the so-called "christological problem" is an illusion of the demon).

24. I owe thanks to George Hunsinger, who in *How to Read Karl Barth* identifies the "Chalcedonian pattern" that characterizes Barth's thought (185–224). While reading Hunsinger, I realized that my excitement over the promise of Taylor's revised transcendental reasoning was not something *new*, but a recovery of reasoning already classic in the Christian tradition. Hunsinger's excellent analysis identifies almost precisely the dynamics I am highlighting. In my opinion, he rightly identifies a key to understanding Barth (see, for instance, his penetrating application of Chalcedonian reasoning to the question of how to understand the relationship of human and divine agency). However, both Hunsinger and Barth saw the Chalcedonian pattern as justified because the Subject of theological ratiocination is uniquely unique. Thus, they mount a defense of the literal incoherence of their affirmations with an appeal to mystery that facilitates

participant, the council of Chalcedon found unmitigated confession of both the full humanity and the full divinity of the Son to be indispensable to full articulation of the Christian faith. Humbly, it refused to allow a presumptuous and premature drive for closure to force any compromise of this confession. Utterly reasonably, it confessed the Son to be fully human *and* fully divine (two distinct conceptual moments, each affirmed with equal strength), "without confusion, without change" ("no" to closure *via* monophysitism or surrogates), and, "without separation, without division" ("no" to closure *via* dualism or surrogates).

❖ ❖ ❖

While never explicitly identified, at decisive moments in the Patristic debates over Trinity and christology, Chalcedonian reasoning triumphed over the demon of closure. In harsh battles characterized by a demand for closure, advocates tended to focus on the most problematic logical implications of their opponents' position while highlighting the most positive aspects of their own. All sides were correct regarding what was *logically entailed* by their opponents' positions. Therefore, as long as the demon of closure prevailed, compromise was impossible.

By contrast, the synod of Alexandria, the Symbol of Union, Leo's *Tome*, and the councils of Constantinople and Chalcedon implicitly exorcized the demon of closure by affirming the most positive affirmations of incommensurable positions insofar as they were indispensable to the faith, while simultaneously condemning problematic logical entailments. For those haunted by the demon of closure, the classic formulae are textbook illustrations of irrationality. "Triangle *and* square *and* circle? Fully round *and* fully cube? Your confessions are literally incoherent," exclaims the demon incredulously. "What could be more irrational, *stupid* frankly, than that?" By Taylor's wholly philosophical standards—no special pleading—they are utterly rational.[25]

---

the quite correct modern objection that theologians, on specious grounds, attempt to insulate themselves from basic and otherwise uncontested principles of rationality that are fundamental to modern thought. This validates the conclusion that central Christian affirmations are irrational. The mistake results from a misplaced appeal to mystery. Barth and Hunsinger's work can easily be modified in accord with Chalcedonian reasoning in order to strengthen their otherwise extremely insightful analyses.

25. Tragically, Kelly, still haunted by the demon, does not recognize the dynamics of Chalcedonian reasoning even as he brilliantly depicts it. Thus, he can only praise Alexandria as, "a practical step of great importance" (Kelly, *Early Christian Doctrines*, 253) and, "statesmanlike" (Kelly, *Early Christian Doctrines*, 254). He can only see Cyril's eventual decision to accept the Symbol of Union as "practical politics" (*Early Christian Doctrines*, 323). He feels compelled to comment that the four theses of Leo's Tome had

The "Problem of Evil"

The agonizing questions provoked by experience of evil are older than Job. But it is only in the modern period that the demon of closure has lured Christians into adopting a self-destructive stance *vis-à-vis* evil. "Theodicy" is the particularly modern affront that quintessentially manifests the haunting of the epistemological demons of certainty and closure. The very idea of "theodicy"—that *we* should set about to justify *God*—displays the arrogant spirit nurtured by the demon of certainty. But it is the demon of closure that presses the dilemma home. The modern problem of evil is concisely and (many have thought) devastatingly summed up in a single question. Affecting a soft, I-can't-dodge-the-obvious tone, the demon says, "But how can one simultaneously confess these three: 1) God's goodness, 2) God's omnipotence, and 3) the reality of evil?"

As the demon of closure is exorcized, the sense of urgency stimulated by this question dissipates utterly. Accompanying this realization is the somewhat stunning recognition that *evil is not even the subject of the modern "problem of evil."* The sole focus of concern lies in satisfying the demon of closure. Consider that two classic solutions to the modern "problem of evil" are: 1) to abandon belief in God's goodness, or 2) to deny God's omnipotence.[26] Note that both "solutions" leave evil utterly alone. The "solutions" in no way help name, prevent, or relieve any concrete evils (reject God's goodness or power and you are still left with exactly the same evil—and now you are without hope in God as well). The "solutions" are useless as guides to ministry, and they offer no direct spiritual or emotional relief.[27] They address only the concern raised by the demon of closure.

---

not "probed the Christological problem very deeply" (Kelly, *Early Christian Doctrines*, 337–38). He can only conclude the Chalcedonian definition is a product of an imperial demand, one which was finally accepted "[o]nly by dint of consummate skill and diplomacy" (*Early Christian Doctrines*, 339–40), and one best characterized as a "settlement" (Kelly, *Early Christian Doctrines*, 338). Kelly's political analyses are all surely right. His descriptions likely exhaust the self-understanding of all involved. But I am suggesting that at Alexandria and Chalcedon the community also made a momentous and brilliant epistemological maneuver and banished the demon from their communal affirmations, if not from their individual hearts and minds. Thus, the Christian can discern in the Conciliar trinitarian and christological definitions not mere pragmatic compromise, but a theologically and philosophically profound triumph of the Spirit.

26. Henceforth, in place of "omnipotence" I will use the theologically more appropriate confession that God's power is "sufficient." This shift in no way mitigates the conceptual tension among the three affirmations.

27. It may, of course, be true either that God is not good or that God is not omnipotent, but the existence of evil in itself does not entail either conclusion.

The third classic "solution" is to deny the reality of evil. While the conceptual dynamics are typically obscure, this is the "solution" I most frequently encounter among lay Christians (often with an allusion to "all things working together for good"). Haunted by the demon of closure, Christians sense vaguely but potently that evil threatens their affirmation of God's sufficiency and goodness. Thus, they struggle to deflect or mute the challenge. Commonly, for instance, they will suggest that many evils must have been *deserved*, and so are just. Other evils, they continue, may be teaching a valuable lesson, while others might be part of a larger plan with good ends. In these cases, too, they contend what *appears* to be evil is ultimately, and hence actually, for the good.

It may be true, of course, that *some* "evils" really are expressions of justice or are necessary pedagogically or as means to higher goods. But even a cursory historical survey of the vast evils perpetuated upon innocent millions to no discernible good renders any attempt to deal with evil by means of such denials morally and spiritually revolting. This third "solution" too in no way helps to name, prevent, or relieve any concrete evils. To the contrary, it aids and abets evil. Its obfuscation inhibits the struggle against evil, and the emotional and spiritual damage wrought upon victims by its machinations cruelly heightens their suffering. Voltaire was *right*—theologically, emotionally, spiritually, and politically—to mock Liebniz and his *Theodicy*. He was *wrong* to think he had mocked, or had even begun to have understood, how Christians actually can stand in the face of evil.

By contrast, Chalcedonian reason facilitates our embrace of two full-blooded but incommensurable Christian confessions: on the one hand, of our profound sense of the faithfulness of a good and sufficient God whose "yes" is reality's alpha and omega; on the other, of our sickening, heart-rending awareness of the unmitigated reality of evil both without and within. Given current understanding, both protest and confession must be full-blooded and uncompromised. Christians simultaneously confess with full confidence and lament with unmitigated ferocity (and, as the Psalms illustrate, such laments are rightly directed *at* God).

For those haunted by the demon of closure, "Where were you when I laid the foundations of the world" sounds like a desperate, irrational dodge. In truth, *Job* is an attack upon an irrational demand for immediate conceptual closure—*Job* attacks the demon of closure. None of this necessitates an abandonment of our demand that there be some ultimate—if currently unfathomable to any but God—explanation for evil. Neither does it mean we must silence those who in frustration and agony cry out at God. Chalcedonian reasoning reasonably prevents us from abandoning any of three powerful, independently attested, and currently incommensurable

Christian convictions: 1) evil exists; 2) God's power is sufficient to ensure the realization of all God's intentions (i.e., the standard, "God is omnipotent"); 3) God is good.

The demon of closure, in a brilliant deception, has tricked even Christians into seeing this threefold affirmation itself as the paradigmatic "problem of evil." Chalcedonian reason dissipates the deception, and in its wake one realizes the threefold affirmation actually reflects the experiential history of Judaism and Christianity. Evil, after all, preceded Jewish or Christian theology. The ancient Israelite confession of God's goodness and faithfulness came not in ignorance or denial but precisely in the face of enduring suffering and evil. Contrary to a common modern prejudice, evil did not arrive as a threat to naive faith. To the contrary, in the actual course of events faith was proclaimed out from the midst of evil (without "theodicy").

Over the past few centuries, then, the demon of closure has successfully tricked mainstream Western theology into a fatal either/or. Either justify fully the existence of evil, or admit that your faith in the ultimacy of God's goodness is irrational. Since justifying the ways of God *vis-à-vis* the existence of evil is evidently beyond our ken, this is a lose/lose proposition.[28] But instead of rejecting the either/or or condemning its presumption, Christian apologists made the fatal mistake of taking up the challenge, of developing "theodicies." Now, it is important to note that modern theological reflection upon evil and suffering has produced great insight. Work on theodicy *per se* is not the problem (though I suggest we drop the arrogant label "theodicy"). But modern philosophers and theologians have typically seen the either/or as an immediate and significant challenge, one which rightly demands an answer, *now*, as a prerequisite to an affirmation of the reasonableness of faith. Thus the demon of closure maneuvered Christians into the rhetorically, intellectually, spiritually, pastorally, and existentially impossible position of having to respond to concrete evils with a complete theoretical explanation.

Christians should respond to evil with aid, compassion, empathy, sheer presence, and eventually (or, perhaps, preemptively), with testimony to the Christian hope that evil does not have the final word. When Karen screams at me over the bruised body of Jenny, her strangled child, "*Why?*

---

28. A form of understanding that synthesizes the three *may* of course emerge over the course of the centuries if we mature spiritually, or such understanding may be utterly beyond our ken. It is premature to draw either conclusion. I maintain only that we cannot currently think the three together, but that this lack does not in any significant way inhibit us in the struggle against evil, and thus that our current inability to achieve conceptual closure should not be the focus of our concern—let alone be given credit as a potential "defeater" of the rationality of Christianity.

Why?" I meet her with my own anguish and sympathy and love. If she presses the question, I give an honest answer: I do not know. In this real-life, heightened emotional context, my tone properly carries a threatening, to-God-directed whiff of, "but there damn well better be some way in which it all works for good *for Jenny*."

I am simultaneously sustained, however, by my incommensurable and enduring faith in God's goodness and power and righteousness, and I am freed by Chalcedonian reason from the suspicion that, in order to retain in all its fullness my faith in God, I must be able to understand, *now*, how to reconcile my faith with the brutal murder of Jenny. Such is not possible. I can retain my (threatening) demand for an explanation. I cannot demand comprehension *now*. But I, and hopefully Karen (though perhaps not on this day), can benefit from both the incommensurables: full-bodied, unmitigated screaming over intractable evil, *and* full-bodied, unmitigated faith in the ultimacy of God's "yes."

Christians are not distinguished by an inability to develop a theory that adequately accounts for evil. *No one* has such a theory. Christians are distinguished by their faith—not conclusion, inference, or knowledge—that a good God is sufficient.[29] Christian hope in the ultimacy of God's grace—not theodicy, and not denial—is what justifiably distinguishes Christians from those tragic souls who, without any such hope, bitterly face the "tears of humanity with which the earth is soaked from its crust to its center."[30] Christians should engage with utmost subtlety, passion, and energy the tasks of naming evil, seeking out its depths even in our own hearts and minds, minimizing its influence, and mitigating its effects. But Christians should abandon confused attempts to defend faith by answering modernity's so-called "problem of evil." Such serves neither God nor neighbor, but only the demon of closure.[31]

29. I cannot here even begin to delineate the faith/knowledge relation in the wake of the exorcism of the demons. I hope to delineate that, along with other dimensions of Chalcedonian reason, in a larger work, in relation to which this essay is something of a promissory note. I fulfill this promissory note in *A Reasonable Belief* and *The Challenge of Evil*.

30. The words of Ivan Karamazov in Fyodor Dostoyevsky's *The Brothers Karamazov* (237).

31. For an example of how one might reflect upon evil after exorcizing the demons of certainty and closure, see above, chapter 1, "Charles Taylor on Affirmation, Mutilation, and Theism."

THE CONTOUR AND SPIRIT OF
CHALCEDONIAN REASON

As the violence which characterized the trinitarian and christological debates illustrates, the demon of closure fosters intolerance. Given its demand for immediate and total conceptual closure, this is not surprising. Under sway of the demon, the ideal of flawless and total systems of understanding becomes an obsession. Incommensurability is fatal. To acknowledge one makes incommensurable affirmations is *always* a major threat—it means one's understanding is incoherent. When adjudicating among various understandings of atonement, for instance, the demon of closure tempts us to suppose that for some one theory to be true all others must be false. Battle lines are clearly drawn and focus is directed upon disagreement and opponents' weaknesses.

If I am to defend substitutionary atonement, for instance, then my goal must be to establish some variety of it as a comprehensive and flawless account of atonement. It seems incoherent to be both Anselmian *and* Abelardian. Not only other atonement theories, but competing varieties of substitutionary theory constitute a threat. Only one of us can be correct. It is them or me. If I can invalidate any aspect of a competing theory, I can safely dismiss it. Likewise, my own theory may collapse by virtue of a single flaw. From within this take-no-prisoners outlook, to affirm isolated strengths in an opponent's account only abets the enemy, for among competing accounts only one can be true. Such are the ideals of rationality that the demon of closure gleefully induces *opponents together to embrace as unquestioned dictates of reason.*

Obviously, this version of "reason" dictates that opponents focus upon points of difference. Efforts to discern and sustain stark boundary-lines among competing communities is ensured. In short, the devastatingly devious fruits of the demon of closure are conceptual brittleness, a constant sense of vulnerability, an unwillingness to compromise, a reflexive denial of the possibility that strong points from competing accounts may supplement weak points in one's own understanding, and an anxious desire to attack. The demon breeds anxiety, defensiveness, and hostility. Witness the trinitarian and christological battles. Witness—among Christians, Muslims, atheists, scientists, politicians, and professors of English, among many others, both liberal and conservative—fundamentalism.

Chalcedonian reason, by contrast, fosters a confident and generous spirit. Chalcedonian reason anticipates conceptual limitation and incommensurability. There is every reason to have utmost confidence on the whole in one's own most certain affirmations. Competing theories—insofar as they allow for valuable affirmations incommensurable with those of your favored theory, and insofar as they rightly isolate problematic areas in your dominant understanding—become sources of helpful, if incommensurable, insights. It is expected and reasonable that one will affirm a few highly attested, internally coherent, but incommensurable vocabularies. In such instances (e.g., mind/mechanism) *incoherence is one's most reasonable extant option.* Furthermore, areas of common affirmation will return to center stage. We will naturally understand ourselves to be by far more linked by our commonly held conceptions than we are separated by our differences. Where the demon of closure tempts us to totalizing affirmations and negations and a divisive, antagonistic mentality, Chalcedonian reason encourages strong affirmation of our theory's strengths, and frank acknowledgment of its weaknesses—all amidst a broad community that by far shares in areas of mutual confession.[32]

Chalcedonian reason, then, facilitates not mere tolerance but *celebration* of incommensurable theories of atonement. The obvious biblical affirmations of incommensurable ideas about atonement, for instance, is not a problem to be overcome, but a gift to be celebrated. In particular social, political, or personal contexts, one theory of atonement may be especially fecund and another damaging. *This most definitely is not "anything goes" relativism.* Some theories may be rejected utterly. Others may retain marginal status. And, as has in fact happened, a few will likely emerge ever more solidly as classics (in the Gadamerian sense).[33]

It is possible that, in time, a single theory of atonement will become ascendant. But once one has truly exorcised the demon of closure one stops *hoping* for such singularity. To the contrary, after the exorcism the possibility of conceptual closure raises the specter of theological reduction, that is,

32. For instance, Chalcedonian reason will quite automatically remember that if one is debating competing accounts of atonement then *everyone in the debate already shares an incredible array of highly specific affirmations*—for example, to name but a few, a personal God exists, God is good, God acts on our behalf, God was in some fashion incarnate in Jesus Christ. There are *lots* of people who reject *all* forms of all these affirmations (though Chalcedonian reason will remember that we still share an incredible array of highly specific ethical affirmations with many of them). The point is that while differences will not be neglected, they will be debated amidst a continual awareness of a multifarious, deeper, and abiding mutuality.

33. A "classic" is a work whose wisdom has been established by virtue of the judgment of generations. No "classic" is absolutely beyond question, but the more enduring the judgment "classic" (e.g., *The Iliad, Macbeth*), the more authority is credited to the judgment (Hans-Georg Gadamer, *Truth and Method*, Second Part, II.b.ii, "The classical example"). In the Christian community, there is also the belief that the influence of the Spirit is subtly inspiring our creation and discernment of classics (e.g., Genesis, the Gospel of John).

of *loss* (especially in light of the possibility that the closure might result from coerced homogenization or a lack of theological creativity). At any rate, the triumph of any single theory of atonement is definitely not itself legitimate as a primary *goal* of inquiry. Such focus serves only the demon of closure. The critical task is to continue refining a variety of theories in the face of new concrete critiques or historical circumstances. We are looking for advance in subtlety across the board. Some theories may be fully eclipsed or rejected, others may newly emerge (perhaps in response to new socio-political or judicial theory, as was the case with Anselm and with Abelard). The enduring insights of the classics can continue to be utilized to the fullest.

Of course, there is no *a priori* way to determine what will happen. There are no meta-criteria by which we can adjudicate among all possible theories. On the other hand, the multifarious but hard-gained wisdom of generations of Christians provides ample contingent but highly reliable criteria by which to adjudicate among theories reasonably and powerfully. And there is *no reason to doubt* that in fact we do marginalize the worst and embrace the best. Loss of certainty does not entail doubt. There remain ample grounds for ascribing degrees of confidence or tentativeness. Even regarding classic accounts, of course, Chalcedonian reason encourages us frankly to acknowledge both strong and weak dimensions, and to acknowledge that in the midst of distinct contexts and challenges, different accounts may appropriately be valued differently. There will be no way to draw absolute lines of demarcation—it is the demon of closure that tricks us with the utterly inane idea that in order to make any judgements one must be able to draw distinct boundary lines. Again, loss of certainty regarding boundaries in no way inhibits judgements with regard to non-borderline cases. Theories of atonement which clearly violate central affirmations (e.g., which see God as petty, vindictive, or hateful) can without hesitation be rejected.

A REASSURING REMINDER

Chalcedonian rationality is alien to our dominant forms of scientific, philosophical, and theological inquiry. Those haunted by the demon of closure may well feel threatened by Chalcedonian reasoning. Fortunately, the demon has not successfully haunted a nearly universal arena of rationality. Comfort may increase when we realize that Chalcedonian reason is virtually identical to ordinary aesthetic reasoning. Within the realm of aesthetics one certainly draws qualitative distinctions. One recognizes the genius of masters like Mozart, Shakespeare, or Dali, and one as easily categorizes rank amateurs. But these judgments are made without any definitive criteria.

Furthermore, we constantly evaluate better and worse without a definition of what is best. It is impossible to adjudicate with any certainty superiority *among* artistic works of genius. "Mozart versus Beethoven" is fine for fun but sophomoric taken seriously. We do not strive to identify *the* best work of art—indeed, the very idea of *a* best work of art (e.g., *a* best "Lord's Supper" rightly strikes us as nonsensical). Furthermore, we easily acknowledge that evaluation of borderline works may long remain uncertain—sometimes the judgment "genius" emerges, or is withdrawn, only after centuries.

Moreover, we readily celebrate incommensurability among both mediums and meanings. Mozart's genius cannot be reproduced with words, nor Shakespeare's with brush strokes, nor Dali's with a symphony. This is not to deny some degree of conceptual overlap, but it is simply confused to think the essence of such distinct expressions of genius can be wholly conceptually coordinated across diverse media (e.g., understanding contributes to our experience of non-linguistic art forms, but full experience of Mozart requires one finally to relinquish words). Similarly, we do not seek to coordinate the meaning of Dali's "Last Supper" with the meaning of da Vinci's "Last Supper," let alone with a Bach mass. We celebrate the uniqueness of Dali and da Vinci and Bach masterpieces—and we hope for the creation of more, equally distinct, masterpieces.

In the realm of aesthetics, then, we operate comfortably and peacefully with no certain foundations, no certain criteria for distinguishing works of genius, no definitive lines demarcating boundaries between "banal," "average," "good," "genius," no possibility of closure regarding *the* best work of art, and with incommensurability among both media and forms of understanding. On the whole, then, within the realm of aesthetics we make confident judgments—decisive at the extremes ("genius" or "utterly banal")—and live comfortably with gradients of plurality and ambiguity. We strive not for finality, but for increase, not for singularity, but for fecundity, not for conceptual narrowing, but for advance into ever more diverse and more complex vistas of beauty, love, and understanding; we strive not for closure, but for invocation of as many incommensurable vocabularies as possible in order to ever more richly contour, enhance, and articulate life.

In theology, likewise, the call to celebrate diverse doctrines of atonement is certainly not a call to celebrate *all* doctrines of atonement. As in art, there will be confirmed classics, confirmed failures, and all manner of efforts in between. We may not be able to draw distinct boundaries, but we can be confident that we know when we have wandered into territories of excellence or deficiency. Our aesthetic reflection, having largely escaped the haunting of the demon of closure, closely mirrors what I am calling Chalcedonian reasoning. Contrary to modern prejudice, the arts, not the sciences, should provide the primary epistemological paradigm for theological reflection (indeed, my argument suggests the arts should provide a primary paradigm for philosophical, ethical, and scientific reflection as well).[34] All this may well frustrate those with a low tolerance for ambiguity, but in fact it accurately depicts the character of our finite and imperfect epistemic capacities.

34. A word regarding ethical judgments, which demand far more careful delineation than is here possible. As should be obvious, ethical relativism is not a consequence of Chalcedonian reason. Just as we are fully confident and unhesitating in judging da Vinci's David a work of genius, we are fully confident in condemning, and, if necessary, jailing, pedophiles. After the exorcism of the demon of certainty, we realize the impossibility of establishing objective and universal ethical truths, but equally false is the reactionary contention that *all* ethical assertions are equally unjustifiable. Also, admitting that ascertaining objectively what is True is beyond our epistemic capacities does not entail that there is no objective and universal Truth, Good, or Evil. It is perfectly reasonable to believe that Good and Evil are matters of Truth (for a Christian such truth would correspond to the judgment of God—and would *not*, notably, be knowledge to which we should *ever even attempt to lay claim*). Even given our finite and imperfect capacities, a host of moral platitudes (e.g., torturing children for pleasure is wrong) can still be affirmed and acted upon without hesitation, even though a host of truly controversial moral questions (e.g., regarding genetic testing and engineering) will remain unsettled for the foreseeable future.

Of course, with regard to the numerous moral quandaries we face in ethics, there are no *a priori* shortcuts. Unlike modern reason, however, which inevitably focuses attention on points of ethical difference among communities, Chalcedonian reason urges us to focus upon areas of commonality while not ignoring points of significant and currently intractable difference—significantly, there is currently considerable global ethical consensus on a host of moral platitudes (e.g., the Geneva Conventions, the Universal Declaration on Human Rights). While Chalcedonian reason does not preclude coercive—and perhaps even violent—action against communities that are acting in accord with incommensurable and what are judged to be evil values, it is far more likely to appeal to violence only in extreme circumstances due to its emphasis on humility and its native impulse to tolerate incommensurability.

Beware a common objection to Chalcedonian reasoning that typically runs like this: if you accept Chalcedonian reasoning then we can never have ethical certainty. This is akin to the student who complained to me, "But if you don't give me an 'A' I won't be able to get into a doctoral program!" Ethical certainty would be nice, but epistemic imperfection and finitude is evidently our lot (this is valid philosophically—as has become obvious in the course of exorcizing the demon of certainty—and valid theologically—following from both our finite ways of knowing and our sinfulness). Note also that ethical relativism, because it is inextricably linked to the dialectic of certainty, *is conceptually exorcised along with the demon of certainty*. We get neither objectivism nor relativism, but ethical judgments about which we can claim far more (e.g., rape is wrong) to far less (cloning zygotes is right/wrong) confidence [cf. chapters on Stout and Hauerwas, below, and my *Agape Ethics*].

CHALCEDONIAN REASON, CHALCEDONIAN SPIRIT

By encouraging carefully modulated judgments, maximum generosity, and a focus on areas of mutual affirmation, Chalcedonian reason fosters a Chalcedonian spirit (in contrast to the bitter spirit which, tragically, characterized so much of the trinitarian and christological controversies). Of particular significance, once the demon of closure is exorcized, Chalcedonian reason inspires in us an intuitive celebration of plurality. We suddenly resonate with rhetorical questions such as: Is it so strange to imagine that the nature of how rightly we are to relate to God is more fully captured by incommensurable Catholic, Orthodox, Baptist, Presbyterian, *and* Quaker conceptions, than by any one singly? Is it not more intuitive, in the face of four historically and theologically incommensurable Gospels, to drop talk of the synoptic *problem* (stifling the demon's chuckles) and instead to celebrate the fecundity of the plurality?[35] Is it not utterly reasonable, while not forsaking frank assessment and argument over relative strengths and weaknesses, to celebrate diverse churches, denominations, polities? Or diverse understandings of the Eucharist, God, Jesus Christ, atonement, christology, or Trinity?[36]

I cannot, of course, simultaneously *be* (in a spiritual/existential sense) Quaker, Catholic, and Baptist, but there is every likelihood that God is more fully glorified by such rich but incommensurable conceptions than would be the case with any one singly. For my finite part, I can *be* Presbyterian and still celebrate and benefit from, if at something less than a full existential level, incommensurable Quaker and Catholic understandings.[37]

35. Recall, in an early rebuke of closure, the Patristic rejection of Tatian's *Diatessaron*.

36. Above I tried to rehabilitate the classic trinitarian and christological confessions by arguing that they preserved the best and excised the worst from the Antiochene and Alexandrian trajectories. It does not follow that these two trajectories *exhaust* valuable possibilities for trinitarian or christological reflection. In this regard, see Daniel Migliore's "The Person and Work of Jesus Christ" for a beautiful example of Chalcedonian reasoning and of a Chalcedonian Spirit (*Faith Seeking Understanding*, 139–64).

37. Though I cannot develop the point here, it is worth noting that Chalcedonian reason would invoke—though with some significant qualifications resulting from the difference in the scale of the incommensurability—the same dynamics that ensue among varieties of Christian theology when dealing with the relationship among religions. To put the point in the most provocative fashion, once one moves beyond certainty and, most especially, closure, one can be a fully convicted Christian apologist while granting the *possibility* that one's friend's incommensurable Buddhist beliefs, insofar as they, like yours, are an indeterminate distance from Truth, are, in their current form, *equally* true (*this* is where it is critical that one remember and take very seriously the category of mystery). Of course, I can sincerely do no other than live within my present understanding. That is, I wholly believe Christianity to be far more true than Buddhism (there is no virtue in pretending otherwise), and would debate a contemporary Buddhist accordingly—but neither of us has unmediated, privileged

For those possessed still by the demon of closure, such celebration of diversity can feel at best irrational and at worst like an abdication of any real conviction and confession. But for those filled with a Chalcedonian spirit, the blending of conviction over one's personal confessions with a humble recognition of finitude, imperfection, and ambiguity, and thus with a celebration of plurality, feels utterly natural. Nor, it is important to note, does it preclude strident or even coercive measures in response to one's most profound, widely shared, and historically deep theological or ethical convictions (see note 34). The Chalcedonian spirit is critical, yet open. A bit more precisely, it is appropriately firm regarding its most firmly supported beliefs (the earth revolves around the sun), dismissive of those judged patently silly (astrological charts), coercive with regard to those judged most certainly evil (pedophilia), appropriately soft regarding highly-prized but non-ethical beliefs (trinitarianism—Christians rightly jail the pedophile, but not the unitarian), and generous in fostering exploration of diverse perspectives in areas of greatest puzzlement (mind/brain relation, contours of a "final theory," ethics of genetic engineering) or mystery (eucharist, incarnation, atonement, God *in se*).[38]

This complex interplay of conviction and humility in our understanding accurately reflects the hard mix of surety and ambiguity in our daily lived experience, and is utterly consistent with biblical assessments of our epistemic potential. The Jewish and Christian Scriptures—in accord with the holy writings of many faiths—stand in stark contrast to the *hubris* to

---

access to the Ultimate, nor can either of us know what might come of either internal developments or inter-faith debates in a millennium or three. Significantly, in the meanwhile, Chalcedonian reason quite automatically inclines one to attend to the vast array of values Christians share with Buddhists (e.g., regarding justice, love, humility, religious freedom, and care for the poor and for the earth).

38. I naturally gloss the distinction between the spheres of ethics and aesthetics. Consistent with the exorcism of the demons of certainty and closure, I would argue that no *a priori* line between the spheres can be drawn, that precise boundaries will always be a matter of debate, but that nonetheless with regard to the vast majority of judgments we can be confident about which are ethical (where "ethical" means simply that we find toleration of diversity unacceptable—e.g., pedophilia), and which are aesthetic (where "aesthetic" means simply that we allow or even celebrate diversity—e.g., Christianity and Buddhism, Beethoven and Liszt). Chalcedonian reason corrects an irrational, historic, and unfaithful tendency for Christians to be most coercive, even murderous, with regard to the *most mysterious* of affirmations (e.g., regarding Trinity, baptism, Eucharist)—obviously, such should be sites of maximal toleration (at these junctures we should quake, stunned at the evil wrought in the name of God by the demon of closure). [I harden the distinction between ethics and aesthetics in later work in terms of the three spheres/rationalities/vocabularies of nature, poetic I's, and agape, correlating aesthetic enjoyment with the sphere of nature, aesthetic creativity with the sphere of poetic I's, and ethics with the sphere of agape].

which the demons of certainty and of closure tempt us: "'For as the heavens are higher than the earth,' says the LORD, 'so are my ways higher than your ways and my thoughts higher than your thoughts.'"[39]

In ways small and historic, the demon of closure has fostered unjustifiable enmity and violence. Its noxious influence endures. But in an age when reason itself has come under unparalleled scrutiny, the demon's subtle contours have been unveiled with unprecedented clarity. Now is the time to still our epistemological *hubris*, to seize this demon, to exorcize it fully from our hearts and our minds, to embrace Chalcedonian reason, and to rejoice with a Chalcedonian spirit.

39. Isaiah 55:9. While many might find the version of reason I am sketching here threatening in its ambiguity, others will recognize my strong dependence upon Gadamer's hermeneutics. The pertinent critique of Gadamer, and in particular of his reliance upon the wisdom of historic communities to generate classics, pivots upon the inherent conservatism entailed in his affirmation of the *status quo*. In brief, I would follow Paul Ricoeur in "Hermeneutics and the Critique of Ideology" by balancing my appeal to Gadamer with Habermas's critique—properly exorcized, as appropriated by Ricoeur, of the haunting that stimulates Habermas's desperate clinging after a metaphysics of certainty and closure. Unfortunately, at the close of this brilliant essay Ricoeur manifests the haunting of the demon of closure. He finds "hermeneutical consciousness" (primarily an "ontology of prior understanding") and "critical consciousness" (primarily an "eschatology of freedom") to be incommensurable (99–100). But whereas Chalcedonian reason would be unsurprised at this antinomy (or, *aporia*), Ricoeur, possessed, feels the lurking threat of incoherence. He declares it a "false antinomy," exclaiming that we should not react, "as if it were necessary to choose between reminiscence and hope!" (100). Ricoeur, unconvincingly compromising the brilliant contrasts drawn to that point in the essay, reacts (caveats flying) by collapsing critique into tradition (that it is a tradition of liberation is no help). Chalcedonian reason facilitates clear admission that the vocabularies of hermeneutics and critical theory are incommensurable, that both must be kept in play, and that frankly acknowledging the antinomy, far from being a descent into incoherence, is *presently our most reasonable course of action*, as is the admission that we cannot but oscillate on an *ad hoc* basis between these two indispensable vocabularies. Ricoeur's brilliant analysis would thereby be simplified and strengthened. I would also follow Ricoeur in drawing the clear parallel within religion to the antinomy between dependence upon the wisdom of the tradition (e.g., Scriptures) and openness to the emergence of the radically new and discontinuous (e.g., the prophetic, or something as unpredictable and wildly improbable as incarnation).

Chapter 4

Cosmodicy

On Evil and the Problem with Theodicy

> The most serious objection to belief in a good and all-powerful
> God has always been an objection based on the presence of evil
> in the world, that vast amount of sin and suffering witnessed
> and experienced in every generation. How, we wonder, can a
> good and all-powerful God allow the savagery and horror of
> disease, starvation, war and death that afflicts our world. This,
> of course, is a classic objection to theistic belief, the well-known
> problem of evil.[1]

Several years ago, a Nobel laureate in physics visited our seminary to discuss science and Christianity. An outspoken atheist, he politely focused his
lecture upon recent developments in theoretical physics. During the Q&A
someone asked him about evil. As he reflected aloud upon the evil afflicting
our world he became increasingly passionate. If God did exist, he finally
burst out, then God would best be compared to an SS *commandant* at a
concentration camp. Such bluntness is unusual, but there is nothing unusual about his sentiment. As the opening quote illustrates, even Christians
consider evil a major obstacle to faith.

As Psalms, Ecclesiastes, Proverbs, and Job illustrate, experience of evil
has long spurred earnest questioning and bitter lament. In the early church,

---

1. Wennberg, "Animal Suffering," 120.

Irenaeus and Augustine famously speculated upon the origins and ontology of evil. But it is only in the modern West that the "problem of evil" finally assumed its current dominant contour—presumed by atheist and Christian alike—as a singular obstacle to faith. The modern "problem of evil" focuses upon the logical incompatibility of three classic affirmations: 1) God is good, 2) God is all-powerful, 3) evil exists.

Tellingly, the focus of the modern "problem of evil" is not any concrete evil, but the inability of human reason to offer a comprehensive explanation of the relation between God and evil. The "problem of evil" thereby becomes an obstacle not only to faith, but to the primordial existential challenge evil presents life. Three centuries after Liebniz coined the term in his famous treatise (*Theodicy*, 1710), the conundrum is not that no theodicy ("justification of God") has prevailed. The (cloaked) conundrum is that theology must now untangle the problem with theodicy before the primordial challenge of evil and its relation to life and faith can be named. We can begin by asking just how theologians got themselves into the curious position of seeking to justify God.

Largely for his seminal work, *Meditations on First Philosophy* (1632), René Descartes is honored as the father of modern philosophy. Descartes dedicated *Meditations* to "the sacred Faculty of Theology at Paris," for it firmly established the Christian faith by logically demonstrating "how God may be more easily and certainly known than the things of this world."[2] The Faculty of Theology at Paris and multitudes of Christians ever since have embraced the still unrealized dream of proving God. In turn, multitudes of atheists imagine they have invalidated Christianity by quashing every proof and, most especially, by invoking the modern problem of evil. By virtue of stimulating this descending dialectic of unwitting hubris, Descartes's *Meditations* deserves credit as one of history's most subtle and effective assaults upon faith.

Charles Taylor discerns how Descartes's proofs—in contrast to the mislabeled "proofs" of Anselm and Aquinas—definitively shifted "the centre of gravity" between divine and human:[3]

> [Descartes's] thesis is not that I gain knowledge when turned towards God in faith. Rather, the certainty of clear and distinct perceptions is unconditional and self-generated. What has happened is rather that God's existence has become a stage in *my* progress towards science through the methodical ordering of

2. Descartes, *Philosophical Writings*, 3–4.
3. Taylor, *Sources of the Self*, 157.

evident insights. God's existence is a theorem in *my* system of perfect science.[4]

Precisely understood, Descartes did not believe in God. God was not the Subject of his faith. God was a conclusion of Descartes's arguments, an object of Descartes's knowledge, a wholly human-generated inference. Descartes articulated a relation to God not in faith through grace, but in knowledge through reason. This profound spiritual confusion—absent from theology (including Anselm and Aquinas) prior to Descartes—afflicts every attempt to prove God.[5]

In this Cartesian/modern conceptual context, where "reason" subtly supplants "faith," the distinctly modern "problem of evil" emerges. In accepting the burden of inferring God, one accepts a criterion of reasonableness that *requires* logical reconciliation of the three classic contentions. So evil appears for the first time not as a potent emotional obstacle to loving God (as in Christian lament), nor as a significant locus for faithful theological inquiry (as in Irenaeus and Augustine), but as a logical obstacle which must be overcome.

Insofar as it adopted the Cartesian pretension, Western Christianity legitimated a devastating twofold either/or. First, either be rational or irrational. If one opts for "rational" (like classic Christianity) then, second, either reconcile the three classic affirmations (i.e., *per impossibile*, develop a theodicy) or eliminate the irrationality by compromising on one of the affirmations (i.e., abandon faith in an all-good God whose power is sufficient to redeem all creation). The snare thus laid is subtle, for each reasonable alternative—offering a theodicy or compromising on one of the affirmations—is caught up in a rationality whose hubris subtly but wholly denies any limits to our reason and elides the legitimacy of faith (i.e., the work of the Spirit). That is, the Cartesian pretension quietly sets up human reason as a wholly capable and exclusive arbiter vis-à-vis God (in theological terms: as an idol). This is how theologians got themselves into the curious position of seeking to justify God.

A good way to begin unraveling the devastating Cartesian distortion is simple but profoundly counter-intuitive. First, Christians should affirm and embrace that physicist's profound offense over the suffering and evil suffusing reality. Second, for the sake of argument, Christians should *simply lose the argument over theodicy* (i.e., grant that God does not exist). In this

---

4. Taylor, *Sources of the Self*, 157.

5. Several lines from this paragraph were published previously in Greenway, "Review of *Faith and Reason*," 922–24.

context the primordial problem, the horrible problem, the problem from which theodicy *shields* us, is revealed.

God does not exist. *But you confront precisely all the same evil.* Now the invective so passionately turned against God must be turned against the cosmos itself and—since we are wholly members of that cosmos, since our existence is purchased only at the price of the existence of that cosmos— upon ourselves. By virtue of our very existence we discover ourselves from the first already complicit.[6] This is the profound if lately obscured heart of the classic Christian confession that we and the world are fallen. Now the primordial challenge of evil re-emerges: not the problem of the justification of God, but the problem of the justification of the cosmos, of life, of ourselves. Not theodicy, but *cosmodicy.*[7]

The existential stance of the morally passionate person who confronts the primordial challenge of evil squarely is brilliantly sketched in Dostoyevsky's *The Brothers Karamazov.* Ivan Karamazov recites a litany of evils that stimulate horror and rage. But Ivan is so supremely sensitive that for the tears of but one child he would give God back his ticket to this world.[8] Ivan illustrates the unprecedented reach of the moral objection in modernity's "problem of evil," wherein evil is more than an obstacle to belief in the existence of God: even if God does exist, absent a conclusive theodicy outrage remains the only moral response (e.g., God as SS *commandant*).

Ivan's excruciating existential stance—of one who finds the cosmos and thus his own existence morally repugnant, and who is helpless to do anything but stand in futile, world and self-condemning protest (even suicide would be an empty gesture)—represents the hopeless and supremely moral endpoint of those who reject belief in God. Our physicist illogically but effectively shielded himself from this excruciating stance by venting— despite his atheism—against God.

Classically, Christians not only *affirm and embrace* Ivan's moral offense, we *enhance* it by turning upon ourselves. We confess ourselves not only complicit (fallen) but guilty from the first (original sin). But Christians also testify to a finite but opening experience of a gracious, accepting "yes" that portends the ultimate fulfillment of our most profound ethical and spiritual hopes. Notably, neither the truth of our spiritual intuitions nor the truth of anyone's moral intuitions is demonstrable on Cartesian grounds (nor, in the classic moral realist sense, on modern scientific grounds—that

6. This is also the sense in which Emmanuel Levinas says, "One comes not into being, but into question" (Levinas, *The Levinas Reader*, 81).

7. "Cosmodicy" is my neologism. Its meaning will become clear in context.

8. Dostoyevsky, *The Brothers Karamazov*, Book V: "Pro and Contra," section 4, "Rebellion."

physicist's science, for example, cannot fully account for the moral realism inspiring his passion). Christian experience of and testimony to the surpassing grace of God is as powerful as people's experience of and testimony to the reality of concrete evils (though in extreme real-life contexts the immediacy of either joy or horror can be overwhelming).

In light of experiences of grace and of evil, and rejecting Cartesian idolatry, Christians *quite reasonably*—if without logical certainty and without a theodicy—live convicted of the reality of evil and convicted of the love of a God able to redeem all creation (i.e., convicted of all three classic affirmations). Questions—appearing again in their classic theological form—endure. If God created *ex nihilo*, where did evil come from? Why would an all-powerful God allow such suffering? But the inability definitively to answer such questions does not preclude reasonable faith. Christians are not distinguished by having a theory that adequately accounts for evil. *No one* has such a theory. Christian hope in the ultimacy of God's grace—not a theodicy, and not denial—is what justifiably distinguishes Christians from those souls who, tragically, live without any such hope.

Christians should confront evil and suffering with confession, resistance, lament, and hope. In the midst of concrete suffering lament may overwhelm hope—the open questions mandate space for full-blooded cries of dereliction and even anguished attacks upon God—but that is a psychological reality requiring great pastoral sensitivity, not a philosophical objection that invalidates the reasonableness of Christian hope. At an opposite extreme, some have testified to overwhelming experiences of joy before God, even amidst profound suffering. Yet such wondrous occasions of hope do not justify denial of the often-overwhelming power of evil and do not rob the yet-open questions of their enduring bite.

Between the extremes, but with no lessening of existential intensity, Christians can experience fully the dynamics of Luther's *simul iustus et peccator* ("simultaneously redeemed and sinner"). Christians who embrace and accentuate Ivan's supreme moral sensitivity can discover the *simul* is directly proportional: unflinching and full-blooded confession of evil only extends the reach and profundity of the redemptive "yes." In direct relation to excruciating consciousness of evil's personal and cosmic dimensions, one can experience the overwhelming reach and power and gift of the *iustus*.

In this theologically proper context, we remember our supremely moral physicist. Now we understand the covert existential protection afforded by his logically absurd but emotionally understandable attack upon a God he thinks nonexistent. We realize that he is a tragic figure. Apart from this flimsy shield he, like Ivan, can experience only *peccator*, only complicity in an ethically irredeemable cosmos. Is that not horrible? Is one not overwhelmed with compassion for a person with such admirable and su-premely moral sensitivity and passion? In the face of this physicist's attack, Christians should feel no defensiveness, should feel no need to go scram-bling after some theodicy. We should feel sorrow. And we should engage in loving evangelical wondering: how to testify, how to bring joy, how to save.

Chapter 5

The Reasonableness of Affirming Free Will

On Kane, Taylor, Dennett, and Honderich

In *Freedom Evolves*, Daniel Dennett calls Robert Kane's *The Significance of Free Will* the "best attempt so far" at a defense of incompatibilism (i.e., in ordinary language, a defense of free will).[1] But Dennett, a preeminent compatibilist, then attacks and dismisses Kane in a single chapter. In *How Free Are You?* Ted Honderich places Kane "at the head of the Free Will regiment."[2] Nonetheless, Honderich, a preeminent hard determinist, not only argues that Kane offers us a "dog's breakfast, a kind of factual absurdity," he deigns to suggest why a professional philosopher might become so confused: "we *want* a certain freedom and the dignity it gives us (Kane), and it seems we want them more as retirement approaches."[3] Dennett and Honderich's critiques do defeat Kane. Nonetheless, Kane is, ultimately, correct. If Kane's argument is purged of one fatal confusion, Dennett and Honderich's critiques are subverted. The antinomy between free will and determinism is tamed, if not resolved, and it becomes clear why presently it is wholly rational to affirm free will and irrational to dismiss it.

---

1. Dennett, *Freedom Evolves*, 99.
2. Honderich, *How Free Are You?* 119.
3. Honderich, *How Free Are You?* 78 (parenthetical in original).

I. CONTRA KANE: THE ILLUSION OF FREE WILL

The incompatibilist understanding of free will constitutes what Kane fairly calls the "natural" incompatibilism of "ordinary persons."[4] As Kane argues, incompatibilism is not only a near-universal understanding, it is prerequisite to ordinary and cherished understandings of self-creation and moral and aesthetic ascription.[5] But defenders of free will are a beleaguered lot among philosophers. Two major objections have elevated determinism (whether hard or compatibilist) over incompatibilism. First, as Thomas Hobbes argued, the objection that free will is unintelligible because it involves either "the 'confusion' of identifying freedom with indeterminism, or the 'emptiness' of unexplained accounts of the self's 'self-determining itself.'"[6] Second, that free will does not fit modern scientific understanding. As Kane concedes, "[b]elief is more widespread than ever today that an old-fashioned incompatibilist free will is essentially mysterious and has no place in the modern picture of human beings emerging in the natural, social, and cognitive sciences."[7]

Kane: Two Tasks for Incompatibilism

Kane claims that at the intuitive core of affirmation of free will one will discern the principle of ultimate responsibility (UR): "*ultimate responsibility* lies where the *ultimate cause* is."[8] Kane argues that this fundamental intuition lies at the root of all the controversies over Frankfurt scenarios, alternative possibilities, or conditional analyses of "can."[9] When incompatibilists explain what distinctive intuition forces them to reject compatibilism, Kane argues, "they will come up with something like UR or *fail to make a convincing case*."[10]

Kane defines U of UR precisely in terms of "sufficient reasons." Sufficient reasons may be:

> (i) (logically) sufficient *conditions*, (ii) sufficient *causes* (i.e., antecedent circumstances plus laws of nature) or (iii) sufficient

4. Kane, "Responsibility, Luck, and Chance," 218.

5. Kane, *Significance of Free Will*, 80; see also 212.

6. Kane, *Significance of Free Will*, 11, with reference to Hobbes, *Works of Thomas Hobbes*, 35.

7. Kane, *Significance of Free Will*, 17.

8. Kane, *Significance of Free Will*, 35.

9. Kane, *Significance of Free Will*, 35.

10. Kane, *Significance of Free Will*, 77.

motives. The first two entail the existence of that for which they are reasons. The third, sufficient motive, applies to actions and is sufficient in the sense that, given the motive, the action for which it is a motive would be performed voluntarily or willingly and would not be omitted voluntarily or willingly.

An act involves some measure of UR only to the degree that *no* sufficient reason obtains: "What U thus requires is that if an agent is ultimately responsible for an action, the action cannot have a sufficient reason of any of these kinds *for which the agent is not also responsible.*"[11] Since UR involves positing effects for which there is in principle no sufficient cause, Kane notes, UR requires indeterminism.[12] Furthermore, if we are to be responsible for such effects, we must be the ultimate cause of actions that do not have any sufficient reasons, that is, the indeterminism must lie in us. Kane calls actions that break the chain of causation by being in-and-of-themselves ultimate causal sources, "self-forming actions" (SFAs).[13] He describes them plainly:

> If free will implies ultimate responsibility and underived origination, then it requires that some free actions must be undetermined. They must be capable of occurring or not occurring, given *exactly the same past and laws of nature.*[14]

That is, "UR requires not only that agents be the ultimate sources or grounds of their actions, but also that they be the ultimate sources or grounds of their *wills*—of their willing to perform the actions."[15] Delineation of UR, then, distinguishes incompatibilist concern over free will, which focuses upon our ability to choose what we will, from compatibilist/hard determinist concern over freedom, which focuses upon our ability to effect what we will (e.g., freedom from political coercion). Compatibilists, incompatibilists, and determinists alike defend freedom, incompatibilists alone defend free will.

Even if we were to have maximum freedom, of course, there would be no such thing as sheer free willing. Kane's UR ("ultimate responsibility") and SFAs ("self-forming actions") do not require uncircumscribed free willing, which would forget our existence as historical beings. Nature and nurture always wield their considerable influence. Our responsibility is

11. Kane, *Significance of Free Will,* 73.

12. Kane, *Significance of Free Will,* 74.

13. Kane, *Significance of Free Will,* 74. I need not distinguish between Kane's SFAs and SFWs (self-forming willings).

14. Kane, *Significance of Free Will,* 106.

15. Kane, *Significance of Free Will,* 113.

never total but is correlated to the degree our self-forming actions are freely willed or "ultimate." Accordingly, we hold people responsible (e.g., in court, in personal allocation of credit or blame) to the degree they or we have *not* been coerced or determined by nature and nurture, to the degree they or we have freely willed. In this way, UR names an intuition indispensable to profound dimensions of most everyone's "natural" understanding.

But why accept UR? Kane confesses that UR is "an incredibly strong and problematic condition."[16] Virtually all philosophers have had the intuition of willing freely. But only, Kane admits, "to reject it in our more reflective moments."[17] For UR *is* apparently unintelligible and unscientific. Kane, however, remains defiantly incompatibilist. He also remains resolute in his fidelity to naturalism. He scorns incompatibilists who have ended with their minds "clouded in mist . . . visited by visions of noumenal selves, nonoccurrent causes, transempirical egos, and other fantasies."[18] He mocks the empty exercise of "putting labels on mysteries."[19] And he rejects contemporary incompatibilists' thinly veiled appeals to mystery:

> Cartesian egos . . . special "acts of will" . . . mental events that exist outside of (but can also intervene within) the natural order . . . causation that cannot be accounted for in terms of familiar kinds of event or occurrent causation. . . . How these special causes or agencies are supposed to operate, or how they are supposed to explain why one choice occurs rather than another, is never well enough explained to allay suspicions that libertarian accounts of free agency are mysterious.[20]

None of these appeals, Kane chides, answers "what most needs explaining for indeterminist theories of freedom," namely, "Why did the agent rationally and voluntarily do A here and now rather than doing otherwise?"[21] Nor do they explain how free will fits in the natural order. The two tasks facing incompatibilists, then, are, 1) to "establish whether a kind of freedom that requires *indeterminism* can be made intelligible," and, 2) to explain "where it might exist, if it does at all, in the natural order."[22]

16. Kane, *Significance of Free Will*, 79.
17. Kane, *Significance of Free Will*, 79.
18. Kane, *Significance of Free Will*, 14.
19. Kane, *Significance of Free Will*, 105.
20. Kane, *Significance of Free Will*, 115.
21. Kane, *Significance of Free Will*, 121.
22. Kane, *Significance of Free Will*, 105.

Free Will in the Natural Order?

Where is free will in the natural order? Kane seizes upon a twentieth-century opening, quantum indeterminacy:

> The crucial differences for *undetermined* free willings (or SFWs) needed for libertarian free agency would be these: (a) the contributing patterns of oscillations of the self-network would *involve chaotic indeterminacies* . . . so the choice outcome would not be determined, and (b) there would be more than one feasible option (A for R or B for R') that the patterns of the self-network might push over the top, thus triggering the choice outcome. Whichever outcome is pushed over the top, however, would be the product of the self-network whose distinctive oscillations would be crucial to its coming about.[23]

This account, Kane contends, appeals to indeterminism in a scientifically acceptable way. Furthermore, he argues, it explains why any of the choices which result from an indeterminate process can be said to be mine: because the indeterminacy obtains among various of *my* options. Our brains allow us to entertain and strive toward a plurality of reasonable and competing options, any one of which, if "pushed over the top" by the self-network, constitutes a reasonable "product" of that agent's decision process.

Unfortunately, Kane here equivocates between the agent being the *location* and the *source* of the ultimate causation. A natural incompatibilist (requiring UR) would judge the product of an indeterminism to be a brute happening, not a free willing/self-forming action. As Dennett argues, Kane:

> has to figure out some way to get the undetermined quantum event to be not just *in you* but *yours*. He wants above all for the decision to be "up to you," but if the decision is undetermined—the defining requirement of libertarianism—it isn't determined by you, whatever you are, because it isn't determined by anything.[24]

Kane's case only deteriorates when he offers detailed neurological description:

> the feeling that certain events in the brain—for example, those corresponding to our efforts or choices—are things we are doing rather than things that are merely happening to us would result from the superposition of the synchronized wave patterns of the self-network upon those neural events. The idea, in other words,

23. Kane, *Significance of Free Will*, 140.
24. Dennett, *Freedom Evolves*, 123.

is that the neural events corresponding to our efforts, choices, and other mental actions would be overlaid by the patterns of oscillations unifying the self-network, so that these patterns and the effort and choice events are coupled, causally influencing and interacting with each other. The effort and choice events would occur, so to speak, "within" the self-network whose distinctive patterns of oscillations were superimposed upon them, and the patterns of the self-network would be contributing causes to choice, pushing one competing reason-network over the top and thus supporting the belief that the choices are *our* doings, the products of ourselves.[25]

Kane here undercuts his own incompatibilism. Of course, *Dennett* could continue, while such neural dynamics explain the "feeling" of and consequent "belief" in free will, rigorous analysis quickly leads to the conclusion that what *feels* like free will is actually a mix of deterministic and indeterministic processes (*sans* UR).[26] Dennett could continue with another quote from Kane:

> [W]hen described from a physical perspective alone, *free will looks like chance*. But the physical process is not the only one to be considered. The indeterministic chaotic process is also, experientially considered, the agent's effort of will; and the undetermined outcome of the process, one way or another, is, experientially considered, the agent's choice. From a free willist point of view, this experiential or phenomenological perspective is also important; it cannot simply be dispensed with.[27]

Indeed, Dennett could concur, the experiential perspective cannot simply be dispensed with, for while "free will" is a confused idea, it wields considerable real-world influence (i.e., it is a potent meme).

Continuing on this unintended determinist trajectory, even Kane's rationale for moral ascription mirrors Dennett's. Challenged to explain how I can be held morally responsible for an action when I "could not have done otherwise," Dennett responds by noting that while I might attempt to deny responsibility by virtue of the fact that the decision was only in me, not mine, it remains the case that all the various options were mine, and thus that the choice—whether determined by my character or the result of an indeterminacy—was mine. At that point, Dennett contends, one can affirm

---

25. Kane, *Significance of Free Will*, 194.
26. Dennett, *Freedom Evolves*, 97–137.
27. Kane, *Significance of Free Will*, 147.

Alfred Mele's, "Default Responsibility Principle: If no one else is responsible for your being in state A, you are."[28]

This begs the question of the connection between responsibility and UR (ask: what sense of "responsible" is Dennett suggesting we not ascribe to someone else?). The sly invocation of "responsible" allows Dennett to avoid articulating his rationale for moral ascription. Since Dennett will not relate the meaning of responsibility to a distinct capacity of agents for UR, the ordinary person's prized, natural incompatibilist understanding of responsibility is elided.

Dennett, for instance, would have to grant that his reasoning is equally valid when applied to a rock: if the rock killed the man, and no one else is responsible for the rock doing so, then the rock is. In a sense, of course, this is true. But, a natural incompatibilist would urge, not in a moral sense. What is missing? UR. Dennett's determinism, by contrast, entails that sufficient reasons for any of our actions flow inexorably out of a past which antedates any choice on our part. So Dennett must talk of "responsibility" without UR—and hence mean "responsible" in a peculiar sense. For determinists, the rock and we are ultimately responsible in the same sense, even if there are differing levels of awareness and even if only humans are subject to mental causes. One can understand how a determinist like Dennett may be forced to this, but it is stunning to hear Kane offer a parallel rationale.

Kane argues that his account allows him to answer this frequent objection: consider two people, Steve and Steve*, who have exactly the same pasts and who make exactly the same efforts up to time t, but at time t Steve chooses A and Steve* chooses B. How, Kane asks, "can it *not* be a matter of chance that one succeeds [say, in prioritizing generosity over greed] and the other does not, in a way that makes them not responsible?"[29] Kane, like Dennett, replies by subtly turning the question:

> if they both succeeded in trying to do what they were trying to do (because they were simultaneously trying to do both things), and then having succeeded, they both *endorsed* the outcomes of their respective efforts (that is, their choices) as what they were trying to do, instead of disowning or disassociating from those choices, how then can we *not* hold them responsible? It just does not follow that, because they made the same efforts, they chose by chance.[30]

28. Dennett, *Freedom Evolves*, 281–83.
29. Kane, "Responsibility, Luck, and Chance," 235.
30. Kane, "Responsibility, Luck, and Chance," 235.

Indeed, given Kane's appeal to indeterminacy, they did not choose by chance. They did not *choose* at all. For indeterminism cannot fund ultimate responsibility (i.e., UR).

At other junctures, Kane acknowledges that indeterminism cannot fund self-forming actions (i.e., SFAs).[31] At these junctures he becomes more cautious. The indeterminism within your brain is not you choosing, he clarifies, it is how "you choosing" *looks* from a physical perspective. Can the "you choosing" be seen any more clearly? Absolutely not, Kane replies, for this "more precisely" is a covert demand for *sufficient reasons*. But to provide sufficient reasons for an SFA is impossible by definition.[32] In this mode Kane is blunt:

> Let's not beat around the bush and postulate special ontological relations to obscure what we must say anyway and can say more simply. At crunch time, the agents just do it; they settle indecision, respond to indeterminacy, and take responsibility then and there for settling their lives on one or another future branching pathway [*N.B.*: an incompatibilist should say: "settle indecision, *decide*, and *are* ultimately responsible . . ."].[33]

Along this trajectory Kane avoids an inadequate appeal to indeterminism, but once SFAs are hidden somehow behind indeterminacies in the "self-network," Kane's fidelity to naturalism is compromised. If the SFA is not the indeterminism itself but is behind it as a cause that is itself of "underived origination," then Kane must be presupposing some special ontological relation. So, Dennett dismisses Kane's SFAs as "magic moments . . . buck-stopping instants in which the universe holds its breath while a quantum indeterminacy permits you to 'do-it-yourself,' creating yourself as a responsible moral agent (and you could have done otherwise)."[34] Kane's appeal to SFAs, concludes Dennett, is:

> a frankly mysterious doctrine, positing something unparalleled by anything we discover in the causal processes of chemical reactions, nuclear fission and fusion, magnetic attraction, hurricanes, volcanoes, or such biological processes as metabolism, growth, immune reactions, and photosynthesis.[35]

Similarly, Honderich argues that neuroscience:

31. Kane, *Significance of Free Will*, 183.
32. Kane, "Responsibility, Luck, and Chance," 236, 239.
33. Kane, *Significance of Free Will*, 193.
34. Dennett, *Freedom Evolves*, 272.
35. Dennett, *Freedom Evolves*, 287, 100.

provides clear and strong support for our theory of determinism. To speak differently, such support is provided by the general fact that neurons are causal. Do you say that a brain and
nervous system has in it a stunningly large number of neurons?
. . . That is true. But can it give you the idea that causation only
works at the bottom level of the brain? Well, it would be an odd
house or machine whose elements were all causal but whose
large substructures were not.[36]

With admirable frankness, Kane anticipates and concedes Dennett and
Honderich's objections. He closes *The Significance of Free Will* with repeated
confession that his theory does not, after all, "eliminate all mystery from free
will." And he concedes that while some sort of agent-causation theory may yet
be resuscitated, "the burden of proof must be on anyone who would do so."[37]

The Intelligibility of Free Will?

It is significant that Kane's inability to avoid appeal to mystery was, in fact,
inevitable, that Kane's conceptual framework rendered him helpless before
Hobbes's classic "intelligibility" objection. Recall three of Kane's critical
contentions. First, that, "what most needs explaining for indeterminist
theories of freedom" is, "Why did the agent rationally and voluntarily do
A here and now rather than doing otherwise?"[38] Second, that free will, and
hence "voluntarily," is defined in terms of UR. And third, that UR requires
the absence of sufficient reasons. The consequence of accepting these three
conditions is that it is no more possible for a decision to be made "rationally and voluntarily" than it is possible for an object to be both "round
and square." That is, the conceptual framework shared by Hobbes, Kane,
Dennett, and Honderich renders Kane's goals inconceivable *ab initio*. I will
attempt to make this point in three ways.

First, imagine a recent decisive free decision (i.e., an SFA). Call the
time of that decision t. Call the decision you made at t, B. Call C what was for
you at t another reasonable choice. Is it conceivable that at t you "rationally
and voluntarily" might have decided C? A determinist would answer, "no."
Kane would have to answer, "yes." But then Kane must explain why, "rationally and voluntarily," he chose B in one world and C in another. Since prior
to t all his experiences, ideas, and impulses—every firing of every neuron,

36. Honderich, *How Free Are You?* 67.

37. Kane, *Significance of Free Will*, 195. See also 150–51: "So I concede that indeterminate efforts are mysterious."

38. Kane, *Significance of Free Will*, 121.

every quantum resolution, all his understanding, all his interpretations, all his preferences—were realized, he cannot give a reasonable explanation for having chosen an alternative action. For, since there is no prior divergence at any level, any valid answer would face the impossible task of providing a rationale for choosing B over C that, simultaneously, could be a rationale for choosing C over B. Even if quantum indeterminacy riddled his past, at time *t* a single history has been realized, so there is no difference that could fund a reason for B versus a reason for C. Since "rational" means having reason for choosing one option over another (i.e., either B *or* C is the more reasonable/preferable option, but not both), and since "voluntary" means either B or C might have been chosen (i.e., B *and* C are both live possibilities), to demand something be "rational and voluntary" is as reasonable as demanding something be "round and square."

Second, note that UR makes free will unintelligible (and unscientific) by definition. Whether we pursue an explanation in terms of causes (science) or reasons (intelligibility), we seek an explanation sufficient to the event or action. If the explanation is not sufficient, then we consider it incomplete, and we continue searching for whatever causes or reasons will yield a sufficient explanation. To the degree no such reason or cause can be discerned (even in theory), we consider the event to be indeterminate and inexplicable. Now, recall that by definition UR requires the absence of sufficient reasons. Recall also that indeterminism cannot fund UR. So, one is left with an either/or: either, 1) a deterministic account, which is scientific and intelligible and explicable (i.e., rational); or, 2) an indeterministic account, which is scientific and a-rational (though not irrational) and inexplicable. In terms of either account, "voluntary and rational" is unintelligible.

Third, consider Kane's description of Steve and Steve* "simultaneously trying to do both things."[39] What, precisely, does "simultaneously trying" mean? There seem to be three possibilities, their efforts are symmetrical, asymmetrical, or indeterminate. If, 1) their efforts are *simultaneous but asymmetrical*, then the outcome is determined (for they inevitably choose that which they try more effectively to choose). If, 2) their efforts are *simultaneous but indeterminate*, then neither is ultimately responsible for either decision (for indeterminism cannot fund UR). If, 3) their efforts are *simultaneous and symmetrical*, then neither option will triumph (as with Buridan's infamous starving donkey, standing exactly equidistant between two piles of hay). None of the three options allows for "voluntary and rational."

In sum, what Kane appears to establish with unprecedented precision is: 1) incompatibilism hinges upon UR; 2) UR is a *sine qua non* in relation

---

39. Kane, "Responsibility, Luck, and Chance," 235.

to ordinary understanding of such cherished ideas as self-creation and aesthetic or moral ascription; and, 3) UR is fantasy, for, exhaustively, our legitimate options include determined decisions, indeterminate happenings (which may *feel*, remarkably and deceptively, like decisions), or an a-rational appeal to the supernatural (i.e., mystery, miracles, magic)—but no account of free will that is rational and voluntary. That is, *contra* Kane's own two requirements: no intelligible account of free will; no account of how free will fits in the natural order. My point, of course, is that this conclusion follows necessarily, *ab initio*, from conceptual presuppositions Kane shares with his opponents.

II. THE UNWITTING CAPITULATION OF DIE GEISTESWISSENSCHAFTEN: CHARLES TAYLOR

Charles Taylor's Defense of Moral Responsibility

In a 1971 essay, "How is Mechanism Conceivable?" Charles Taylor, a famed defender of *die Geisteswissenschaften* (i.e., the "sciences of spirit/mind"), notes that it is natural to assume that there "is no upper limit" to our ability to give a neurophysiological account of our every movement, and that "it is equally natural to assume that that account will be mechanistic.[40] But, Taylor says, "common sense is alarmed" by these assumptions, for it seems that, "somehow a complete mechanistic explanation would radically undermine our whole complex of notions which centre around freedom and moral responsibility."[41] Taylor refuses to abandon freedom and moral responsibility, and this on the basis of "an argument which seems to have no parallel elsewhere in philosophy. It is just that this supposition is *too preposterous to be believed*."[42] Any acceptable theory must "save the phenomena," must "be rich enough to incorporate the basis of . . . distinctions which, at present, mark the intentional world of human agents and which are essential to understand their behaviour."[43] It is simply "unthinkable" that "we have been talking nonsense all these millennia."[44]

   Taylor is not nearly so radical as he sounds. The basic concern over freedom and moral responsibility, he explains, arises because the "model of explanation in natural science which has been applied in physiology has

40. Taylor, *Human Agency and Language*, 164.
41. Taylor, *Human Agency and Language*, 164.
42. Taylor, *Human Agency and Language*, 169 (emphasis mine).
43. Taylor, *Human Agency and Language*, 174, 177.
44. Taylor, *Human Agency and Language*, 169, 170.

no place for ascriptions of bent or inclination; at the same time, it shies away from meaning relations as from the plague."[45] That is, mechanistic explanation "eschews all teleological and intentional concepts."[46] This raises a problem, Taylor continues, because these features "are an essential part of our notion of ourselves. If we can give a complete mechanistic explanation of our behaviour and feeling, then, we feel obscurely, this will amount to saying that these features are not essential after all. We are thus torn apart by the warring tendencies of our intellect."[47]

However, Taylor argues, we can retain teleological and intentional concepts *and* remain faithful to mechanism. We do not need ontological dualism or any bifurcation in our understanding of "cause." The "warring tendencies" can be displaced because "our ordinary accounts of action are causal in a perfectly straightforward sense, even if they are not mechanistic. . . . To know the purposes, desires, feelings or whatever, that condition people's behaviour is to know the causal background of their actions."[48] For instance, "want" within an intentional vocabulary invokes "cause" in a perfectly ordinary sense:

> if A wants G and sees that he can get it by B, then if there are no deterrents or obstacles . . . he does B of necessity: that is, this is what we mean by "want," for it ascribes a bent of the agent toward a certain consummation, and if with no obstacles or deterrents he fails to move in this direction, we cannot go on ascribing it to him.[49]

There is, Taylor concedes, an incommensurability between physical and intentional vocabularies, but this entails no ontological divide. The two vocabularies are not "talking about different things in any relevant sense, for identity-relations can easily be mapped between the two ranges of things described."[50] Of course, Taylor agrees, there would "be nothing in the neurophysiological theory like the concept 'want,'" which is a central category in talk of agency:

> but this would not prevent us from using connecting propositions such as 'the state Px is the state of the CNS [i.e., central

45. Taylor, *Human Agency and Language*, 166.

46. Taylor, *Human Agency and Language*, 186.

47. Taylor, *Human Agency and Language*, 166 (paragraph break between final two sentences of quote).

48. Taylor, *Human Agency and Language*, 166–67.

49. Taylor, *Human Agency and Language*, 172.

50. Taylor, *Human Agency and Language*, 167.

nervous system] which corresponds to what we call "wanting peanuts." We could indeed never show why wanting peanuts is followed by trying to get peanuts, but we could show why this behaviour follows Px; and this contingent nomological regularity would be what underlies (all unknown to us at present) our present use of the concept "wanting peanuts."[51]

But does not appeal to both conceptual (e.g., intentions) and physical (e.g., gravity) causal forces entail ontological dualism insofar as it invokes two incommensurable forces? No, answers Taylor. Consider the contrast between electromagnetic and gravitational forces in physics. Both forces are needed to explain certain events (e.g., "one can lift things with a magnet that otherwise would fall to the ground"), but no ontological dualism is implied.[52] Admittedly, an awkward conceptual incoherence obtains—sparking dreams of a final theory. But it makes no sense to affirm only one of the two vocabularies. Analogously, the antinomy between scientific laws and explanations and intentional concepts:

> reposes in the end on the identification of scientific laws and explanation in general with laws and explanations currently in vogue, viz. mechanistic ones. It is only by accepting this identification that we can show that the only alternatives to reductionism are dualism and exceptionalism.[53]

It is, however, "perfectly conceivable that we may move towards a neurophysiological theory which will not be reductive, in the sense that it will not show teleological and intentional concepts to be eliminable at a more basic level."[54] This, Taylor contends in answer to his title question, shows us how mechanism is conceivable. Abandoning the "preposterous" eschewal of intentional concepts, we can conceive of a neurophysiological "final theory." That is, we can "point towards a dissolution of the alternative mechanism-dualism" and work toward a "non-dualistic conception" that nevertheless does not entail a reductivist notion of the human sciences, thereby, "surmounting the antinomy of mechanism."[55]

51. Taylor, *Human Agency and Language*, 173.

52. Taylor, *Human Agency and Language*, 184.

53. Taylor, *Human Agency and Language*, 185.

54. Taylor, *Human Agency and Language*, 179.

55. Taylor, *Human Agency and Language*, 186.

Unintentionally Ceding Free Will and Moral Ascription

In light of Taylor's 1972 essay, the significance of Dennett, Honderich, and most especially Kane's work in the intervening decades is clarified. First, Taylor's call for a theory that retains a role for intentions and meanings while offering "accounts of action" that are "causal in a perfectly straight-forward sense," is answered by both Honderich and Dennett, who remain deterministic while invoking intentions and meanings (think, for instance, of Dennett's invocation of "memes" or of Honderich's defense of the "mental" and talk of "reasons"). Second, as is painfully clear in the wake of Kane's delineation of the significance of UR, Taylor's deterministic specifications for an enriched mechanism do not "save the phenomena" with which he is concerned (namely, free will and moral responsibility).

This leads to a startling conclusion: it is Taylor, not Dennett or Honderich, who best illustrates the modern conceptual dynamics that make free will unthinkable. For it is Taylor—who means to defend that "whole complex of notions which centre around freedom and moral responsibility"—who unintentionally elides the conceptual space this complex of notions requires.[56]

Again, determinism simply follows from the modern idea of "cause" (and the associated idea of "explanation") common to the *Natur-* and the *Geisteswissenwschaften*. To give an explanation is to provide sufficient reasons/causes such that an event can be seen to follow necessarily given the existence of the reasons/causes. To the degree one's explanation does not provide sufficient reasons, it is incomplete. To the degree sufficient reasons cannot be provided, the event is, to the best of our knowledge, indeterminate. Since UR excludes sufficient reasons and cannot be funded by indeterminacy, modern analysis *inevitably* ends with incompatibilism (i.e., affirmation of free will) appealing to something that appears magical, mysterious, or miraculous.

As Taylor, a classic defender of the *Geisteswissenschaften*, illustrates, the price Diltheans (if not Dilthey) ended up paying to purchase scientific respectability for the human sciences was the equating of "reasons" and "causes" in this sense.[57] Thus even defenders of the *Geisteswissenschaften* have presumed a rationality that makes free will unintelligible. It is not

---

56. Taylor, *Human Agency and Language*, 164.

57. Notably, this was not the case for Dilthey himself, whose defense of incommensurable *weltanshauung* specifically, and in a fashion not dissimilar to my argument here, defended the reasonableness of affirming a world in which free will in Kane's sense obtains (see Dilthey, "The Types of World-view and Their Development in the Metaphysical Systems"; and Dilthey, *Wilhelm Dilthey, Selected Works*, 55–72).

surprising, then, that even in departments of literature purportedly irrational and anti-scientific deconstructionists have brought the implications of the deterministic logic of the *Geisteswissenschaften* to the surface, ending rigorously with the "disappearance of the subject" ("we do not speak language, language speaks us"). It is not surprising that even Richard Rorty—commonly declared an anti-scientific prophet of poetry—applauded Dennett's compatibilism and affirmed that, "Physicalism is probably right in saying that we shall someday be able, 'in principle,' to predict every movement of a person's body."[58]

As Wayne Proudfoot, professor of religion at Columbia University, illustrates in discussion of the moral/religious thought of William James, the same presumptions are potent even within religious studies:

> The inquiries into language and culture that have occupied the humanities and the social sciences for most of the twentieth century, along with progress in the natural sciences, have led to beliefs that conflict with what James took to be the religious hypothesis. Any moral order, any *more* that is continuous with the higher parts of the self, any forces that might help to bring our ideals about, can be understood only as the emergent social products of the beliefs, desires, and actions of men and women. At the end of the nineteenth century, a number of thinkers subscribed to a kind of panpsychism, which they took to be compatible with the science of their day. At the end of the twentieth century, that belief is no longer plausible.[59]

Proudfoot goes on to explain that while there "is an unseen moral order," it, "consists of the social and cultural world that is a product of history."[60] All this, Proudfoot explains, is why for the past century "the humanities and social sciences have been preoccupied with the ways in which language is constitutive of agency, experience, social practices, and everything identified with *Geist* in the *Geisteswissenschaften*."[61]

In light of all this, it is not surprising that a naturalistic understanding of causation and explanation now seems as natural to "ordinary persons" in the West as their natural incompatibilism. Most every high school senior in the United States, for instance, has absorbed the idea that when it comes to our actions, the great debate is "nature or nurture?" (or, "genes or memes?")—an either/or that elides any conceptual space for "freely chosen."

---

58. Rorty, *Philosophy and the Mirror of Nature*, 355.
59. Proudfoot, "Religious Belief and Naturalism," 85.
60. Proudfoot, "Religious Belief and Naturalism," 85.
61. Proudfoot, "Religious Belief and Naturalism," 85.

So university professors can quickly demonstrate to startled Philosophy 101 students that, in obvious accord with understandings of cause and explanation they all already accept, free will and ordinary understandings of moral responsibility are chimeric.

III. THE REASONABLENESS OF FREE WILL

Zeno's paradoxes are easily refuted. Simply walk out of the room. Of course, that would miss the point. Zeno's paradoxes were significant because they unveiled previously undetected epistemological and ontological lacuna in contemporary thought and so served as cautions and as stimuli to creative new ways of thinking through fundamental epistemological and metaphysical questions. The arguments of determinists from Hobbes to Honderich and Dennett should serve similarly.

Admittedly, choosing something freely is not as compelling a refutation as walking out of a room. But, ultimately, precisely and nothing other than such first-person intuitions of ultimate responsibility (UR) and self-forming actions (SFAs) lie at the heart of lay and professional rejection of determinism from Bishop Bramhall to Robert Kane.[62] As is now evident, however, the conceptual terrain required to make incompatibilism intelligible has long been ceded not only by analytic philosophers like Kane, but even by defenders of the *Geisteswissenschaften* like Taylor. That is, given the conceptual power in the West of our natural naturalism, our natural incompatibilism has become literally unthinkable. Simultaneously, our natural incompatibilism has remained so fundamental to societal and self understanding that Taylor rejects the unthinkability itself as "unthinkable."

Determinism is not unthinkable. But given the collective weight of human consensus and practice, Taylor is right to conclude that it is, *prima facie*, too preposterous to be believed. Only a very strong argument should convince us of the falsehood of incompatibilism. Contrary to common presumption, no such argument exists. There exists only a weakly supported premise, which has surreptitiously evolved into a dogma.

The Dogma

The premise is obvious but typically suppressed: the modern scientific (i.e., naturalistic, empiricist, "efficient") notion of cause is not only accurate but exhaustive. Clearly, as the incredible success of modern science attests, the

---

62. See Kane, *Significance of Free Will*, 77, 79–101.

naturalistic notion of cause is accurate. But no landmark argument has established that it is exhaustive. What triumphed between the time of Hobbes and ourselves was not an argument but, thanks to the stunning advance of modern science, a slowly emerging background consensus. "Why did you do that?" came to be considered equivalent to "what caused that?" That is, the action vocabulary of reasons (initially endemic to Descartes or Kant's mental or noumenal spheres) came to be interpreted as a verbal variation *within* the event vocabulary of causes (initially endemic to Descartes or Kant's material or phenomenal spheres). The suppressed premise has evolved into an unspoken and virtually unquestioned dogma of modern reason in English-language academia—presumed by Dennett, Honderich, Taylor, and Kane alike.

Bowing to the dogma, Kane demands we delineate free will within the natural order and chastises those who end with their minds "clouded in mist." Bowing to the dogma, Taylor calms the "warring tendencies of our intellect" by stressing that action accounts are causal in a straightforward sense. By dint of the dogma, Honderich, when confronted with Kane's appeal to our immediate intuition of willing freely, bluntly asserts, "this kind of supposition cannot be right . . . since it offends against the fact that causal enquiry and causal reasoning are in an essential way general. All clear and arguable accounts of it agree."[63] By dint of the dogma, Dennett flatly confesses that his "fundamental perspective is naturalism" and proclaims, "the proper job for philosophers . . . is to clarify and unify the often warring perspectives [i.e., of the natural sciences and of philosophy] into a single vision of the universe."[64] The dogma even encourages Dennett to ridicule those who reject naturalism (they are "alarmist," desperately invoking "obscure and panicky metaphysics" and "mysterion doctrines").[65]

There is, Dennett simply proclaims, no "God-like power to exempt oneself from the causal fabric of the physical world," but, he continues incredulously, "unrepentant dualists and others actually embrace the idea that it would take a miracle of sorts for there to be free will."[66] For example, he notes, Roderick Chisolm posits we can act as "a prime mover unmoved." But, Dennett retorts:

63. Honderich, *How Free Are You?* 78.

64. Dennett, *Freedom Evolves*, 15.

65. Dennett, *Freedom Evolves*, 14–15, 16, 21 ("obscure and panicky" he credits to P. F. Strawson). Due to the strength of the dogma, even a sympathetic reviewer in *The Philosophical Review* feels bound to acknowledge that the sort of causation Kane and Timothy O'Conner invoke is "spooky" (Huemer, Review of *The Oxford Handbook of Free Will*, 280).

66. Dennett, *Freedom Evolves*, 100.

> How do "we" cause these events to happen? How does an *agent*
> cause an effect without there being an event (in the agent, pre-
> sumably) that is the cause of that effect (and is itself the effect of
> an earlier cause, and so forth)?[67]

Dennett treats this as an obviously devastating argument against Chisolm (and Kane). But this is no argument. Dennett's rhetorical questions
simply presuppose the dogma. When Dennett gestures toward an argument
for the dogma, he succeeds only in exposing its vulnerability:

> Agent causation is a frankly mysterious doctrine, positing some-
> thing unparalleled by anything we discover in the causal pro-
> cesses of chemical reactions, nuclear fission and fusion, magnetic
> attraction, hurricanes, volcanoes, or such biological processes as
> metabolism, growth, immune reactions, and photosynthesis.[68]

This stupendous extrapolation (i.e., from volcanoes to brains/minds)
has long stood in the stead of any focused argument for the dogma. Dennett
cites the classic formulation of Pierre-Simon Laplace:

> An intellect which at any given moment knew all the forces
> that animate Nature and the mutual positions of the beings that
> comprise it, if this intellect were vast enough to submit its data
> to analysis, could condense into a single formula the movement
> of the greatest bodies of the universe and that of the lightest
> atom: for such an intellect nothing could be uncertain; and the
> future just like the past would be present before its eyes.[69]

Laplace presumes that the idea of causation inferred from study of
objects such as planets was accurate not only in relation to those objects,
but exhaustively. Given the limitations of physics, let alone biology and
chemistry, in 1814, it is remarkable that Laplace's claim never emerged as a
textbook example of the fallacy of hasty generalization.

"Perhaps Laplace's claim was premature," one may retort, "but Dennett
speaks after two more centuries of stunning scientific advance." Certainly, but
the increase in knowledge has not resulted in an unqualified increase in confidence—especially vis-à-vis so fundamental a phenomena as causation. To
the contrary, duly impressed physicists now commonly voice their suspicion
that the world may be not only stranger than we did imagine, but stranger
than we *can* imagine. In this context, the audacity of Dennett's stupendously

---

67. Dennett, *Freedom Evolves*, 100.

68. Dennett, *Freedom Evolves*, 100.

69. Dennett, *Freedom Evolves*, 28, citing Laplace, *A Philosophical Essay on Probabilities*.

hasty generalization from photosynthesis to brainwaves, from hurricanes to consciousness, from immune reactions to free will, should be patent.

Honderich, as we saw, makes the same hasty generalization at the critical juncture in his argument: "it would be an odd house or machine whose elements were all causal but whose large substructures were not."[70] The audacity of his leap from houses to brains/minds is patent when the same appeal is made relative to the question of consciousness: "it would be an odd house or machine whose elements were all lacking consciousness, but whose large substructures were not." True enough. But it hardly follows that we lack consciousness. Nor, likewise, does it follow that we lack free will. To the contrary, the case of consciousness indicates that when it comes to structures as incredibly complex as brains, emergent properties not predicable of the parts may reasonably be predicated of the whole. Or indeed, the case of consciousness may indicate that entirely different (i.e., other than naturalistic) vocabularies and background conceptualities might be required.

Hume's Critical Reminder

It is helpful to recall, as Hume pointed out, that "necessary connection," the idea at the core of the pertinent notion of "cause," is derived neither from an *a priori* deduction nor from direct observation. It is an abstraction derived from observation of regularities in nature. Dennett cites Hume's argument but tames it, reducing Hume's point to the contention that there are no logical guarantees that the regularities of nature will forever obtain. He then promptly interprets Hume's point within a determinist/indeterminist paradigm that presumes the very idea of necessary connection that Hume brings into question:

> Bearing in mind Hume's ominous discovery that we can never prove that the future will be like the past, we can nevertheless set out to find what regularities we can and make the huge but tempting wager—what do we have to lose?—that the future *will* be like the past, that we are not in one of those bizarre universes that leads us down the garden path only to disappoint us by going haywire after a longish period of regularity.
>
> We now have a way of sorting Democritean universes into the deterministic, the indeterministic, and then all the junk.[71]

---

70. Honderich, *How Free Are You?* 67.
71. Dennett, *Freedom Evolves*, 35.

Hume's argument, however, undercuts the background dogma which delimits these three as the only conceivable options. Hume's argument is more penetrating than Dennett acknowledges.[72] It opens the possibility that there might be "universes" (e.g., like our own) with wholly other types of causation. For instance, universes in which we infer the character of causation partly from consideration of our experience of making rational and voluntary choices (as did Aristotle); universes, that is, which include understanding of a type of "cause" that describes decisions that are *rational and voluntary* (e.g., correlate with the way ordinary persons think of the relation between reasons and actions). That is, universes that include an understanding of "cause" that is for us, insofar as we accept the dogma, unthinkable.

Dennett's, "what do we have to lose?" then, pertains not to the mundane question of whether or not we should gamble on the endurance of past regularities, but to our acceptance of the dogma. Since this truly huge wager involves UR and free will, the answer to "what do we have to lose?" is, "a lot," namely, that whole prized complex of notions associated with our natural idea of free will and moral responsibility. We should ask, rather, "What do we have to lose if we reject the dogma, gamble on the accuracy of the deterministic, scientific notion of cause as it pertains to gross physical objects (e.g., hurricanes, houses, planets), but bet that when it comes to incredibly complex physical objects like human brains, or to realities such as consciousness, the explanatory concepts of scientific naturalism are stretched beyond their sphere of valid application, and affirm free will?"

Reasonable Incommensurability[73]

Given their arguments, in response to my substitute question Kane and Taylor, no less than Dennett and Honderich, would respond, "What do we have to lose? Coherence! Rationality!" In the "Introduction" to his *Essays on Actions and Events*, Donald Davidson dramatically declares:

> Cause is the cement of the universe; the concept of cause is what holds together our picture of the universe, a picture that would otherwise disintegrate into a diptych of the mental and the physical.[74]

72. Perhaps, given his compatibilism, more penetrating than even Hume acknowledges.

73. For my argument in this section, and indeed, for the most critical elements of the entire argument, I am profoundly indebted to Taylor's later essays, "Revised Transcendental Reasoning" and "Overcoming Epistemology" (*Philosophical Arguments*), and to the historicist form of rationality he practices in *Sources of the Self*.

74. Davidson, *Essays on Actions and Events*, xi.

Note the subtle but critical shift from cause being "the cement *of the universe*," to cause being "what holds together *our picture* of the universe, a picture that would otherwise disintegrate into a diptych of the mental and the physical." Talk about panicky metaphysics. Davidson gives no argument against the diptych; all his essays simply presuppose the dogma.

Davidson, of course, is assailing the infamous Cartesian mind/matter dualism. This dualism (and variants like Kant's noumenal/phenomenal) has been judged irrational because it simultaneously posits two wholly distinct ontological realms that, it also affirms in direct self-contradiction, interact. This is obviously incoherent. Thus not only Kane but even Taylor, who explicitly warned us not to identify explanation in general with the forms of explanation now in vogue, explicitly identifies cause in general with the modern scientific idea of cause now in vogue (i.e., he accepts the dogma). Taylor cites the classic objection to any mind/matter dualism. It is "particularly implausible," he concludes, "since it involves non-interference between the two realms."[75] But this classic objection should be reassessed in light of the historicist, evolutionary epistemology one might reasonably expect of any empiricist. For it turns out that "incoherent" does not necessarily mean "irrational"—to the contrary.

Descartes's basic mistake was not his embarrassing "pineal gland" speculations, but his overly-ambitious presumption that his reasoning isolated two distinct substances out of which all reality was composed. It is more appropriate to acknowledge that we are faced not with two wholly distinct substances, but with two mostly distinct and imperfect vocabularies, not with a diptych in reality, but with a diptych in our picture of reality. In our millennia-old and ongoing struggle to describe accurately the ultimate contours of the reality we partly constitute and inhabit as conscious beings, we have developed (at least) two indispensable and highly sophisticated vocabularies (e.g., mental, physical) that are not commensurable.

The determinist idea of cause and effect was isolated and developed specifically in relation to our dealings with "nature." Notably, this was not the Aristotelian "nature" of the medieval period, but "nature" as it came to be defined through the scientific revolution, namely, "nature" as the sphere in which explanations were framed exclusively in terms of what, speaking roughly, had been the Aristotelian spheres of material and efficient "causation." This is the modern meaning of nature aligned with Descartes's "matter" or Kant's "phenomenal" spheres and with today's naturalistic science. Within "nature" in this modern sense one isolates mechanistic,

---

75. Taylor, *Human Agency and Language*, 181–82.

deterministic/indeterministic events that are, if not random, explicable in terms of sufficient causes.

Over the millennia, however, our experiences led us to develop another significant sphere of vocabularies that remain indispensable to our ordinary understanding of free will and moral and aesthetic ascription. The sphere delineated by these vocabularies corresponds with Descartes's "mind," Kant's "noumenal," and with the SFAs and UR of our "natural" incompatibilism. Within this sphere one finds voluntary and rational actions (i.e., SFAs) that are explicable in terms of reasons. Even when the action is seen to follow clearly from the reasons, the connection is not considered to be necessary (i.e., for it to be an action, there must be some measure of UR). To reiterate, an agentival vocabulary of, for example, moral praise or culpability and of poetic creativity, is virtually indispensable to current human understanding, and is the collective product of generations upon generations among a multitude of cultures. We should be persuaded to abandon it only if compelled by a very powerful argument.

Given our ever-increasing wonder before the incredible complexity of reality, there is nothing inconceivable, or even particularly surprising, about the fact that over the millennia we have developed two incommensurable vocabularies.[76] At this early stage in humanity's intellectual journey, moreover, to embrace incommensurable vocabularies that leave us with an incoherent yet critically comprehensive picture of reality is clearly more rational than to embrace a single vocabulary that, while yielding overall coherence amongst our vocabularies, renders us unable to articulate our experience of critical phenomena.

At present, however, the conceptual reduction of reasons to causes is so thorough that English-speaking Western intellectuals tend simply to equate thinking rigorously with thinking in terms of the dogma. For instance, Kane comments that though we ordinarily believe in free will, we "reject it in our more reflective moments." Quite so, but only because "more reflective" here translates into "more naturalistic," for once the vocabulary of reasons is reduced to the vocabulary of causes, our everyday talk of free will becomes literally unintelligible. Since this reduction depends upon the dogma, however, our supposedly "more reflective moments" are, *vis-à-vis* mental phenomena, profoundly confused (and, *vis-à-vis* the debate over free will, question begging).

---

76. Note that "incommensurable" means simply that no common coordinate system can currently be found to coordinate among vocabularies. It does not follow that we are incapable of *understanding* more than one incommensurable vocabulary, or to switch from one to the other in response to real-time needs or desires.

By contrast, a rigorous empiricist, evolutionary epistemology will remember that the contours of rationalities themselves, including their most basic construal of logic or causality, are a product of our experiences and are carried within vocabularies developed in conversation with various streams of experience. Accordingly, it will retain and rigorously distinguish a vocabulary that accounts for our experience of SFAs and UR.[77] That is, a rigorous empiricism will strictly delimit the usage of terms and their correlate rationalities as they are inscribed in various vocabularies (e.g., physical vs. psychical). For instance, it will note that to ask "what *caused* you to *choose* A?" is precisely as confused as asking "for what *reason* did that rock *decide* to fall?" It will distinguish talk of "sufficient reasons," which pertain to the reasonableness of SFAs, from talk of "sufficient causes," which pertain to deterministic relations between cause and effect. It will say not "ultimate responsibility lies where ultimate *cause* is," but "ultimate responsibility is correlate to the degree of one's exercise of free will (relative to nature, nurture, and/or coercion)." It will pierce the confusion structuring the reasoning of the following argument, from philosopher Saul Smilansky—which, to those bewitched by the dogma, looks unassailable:

> The reason why I believe that libertarian free will is impossible, in a nutshell, is that the conditions required by an ethically satisfying sense of libertarian free will, which would give us anything beyond sophisticated formulations of compatibilism, are self-contradictory, and hence cannot be met. This is so irrespective of determinism or causality. Attributing moral worth to a person for her decision or action requires that it follow from what she is, morally. The decision or action cannot be produced by a random occurrence and count morally. We might think that two different decisions or actions can follow from a person, but which of them does, say, a decision to steal or not to steal, again cannot be random but needs to follow from what she is, morally. But what a person is, morally, cannot be under her control. We might think that such control is possible if she

---

77. Notably, SFAs and UR are evidently functions of an emergent reality. So, like consciousness, they are not experienced directly *via* the five senses. Insofar as we are conscious, the conclusion that all reality must be directly perceptible through the five senses is false. Just as the inability to sense consciousness directly through the five senses does not entail that consciousness is illusory, like inability to sense free will does not entail that free will is illusory. To insist that "experience" by definition excludes UR or consciousness or anything else not sensed directly through the five senses is to beg the question by defining experience, and thereby the parameters of any possible metaphysics, *ab initio* in terms of a naturalistic vocabulary (i.e., to treat an *a posteriori* vocabulary as if it were *a priori*). For a good beginning along another trajectory, see Levinas, *The Theory of Intuition in Husserl's Phenomenology*.

creates herself, but then it is the early self that creates a later self, leading to vicious infinite regress. The libertarian project was worthwhile attempting: it was supposed to allow a deep moral connection between a given act and the person, and yet not fall into being merely an unfolding of the arbitrarily given, whether determined or random. But it is not possible to find any way in which this can be done.[78]

Once the dogma is unveiled, it is clear that such reasoning does not hold "irrespective of determinism or causality." To the contrary, a scientific conception of causality, taken to be metaphysically exhaustive (i.e., the dogma), decisively structures such understanding. Since the dogma is presumed, only two options for understanding the origins of a moral decision emerge. They are: 1) "random," (i.e., indeterminism) or, 2) "the early self that creates a later self" (i.e., determinism). The deterministic/indeterministic understanding of causality endemic to the vocabulary of modern science thereby structures this understanding. Since the deterministic/indeterministic either/or is presumed to be exhaustive (the dogma), free will is rendered incomprehensible. But insofar as the dogma is neither identified nor defended, the critical question is begged.

Hobbes's classic objections, likewise, constitute an invitation to beg the critical question. Kane accepts the invitation with his fateful fidelity to the dogma. Believing that incompatibilists must meet Hobbes's objections, he insists that incompatibilists complete two tasks that are impossible by definition. For, first, one cannot make SFAs intelligible within a naturalistic vocabulary, for they are endemic to another vocabulary. The explanatory parameters of naturalism entail that, given the dogma, every naturalistic attempt to explain SFAs in a naturalistic vocabulary will appear empty or confused. As was illustrated in every critique of Kane in Part I, the naturalistic options always reduce to determinism, indeterminism, or mystery. For the same reason, second, one cannot give an account of SFAs in the natural order (where "natural" is construed exhaustively in accord with the dogma). Thus, Kane's starting points subvert his arguments. Once freed of the dogma, Kane can eliminate the ambiguities and tensions which now haunt his otherwise brilliant delineation of the contour and significance of free will.

78. Saul Smilansky recounting a critical aspect of his argument from *Free Will and Illusion* at Ted Honderich's "Determinism and Freedom Philosophy" website ("Why Not Libertarian Free Will"—see https://www.ucl.ack/uk/~uctytho/dfwVariousSmilansky.htm).

Vocabularies and Reality: Realistic Realism

This argument suggests no ontological dualism (it is more modest than that). It does not posit the existence of some mysterious, non-material essence that floats somewhere behind our brains. It does not recommend embrace of self-contradictory vocabularies. It certainly does not suggest the disintegration of reason. But it does acknowledge that we have not yet developed a vocabulary that perfectly and exhaustively describes all dimensions of reality. It thereby avoids the standard critiques Honderich levels against dualism:

> A distinction between two worlds or two conceptions of *the world* is of course possible. . . . But there seems no hope whatever of locating indeterminism and freedom significantly in only one of them, and certainly no hope for taking it out of the experienced world entirely. In any case, since what is undetermined and free must in some sense turn up in both worlds, it is impossible to see that the contradiction is actually escaped. Certainly there can be no good sense in the sort of philosophical speculation that supposes there can be two ways of seeing the same things, two perspectives on them, such that what is true about these same things in one perspective can be safely contradicted in the other perspective.[79]

Of course, the contradictions between the vocabularies of nature and free agency have not been escaped, but that indicates only that our understanding is yet imperfect. Moreover, we do locate free will within naturalism, and it does not appear as a contradiction. As Kane said, "when described from a physical perspective alone, *free will looks like chance*."[80] Likewise, determinism appears within incompatibilism as the physical, psychological, and/or socio-cultural structures/conditioning that circumscribe the range of all our free willing. At such junctures what appears are not contradictions but gaps or limits indicating aspects of reality where a vocabulary exceeds its sphere of valid application.

Honderich's fear about the irrationality of making contradictory remarks about "the same things" is likewise assuaged by humility. The classic example, now dated, obtained when light, the "same thing," was most

79. Honderich, *How Free Are You?* 146.

80. Kane, *Significance of Free Will*, 147. Ironically, Dennett was right that from a naturalistic perspective Kane's SFAs look like, "magic moments . . . buck-stopping instants in which the universe holds its breath while a quantum indeterminacy permits you to 'do-it-yourself,' creating yourself as a responsible moral agent (and you could have done otherwise)." Apart from the dogma, however, this is no objection to SFAs.

reasonably described in terms of waves or particles. The two vocabularies were incommensurable. But no "wave" advocates castigated "particle" partisans for creating a diptych. There was no fretting over ontological dualism because no one was silly enough to declare that they had isolated two wholly distinct substances. What was manifest was not any ontological dualism but the limits of two vocabularies. Given the evidence, it was most rational to retain both vocabularies, to oscillate on an *ad hoc* basis between them in accord with one's objectives, and to remain open to the possibility of a new vocabulary that would allow one to transcend the incommensurability.

We face an analogous situation *vis-à-vis* our understanding of the ultimate character of reality. Given first the power and universality of human intuitions of SFAs and UR, and second the frailty of the dogma, it is currently more rational to maintain that human actions are better described using both physical and agentival vocabularies and, more specifically, to affirm that the human brain is better described using both vocabularies. We should not posit the existence of some non-material soul that is ontologically distinct from the brain yet in causal relationship with it. That *would* be absurd. Incompatibilists need only point out that evidently the naturalistic vocabulary is accurate but not exhaustive *vis-à-vis* brains.[81] Agentival descriptions are also essential, for they describe aspects of the ultimate character of "brains" that current science cannot fathom.

Science may someday advance to the point where it can give an account of free will. To appropriate Taylor: it is perfectly conceivable that we may move towards a neurophysiological theory that will not be reductive, in the sense that it will not render free will inconceivable. But that highly advanced vocabulary is at least as distant from our current forms of understanding as Aristotelian physics was from quantum theory. Of course, however preposterous it now seems, the dogma may ultimately be proven correct, free will may be an illusion. It is also possible that the universe *is* stranger than we can imagine, and that embrace of incommensurable vocabularies is forever our lot. It is simply too soon to tell.

---

81. Incompatibilists are typically driven toward the absurdity because, conceding the dogma, they allow determinists to define "brain" exhaustively in naturalistic terms. This leaves incompatibilists with no choice but to posit something "supernatural" behind the brain. This would be no problem if "supernatural" were understood rigorously as meaning merely: "outside 'nature' as circumscribed by the vocabulary of scientific naturalism." In the wake of the influence of the dogma, however, "supernatural" is commonly interpreted pejoratively among intellectuals as "otherworldly," "magical," "miraculous," or "God-like." That is, given the dogma, any labeling of the source of free will will inevitably appear to invoke a "ghost in the machine." To exorcise the "ghost" by rejecting all non-naturalistic predication is not a philosophical advance, but a question-begging rejection of any non-naturalistic vocabulary.

In the meantime, it is most reasonable to retain the families of both psychical and physical vocabularies, to oscillate between them on an *ad hoc* basis according to our purposes, and to continue to advance the subtlety and power of each within its distinct conceptual parameters. Incompatibilists like Kane, moreover, should not (*contra* Kane) assume the burden of proof: it currently rests upon determinists. Determinists like Dennett and Honderich have greatly enhanced our understanding of freedom and free will and their inquiries may continue to bear fruit. But they can, at best, embrace the dogma as a working hypothesis.[82] Otherwise, it is most reasonable to adopt a Davidsonian principle of charity and to expect that the basic affirmations of both our physical and agentival vocabularies will someday be taken up in some as-yet undreamt vocabulary (i.e., preserved if somewhat modified as recontextualized). Ideally, this new vocabulary would not only unify the still incommensurable sub-vocabularies that now articulate the fundamental forces of physics, it would unify the vocabularies of all the natural sciences with all our existential, ethical, and aesthetic vocabularies. Now *that* would be a final theory—and may well be forever beyond human imagining.

❖ ❖ ❖

Once the frailty of the dogma is unveiled and a properly historicist, non-reductive, evolutionary epistemology is invoked, the antinomy between determinism and free will is tamed, if not resolved, and it becomes clear that currently it is rational to affirm free will and irrational to dismiss it. It turns out that all Kane's "natural incompatibilists"—"ordinary persons" innocent of philosophy's dogmatic critiques of free will and in their daily lives blithely oscillating on an *ad hoc* basis between incommensurable agentival and physical vocabularies—have pretty much been following the most reasonable course all along.

---

82. Dennett's contention that all freedoms "worth wanting" are compatible with determinism has, to say the least, failed to convince either incompatibilists (including most every "ordinary person") or even many determinists (e.g., hard determinists). Moreover, Dennett's arguments trade heavily upon the dogma. Once the dogma is disarmed and it becomes clear that free will and associated ideals (e.g., moral ascription) can reasonably be predicated, Dennett's contention that such predication is not "worth wanting" loses most all of its already limited force.

Chapter 6

On Ted Honderich's *Actual Consciousness*

Actual Consciousness is the latest version of Ted Honderich's new and widely discussed theory of consciousness. In an earlier iteration he called his theory—the focus of a double issue of *Journal of Consciousness Studies* in 2006—"Radical Externalism." Honderich's audience is fellow analytic philosophers (who work in accord with what Honderich calls "mainstream philosophy"). For theologians, this clear but technical book provides a reliable road map to the five leading "mainstream" ideas about consciousness (namely: "qualia, something it is like to be a thing, subjectivity, intentionality, or aboutness, and phenomenality" [xiii]), and also to the various problems that have kept any of these theories, each of which is highly developed, from general acceptance. Moreover, Honderich maps and in many instances briefly summarizes the essential contributions of every major, English-language participant in the mainstream debate. The summaries are necessarily and admittedly insufficient, but are accurate as far as they go, and also help to map the mainstream conceptual landscape.

In a word, Honderich's goal is to give a complete explanation of what consciousness *is*. In contrast to what Honderich takes to be ongoing confusion over the existence of free will, which for him simply does not exist, there is no denying that consciousness actually is. So the mainstream challenge is to explain consciousness while remaining within the parameters of modern science, which means explaining how consciousness is physical. More precisely, for Honderich this means that consciousness must be: in the inventory of science, open to scientific method, in space and time, and in particular and categorical lawful connections with other realities (these are essential criteria of "physical").

Honderich suggests that working within the parameters of the physical in this modern scientific sense allows one to avoid trafficking in metaphysics. This illicit and all-too-common suggestion insulates mainstream philosophy by masking the fact that its metaphysic is asserted, nowhere established. Insofar as free will and creativity (in the ordinary senses), moral reality and personal responsibility, let alone God, are essential to theology, what Honderich asserts as basic to any credible understanding forecloses upon the credibility of theology (for none of these fit in Honderich's "mainstream" ontology).

Honderich argues that reality (i.e., "physicality") has two aspects. There is an *objective physical world* and also (his startling, novel move) *subjective physicality*. Consciousness is endemic to/*is* subjective physicality and has two parts, the *subjective physical worlds* of *perceptual consciousness* and the *subjective physical representations* of *cognitive consciousness* and *affective consciousness*. Honderich's theory may well become the sixth leading idea about consciousness, but it is far from clear it can eliminate even mainstream philosophers' fear that the essence of consciousness remains elusive.

Honderich's idea of "subjective physicality" is oddly reminiscent of Heidegger's idea of "world," but since for Honderich consciousness remains *in* time, he never escapes what Heidegger identifies as a "crass" understanding of time. So Honderich never approaches Heidegger's far more revolutionary understanding of the relation among time, *Dasein*, physicality, cause, reality, and truth. Honderich has only disdain for metaphysicians such as Heidegger, but as one recognizes the insufficiencies not only of the five leading mainstream ideas about consciousness, but also the insufficiency of Honderich's theory, it is hard not to be reminded of Husserl, who, precisely because of his brilliance and rigor, in failure stimulated the revolutionary philosophies of Heidegger and Levinas, which derail the naturalistic metaphysics of "mainstream philosophy" and set us on the path to rigorous (i.e., clear [if difficult], consistent, complete, and general) and far more illuminating understandings of consciousness, free will, creativity, and moral reality and, in good "love of wisdom" fashion, remain in dialogue with the world's classic wisdom traditions.

Chapter 7

Christian Ethics in a Postmodern World?

Hauerwas, Stout, and Christian Moral Bricolage

SETTING THE STAGE

Cartesianism and the Dream of Modernity

Jeffrey Stout traces the origin of modernity to the philosophy of René Descartes.[1] Responding to an age when the diversity of authorities was leading to violent civil strife and to conflict between the church and respected scientists such as Galileo, Descartes initiated a pivotal move away from authority and tradition. He turned instead to the natural light of reason and defined knowledge as that which could not possibly be doubted.

The flight *from* authority, therefore, was simultaneously a flight *to* objective reason and certitude. Philosophical method underwent significant permutations in the following centuries, but the modernist dream of attaining certain knowledge through a foundationalist epistemology endured.

---

1. Stout, *Flight from Authority*, 31–65.

The Eclipse of the Ethical Dream of Modernity

The *ethical* dream of modernism is to delineate universal ethical criteria. As Stanley Hauerwas notes, "contemporary ethical theory has tried to secure for moral judgments an objectivity that would free such judgments from the subjective beliefs, wants, and stories of the agents who make them."[2] The undergirding assumption of the modern approach is that morally justifiable reasons must be completely objective.[3] Only such objective judgments, the modernist believes, can ensure that we do not slide into an abyss of nihilism, skepticism, or relativism.

We have, however, begun to understand the implications of the insight that one's prejudices, far more than one's judgments, constitute the historical reality of one's being.[4] The long-idolized appeal to an objective, neutral reason, to a reason free from preconceived opinions, has been exposed as whimsy. This historicist insight, emerging simultaneously in diverse disciplines, signals "postmodernity."[5]

Ethics After Modernity

Alasdair MacIntyre's *After Virtue* (1984) presented the first widely influential account of the implications of the postmodern condition for ethics.[6] MacIntyre contends that moral debate today takes place in largely incommensurable (*not* "untranslatable") languages, which are the unrecognized fragments of previously coherent ethical wholes. Consequently, public ethical discourse has degenerated into an "emotivism."

MacIntyre argues that the Enlightenment project of justifying morality *had* to fail because Enlightenment thinkers failed to notice the three distinctive developments of the moral scheme that they had inherited: "untutored human nature, man-as-he-could-be-if-he-realized-his-*telos*, and the moral precepts which enable him to pass from one state to the other."[7] Consequently, they did not discern that "the joint effect of the secular rejection of both Protestant and Catholic theology and the scientific and

---

2. Hauerwas, *Truthfulness and Tragedy*, 16.

3. Hauerwas, *Truthfulness and Tragedy*, 17; and Hauerwas, *The Peaceable Kingdom*, 11.

4. Gadamer, *Truth and Method*, 245.

5. Bernstein, *Beyond Objectivism and Relativism*.

6. MacIntyre, *After Virtue*.

7. MacIntyre, *After Virtue*, 54–55.

philosophical rejection of Aristotelianism was to eliminate any notion of man-as-he-could-be-if-he-realized-his-*telos*."[8]

This rejection, MacIntyre explains, amounted to the "invention" of the truly autonomous individual.[9] With this invention, the functional concept of "man"—variants of which both Aristotelian and Christian ethics depended on to justify the logic of the move from "is" to "ought"—was destroyed.[10] For example, while for Aristotle freedom was not an end in itself but intrinsically related to the *telos* of humans, in the modern period the stress centered on freedom as an end in itself.[11] Freedom became a trans-cultural, trans-historical foundation of ethics. It is our recognition of the impossibility of sustaining modernist projects of this sort that has spawned a sense of chaos.

A Sense of Chaos

The historicist seeds of postmodernity are rooted in modern thought. Postmodernism, therefore, does not signal a distinct philosophical period as much as a community-wide recognition of the depth and implications of Lessing's infamous ditch. The term *postmodernism* is largely a heuristic device for naming the ethos that accompanies the shock of this recognition.

The failure to establish an objective basis for rational discussion has bred the postmodern ethos, for we have been weaned on the modernist confidence that our most fundamental ethical convictions can be objectively established.[12] We have held our most fundamental ethical assumptions as unquestionably objective and universal. They have been so basic that they are "like the air we breathe."[13]

As we become aware that all "ethical reflection occurs relative to a particular time and place," however, we recognize that even fundamental questions about the good or the right necessarily draw "on the particular convictions of historic communities to whom such questions may have significantly different meanings."[14] We experience a "feeling of chaos" because the "very 'air we breathe' is being questioned."[15]

8. MacIntyre, *After Virtue*, 54.

9. MacIntyre, *After Virtue*, 60–61.

10. MacIntyre, *After Virtue*, 58.

11. Hauerwas, *Peaceable Kingdom*, 8.

12. Hauerwas, *Peaceable Kingdom*, 10.

13. Hauerwas, *Peaceable Kingdom*, 4.

14. Hauerwas, *Peaceable Kingdom*, 1.

15. Hauerwas, *Peaceable Kingdom*, 4.

Richard Bernstein in *Beyond Objectivism and Relativism* aptly labels the sense of chaos which accompanies the dashing of our Cartesian ambitions "Cartesian anxiety."[16] This Cartesian anxiety is most powerfully felt within the realm of ethics. If there is no objective basis for rational discussion, how are we to avoid the spectres of skepticism, nihilism, or relativism? How do we justify our struggle against injustice, oppression, and prejudice? In the face of these concerns, Jeffrey Stout and Stanley Hauerwas offer two distinct and influential ethical alternatives for our postmodern age.

THE ETHICS OF A POSTMODERN PRAGMATIST: JEFFREY STOUT

Modern Virtue for a Postmodern Age

In *Ethics after Babel*, Jeffrey Stout extends a pragmatic plea that we accept our finitude and seek out practical wisdom. Where MacIntyre laments the "new dark ages which are already upon us," Stout searches for "Virtue among the Ruins."[17]

The invaluable insight that the modernist legacy has bequeathed us is "the recognition, born of *phronesis* and forged in the religious strife of early modern Europe, that the good life for us must make allowances for our inability to achieve perfect agreement on the good life."[18] This recognition signals Stout's decisive departure from MacIntyre, for where MacIntyre sees "the social embodiment of emotivism," Stout sees an "implicit commitment to a provisional, self-limiting, conception of the good."[19]

MacIntyre, argues Stout, correctly asserts that we no longer share a Christian or Aristotelian teleology, but there is still wide consensus regarding a "provisional *telos*."[20] While modern thinkers were unsuccessful in their quest for certainty, they were successful in facilitating a vocabulary independent of specific understandings of God for a population that had come to the implicit consensus that "putting an end to religious warfare and intolerance" by compromising on detailed visions of the good was morally superior to violently instantiating one's own detailed vision through violence.[21]

---

16. Bernstein, *Beyond Objectivism and Relativism*, 16–20.

17. MacIntyre, *After Virtue*, 263; and Stout, *Ethics after Babel*, 191.

18. Stout, *Ethics after Babel*, 238.

19. Stout, *Ethics after Babel*, 238.

20. Stout, *Ethics after Babel*, 212.

21. Stout, *Ethics after Babel*, 212, cf. 161, 222–24.

Essential to modern polemics was an appeal to "public" knowledge. By moving away from private appeals to tradition or authority and to appeals to public argumentation, modern thinkers negated the need to resort to violence when authorities clashed. Differences were in principle resolvable through public argumentation. Stout's appeal to our "provisional *telos*" is an attempt to reaffirm the value of this public domain in order to prevent the strife likely to ensue from a sectarian ethos.

Stout's explicitly pragmatic emphasis, however, signals a shift in the nature of the appeal to the "public." For modern thinkers, the appeal to public reason was simultaneously an appeal to the natural light of reason, a means to necessary truth. Since this appeal is abortive, Stout substitutes this appeal to the public with an appeal to consensus, to the lack of real doubt among the populace.

Stout's appeal embraces the pragmatic response to modernity initiated by C. S. Peirce, who scorned the contrived doubt of the Cartesians and their understanding of knowledge as that which no reasonable person could possibly doubt. Peirce emphasized *real* doubt and defined knowledge as that which no reasonable person would even think to doubt.[22]

In the same pragmatic spirit, Stout, speaking in the realm of ethics, defines a platitude as "a judgment that only the philosophers (and the morally incompetent or utterly vicious) among us would think of denying."[23] Consequently, our shared conception of the good can be defined as "the set of all platitudinous judgments employing such terms as *good, better than,* and the like."[24] Naturally, there is still disagreement on significant issues and even shared judgments are justified differently, but neither of these factors makes the "consensus ineffective or insignificant."[25]

It is premature, therefore, to conclude that "the new dark ages are upon us" (MacIntyre) or that ours is a history proceeding in "a downward spiral toward ruin."[26] As we participate in the deconstruction of the Cartesian ambitions of modernity, however, we must keep watch lest a reactionary response vitiate the great achievement of modern thought and cast us back into sectarian conflict.

---

22. Peirce, "Some Consequences of Four Incapacities," 39–40.
23. Stout, *Ethics after Babel*, 212–13.
24. Stout, *Ethics after Babel*, 212.
25. Stout, *Ethics after Babel*, 213.
26. Stout, *Ethics after Babel*, 219.

The Threat of the Postmodern Ethos

The postmodern ethos threatens to undo the peaceable moral discourse achieved by modernity. Skepticism, nihilism, and relativism are the "three spectres" that "haunt the philosophy of moral diversity."[27] These spectres are dangerous because they undermine confidence in "our talk of moral truth and justification, and each can have worrisome effects on how we live our lives."[28] Modernists and theists each countered these spectres with a "God's-eye view." "After Babel" these approaches must be abandoned, but a "complete loss of confidence" must be avoided or we do indeed risk the loss of what is good and valuable in our modern tradition of moral discourse.[29]

Bernstein's diagnosis helps us understand our anxiety as a function of false expectations. Only because we have been nurtured within a culture obsessed with the Cartesian quest for certainty are we gripped by a fear that without absolutes we must slide into an abyss of skepticism, relativism, and nihilism. If one did not have Cartesian expectations, a Cartesian anxiety would not arise.

This critical insight rests at the core of Stout's position, for it allows him to shift the "burden of proof" regarding the questions of nihilism and skepticism.[30] "Instead of asking, 'why *not* be a moral nihilist or skeptic, given the fact of moral diversity?' I intend to ask, 'Why feel one *must* be?'"[31] If one assumes that we would not embrace nihilism or skepticism "unless we felt we had to" and that "moral diversity" is a "leading cause . . . of nihilistic or skeptical compulsions in ethics," then shifting the burden of proof, a shift that reflects a transition from a Cartesian to a postmodern mentality, allows us more easily to assuage our fear of moral chaos.[32]

If we move into a conceptual framework that is genuinely beyond objectivism and relativism, we will be enabled to accept a modest pragmatism that indwells openly the contingent time and place that we inescapably and fully inhabit. We will recognize that "the facts of moral diversity don't *compel* us to become nihilists or skeptics, to abandon the notions of moral truth and justified moral belief."[33]

27. Stout, *Ethics after Babel*, 3.
28. Stout, *Ethics after Babel*, 3.
29. Stout, *Ethics after Babel*, 3.
30. Stout, *Ethics after Babel*, 15.
31. Stout, *Ethics after Babel*, 15.
32. Stout, *Ethics after Babel*, 15.
33. Stout, *Ethics after Babel*, 14.

Dispelling the Spectres of Postmodernity

Stout begins addressing the spectres of moral diversity by combating the notion of radical incommensurability. Utilizing Davidson's famous argument from "On the Very Idea of a Conceptual Scheme," Stout argues that any disagreement presupposes a more fundamental common understanding. The very recognition of disagreement entails a deeper level of agreement by virtue of which the disagreement is identified. If this were not the case, the disagreement would be purely verbal, for the two sides would simply be talking about different things.[34] Anxiety over sheer relativism, therefore, is nullified.

Different societies and cultures, however, have substantial moral disagreements that are neither verbal nor capable of resolution by appeal to common rationales. The concept of a radical relativity is incoherent, but our judgments are indeed relative to particular historical and social locations (i.e., the incoherence of *conceptual relativity* does not preclude *moral diversity*). Davidson's argument helps us understand that an admission of the relative nature of our judgments does not force us down a slippery slope to skepticism and radical relativity, but sets us on a spectrum of relativity.[35] We must learn how self-consciously to inhabit this spectrum. The peaceable continuity of our society depends upon our ability to forge a path between the "false unity" of modernism and those forms of postmodernism that end in "sheer chaos."[36]

In *The Consequences of Pragmatism* we find Rorty's infamous statement that a pragmatic understanding of truth entails affirming Sartre's contention that fascism, if it triumphs, will be "the truth of [humanity]."[37] Citing this example, Stout asks whether pragmatism can provide any "moral response to the Terror. Can morality itself survive widespread acceptance of such thoughts? Or will the dissemination of pragmatism lead, in practice, to the demise of morality?"[38] Stout's answers are, respectively, "no" and "yes." The demise of morality is a very real danger for a pragmatism overly influenced by the modernist existentialism of a Sartre, for it accepts "forms of moral nihilism, epistemic reductionism, and radical relativity that a fittingly

34. Stout, *Ethics after Babel*, 19–20.

35. Stout, *Ethics after Babel*, 82–105.

36. Stout, *Ethics after Babel*, 21.

37. Rorty, *Consequences of Pragmatism*, xlii.

38. Stout, *Ethics after Babel*, 257.

modest pragmatism shuns."[39] Accordingly, a modest pragmatism "needs to publicize its antireductive intent."[40]

A modest pragmatism steps beyond the opposition between the subjectivity of the poet and the objectivity of the scientist. It develops a language "in which it makes sense to say that making and finding are equally present in the work of the poet, the scientist, and the moralist."[41] In this language the poet, the scientist, and the moralist would each lay equal claim to truth and objectivity and would each remain equally dependent on "the invention of linguistic artifacts that bring into being new tropes—and eventually new truths . . ."[42] A modest pragmatism, therefore, while depriving us of metaphysical or epistemological comfort, still demands that we "judge moral positions true or false. . . . Its doubts about philosophical theories leave the notions of moral truth and justified moral belief intact."[43]

The crux of Stout's modest pragmatism, the philosophical nuance that enables us to acknowledge the contingency of our judgments while retaining confidence in moral truth, lies in his drawing of a distinction between moral justification and moral truth.[44] While justification for our moral beliefs is indeed relative it "doesn't follow . . . that the truth of a given proposition is relative."[45] Hence we can hold our beliefs as "true" and assert that people who disagree have beliefs that are "false," because this is precisely what "to hold our beliefs" means (i.e., that we accept them as true).[46] This guards us from stumbling into the Terror, because doubts about explanation or criteria of moral truth are not necessarily doubts about moral truth.[47]

Likewise, it is in this usage of the word *true* that its definition is exhausted. Philosophical attempts to further define truth in terms of statements' correspondence to some "culture-transcendent thing-in-itself" are pointless for culturally bound creatures.[48] We use "true" to signify that which we do not doubt: the platitudinous scientific, social, and cultural affirmations we never even think to make explicit.

---

39. Stout, *Ethics after Babel*, 260.

40. Stout, *Ethics after Babel*, 263.

41. Stout, *Ethics after Babel*, 262.

42. Stout, *Ethics after Babel*, 262, cf. 249–50.

43. Stout, *Ethics after Babel*, 265.

44. Stout, *Ethics after Babel*, 25–26.

45. Stout, *Ethics after Babel*, 27–29.

46. Stout, *Ethics after Babel*, 23.

47. Stout, *Ethics after Babel*, 23.

48. Stout, *Ethics after Babel*, 24.

We do not choose to believe these affirmations; they are affirmations we cannot help but believe. What is true is that which is the case independent of our believing it to be the case. That is what we use "true" to signify. Relativity of justification, therefore, does not entail relativity of truth.

Stout's distinction between justification and truth leads to a complex understanding of the inter-relationship of truth, justification, evil, and blameworthiness. For instance, Stout holds that it is, has been, and always will be true to say, "slavery is wrong."[49] It is true because we can give a moral justification for that conclusion. The moral justification is relative to our time and place, but the truth "slavery is wrong" is not relative.

We might, for example, imagine a time (e.g., third-century Athens) when there was no justification for believing slavery wrong. Given their context, the Greeks justifiably believed the assertion "slavery is condonable" to be true. But that does not mean that the assertion "slavery is condonable" was in fact true. In fact, "slavery is wrong" was always true. Slavery, then, is and always has been evil. If the third-century Athenians had no way of justifying the assertion "slavery is wrong," however, then they are not "blameworthy" on this count, though what they participated in was evil.[50]

Stout anticipates the objection that he has in fact done away with a "reality that transcends us as knowing beings."[51] Stout replies, "to say that testing or justifying beliefs always involves appeal to further beliefs and not appeal to things as they are in themselves, independent of all human description, is an epistemological, not an ontological remark."[52]

Stout takes this epistemological/ontological distinction so seriously that he is willing to allow the idea of "a culture-transcendent Moral Law if it commits us merely to such notions as these: That there are moral truths; that any given moral proposition may in fact be true even though none of us knows that it is . . ."[53] It is Stout's willingness to entertain such ideas, his refusal to countenance the standard split between *finding* and *making* truth, which points to the unique realist edge, the "modesty," of his pragmatism.

49. Stout, *Ethics after Babel*, 28.

50. Stout, *Ethics after Babel*, 30–31.

51. Stout, *Ethics after Babel*, 33.

52. Stout, *Ethics after Babel*, 33.

53. Stout, *Ethics after Babel*, 34.

Moral *Bricolage*

Recognizing the contingency of our thought and existence "is the beginning, not the end, of critical thought."[54] Admitting that our justificatory structures are relative to historical and cultural factors does not issue in a cultural determinism that frees us from moral responsibility. It is still our task to judge what in our moral tradition "is worth preserving, what requires reformulation, and what must be left behind."[55] Utilizing the critical resources of tradition, history, anthropology, and creative art, we labor to generate as many "new 'candidates for truth and falsehood'" as possible and to develop a coherent moral language adequate to the needs of the moment.[56] Stout calls this effort "moral bricolage."[57] He concludes his entire work with a poetic call to this task:

> The languages of morals in our discourse are many. . . . But they do not float in free air, and their name is not chaos. . . . It is a motley: not a building in need of new foundations but a coat of many colors, one constantly in need of mending and patching. . . . Our task, like Thomas Aquinas's, Thomas Jefferson's or Martin Luther King's, is to take the many parts of a complicated social conceptual inheritance and stitch them together into a pattern that meets the needs of the moment. It has never been otherwise. The creative intellectual task of every generation, in other words, involves moral *bricolage*.[58]

According to Stout's understanding of moral truth and justification, admitting that moral *bricolage* is a "creative human effort" is not to deny that the moral truths "thus brought into being really possess truth-value or can be discovered to be true or false by rational means."[59] Honesty demands that we acknowledge our facticity; we begin "already immersed in the assumptions and precedents of a tradition."[60] Our cognitive capacities are demonstrated through the creativity with which we move from this inescapable beginning, as we subject "this or that assumption or precedent to

---

54. Stout, *Ethics after Babel*, 73.
55. Stout, *Ethics after Babel*, 73.
56. Stout, *Ethics after Babel*, 67, citing Hacking, "Language, Truth and Reason," 60.
57. Stout, *Ethics after Babel*, 73–75, 293–94.
58. Stout, *Ethics after Babel*, 291–92.
59. Stout, *Ethics after Babel*, 77.
60. Stout, *Ethics after Babel*, 77.

criticism as *real doubts* arise, employing old vocabularies or inventing new ones, *the better to think and live well.*"[61]

Creativity and critical distance is obtained in this fully immanent ethical criticism through "stereoscopic social criticism," a criticism which brings social practices and institutions, internal and external groups, into focus at the same time.[62] As a doctor struggles in concrete ways with the conflict between the good of her patient, the good of her practice, the good of medicine, the good of the insurance industry, and the good of her family, she will, in multiple concrete instances and in dialogue with her peers, put these conflicting goods into creative interplay and formulate justifiable and creative moral judgments which best meet the diverse needs of the moment. She will, in short, engage in moral *bricolage*.

Some may fear the relativity of ethical judgments thus formulated. However, Stout fears still more those who insist on the priority of abstract theory and who divisively use categories such as "communitarian" or "liberal." Noting the very similar social judgments of theorists as diverse as Rorty, West, Bellah, and even MacIntyre, Stout avers that this theoretical diversity threatens us only if it distracts us from the real-life unity of theorists' practical judgments.[63] The real tragedy would be if we were distracted from accomplishing real social change due to these differences. For what threatens moral discourse in our society are "the acids of injustice, which eat away at the moral fiber of privileged and victimized alike, and . . . the possibility of nuclear war . . . [and] habits . . . appropriate to the marketplace."[64] Most communitarians and liberals would agree with this diagnosis. Focusing on this agreement and working to address its concerns is the continuing task of the pluralistic tradition and its moral *bricoleurs*.[65]

TAKING NARRATIVE SERIOUSLY: STANLEY HAUERWAS

Hauerwas argues that the modernist search for foundations harmed religious ethics, for foundations cannot but make "religious convictions morally secondary."[66] While the search for an unqualified ethic has the admirable goal of "securing peace between people of diverse beliefs and histories," it is unacceptable because it makes "irrelevant the essential Christian convictions

61. Stout, *Ethics after Babel*, 120, emphases mine.

62. Stout, *Ethics after Babel*, 279.

63. Stout, *Ethics after Babel*, 277–78.

64. Stout, *Ethics after Babel*, 277.

65. Stout, *Ethics after Babel*, 287–88.

66. Hauerwas, *Peaceable Kingdom*, 11.

about the nature of God . . ."[67] Hauerwas, therefore, unblinkingly pursues a self-consciously Christian ethic.[68]

Narrative as the Form of Rationality

The standard (modernist) account tries to establish basic moral principles according to which all others are justified. However, "it is profoundly misleading to think that a rational explanation needs to be given for holding rational beliefs, for to attempt to provide such an account assumes that rationality itself does not depend upon narrative."[69] Hauerwas emphasizes the failure of modern thinkers to consider that our very language is embedded in a particular narrative. We cannot but understand our behavior and intentions according to this narrative. The appeal to objective reason is chimeric, for rationality itself depends on a particular narrative.[70] Furthermore, since all rationality is narrative-dependent, "there is no neutral story that insures the truthfulness of our particular stories."[71]

This recognition strips us of the security that the standard account promised, but truthfulness consists in accepting the "many claims on our lives without trying to subject them to a false unity of coherence."[72]

Narrative, Practical Understanding, and Character

This understanding of narrative as a form of rationality is useful with regard to practical reason, because life situations proceed contingently, not with necessity. However, it is also true that our actions are predictable despite their contingency. By observing how stories evolve and attending to the multiple stories any given situation involves, we determine what may be characteristically expected in concrete instances.[73] Since this allows us to answer plausibly the question of what may happen next, narrative offers a fitting intelligibility for determining the proper course of action.[74]

---

67. Hauerwas, *Peaceable Kingdom*, 22.

68. Hauerwas, *Peaceable Kingdom*, 69.

69. Hauerwas, *Truthfulness and Tragedy*, 22–23.

70. Hauerwas, *Truthfulness and Tragedy*, 20–21.

71. Hauerwas, *Truthfulness and Tragedy*, 24.

72. Hauerwas, *Truthfulness and Tragedy*, 27–28.

73. Hauerwas, *Truthfulness and Tragedy*, 28–29.

74. Hauerwas, *Truthfulness and Tragedy*, 29.

We generate a conception of character by observing various individuals in different situations and noting what actions or passions ensue. Reflecting on the progression of various characters in their stories, we "learn to recognize different configurations and to rank some better than others."[75] We can then "consider the set of expectations associated with a developing character as a 'language,' a systematic set of connections between actions which offers a setting or syntax for subsequent responses."[76] Narrative rationality's ability to understand characters, therefore, "offers insight into human conditions, which recommends narrative as a form of rationality especially appropriate to ethics."[77]

Modernist and Narrative Theology

Christian absolutists have tried to deny the contingency of our being by establishing Christian foundations from which moral judgments can be derived. They fail to realize that "the task of Christian ethics is to help us to see how our convictions *are* in themselves a morality"—we do not believe and then act; "our convictions embody our morality; our beliefs are our actions."[78] In the face of a foreboding of chaos, the "task of Christian ethics is not to relieve us of the ambiguity but to help us understand rightly what it means to live in the world we do—that is, to live truthfully in a world without certainty."[79]

Once we understand this, we can understand why the "nature of Christian ethics is determined by the fact that Christian convictions take the form of a story or, perhaps better, a set of stories that constitutes a tradition, which in turn creates a community."[80] This technical understanding of the contingency of our existence in the meaning of story entails our acceptance of the "narrative character of Christian convictions."[81] When we realize that there is "no point outside our history where we can secure a place to anchor our moral convictions," we realize that we "must begin in the middle, that is, we must begin with a narrative."[82]

75. Hauerwas, *Truthfulness and Tragedy*, 29.

76. Hauerwas, *Truthfulness and Tragedy*, 30.

77. Hauerwas, *Truthfulness and Tragedy*, 30.

78. Hauerwas, *Peaceable Kingdom*, 16, 22–23.

79. Hauerwas, *Peaceable Kingdom*, 16.

80. Hauerwas, *Peaceable Kingdom*, 24.

81. Hauerwas, *Peaceable Kingdom*, 24–25.

82. Hauerwas, *Peaceable Kingdom*, 62–63.

Christianity proffers a narrative beginning that includes God's saving action in the history of Israel and the life of Jesus Christ. Since we are the creatures of the Christian God, to engage in this work with God completes our nature, aligning us with our created *telos*.[83]

Christian ethics, therefore, does not have a methodological starting point. There is no foundational reply to the question, "how do we know that Christianity is true?" This question, like the question "why be good?" is misleading.[84] Christian ethics does not begin with a logical inference derived from abstract principles but "in a community that carries the story of the God who wills us to participate in a kingdom established in and through Jesus of Nazareth."[85] Belief, the "assent *of* faith," is the mode of our participation in this reality.[86] Because we are "people of a book," people who live through the passing on of the memory and meaning of the God of Israel and Jesus, the "truth" of Christianity is "inherently contingent," for "it can only be passed on from one generation to another by memory."[87]

Much as philosophers nurtured in the modernist tradition react violently to attacks on the quest for certainty, Christians often react passionately against the assertion that the truth of Christianity is inherently contingent. There is both a philosophical and a theological response to these fears.

First, just as philosophers can be made to see their anxiety as the function of false Cartesian expectations, Christians should shed the modernist assumptions that inspire their desperate search for absolutes. Hauerwas, like Stout, shifts the burden of proof: the "charge of relativism is dependent on the assumption that moral reflection is only secured by providing a knockdown argument against relativism."[88] That assumption, however, is part of the discredited modernist perspective. Hauerwas does not combat relativism through a Davidsonian philosophical argument but, abiding by the dictum that "practical arguments may be best in a practical discipline," is "content to challenge the relativist or subjectivist to try to live out the implications of [his or her] position."[89]

Second, theologically we can accept with equanimity the contingency of Christian truth because it is consonant with the biblical understanding

83. Hauerwas, *Peaceable Kingdom*, 62.

84. Hauerwas, *Truthfulness and Tragedy*, 39.

85. Hauerwas, *Peaceable Kingdom*, 62.

86. Hauerwas, *Truthfulness and Tragedy*, 35.

87. Hauerwas, *Peaceable Kingdom*, 70.

88. Hauerwas, *Truthfulness and Tragedy*, 2.

89. Hauerwas, *Truthfulness and Tragedy*, 2.

that we yet see through a glass darkly. Awareness of the contingency of our knowledge issues in humility as we strive to share in God's saving action.

Church and Society

Christian ethics claims universal relevance, for "Christians claim that by learning to find our lives within the story of God we learn to see the world truthfully."[90] Despite this unequivocal claim to universal significance, however, the nature of the Christian ethic as intrinsically "qualified" has significant ramifications for the relationship of Christians to secular society.

A tragic consequence of the notion of an unqualified ethic, that is, one based on reason itself or another "'inherent' human characteristic," is that it "underwrites coercion."[91] If one understands one's own ethic to be absolute and universal and unqualified, then one can argue that dissenting groups or individuals should be forced to "be true to their 'true' selves."[92] A qualified ethic, by contrast, offers no absolute grounds by which such coercion can be justified. This is as close as Hauerwas comes to opening a purely philosophical argument for his pacifism; his primary response is theological.

Intrinsic to Christian understanding is a confession of dependence on God's power. This, argues Hauerwas, entails the recognition that "peace is not something to be achieved *by our power*. Rather peace is a gift of God that comes only by our being a community formed around a crucified savior—a savior who teaches us how to be peaceful in a world in rebellion against its true Lord."[93] Because of the distinctiveness of the Christian narrative, and because Christians cannot make appeals to extra-theological, universal starting points in arguing their case, Christians can neither coerce others to adopt their point of view nor find a common basis from which to advance a modernist argument. For this reason, the category of "witness" becomes critical. The task of Christians is to be "nothing less than a people whose ethic shines as a beacon to others illumining how life should be lived well."[94]

90. Hauerwas, *Peaceable Kingdom*, 34.
91. Hauerwas, *Peaceable Kingdom*, 12.
92. Hauerwas, *Peaceable Kingdom*, 12, 60–61.
93. Hauerwas, *Peaceable Kingdom*, 12.
94. Hauerwas, *Peaceable Kingdom*, 34.

The Individual and the Community

On the individual level, the fact that our character is derived from a community entails the recognition that our freedom is in the hands of others. The meaning of my action, the development of my character, the purpose and direction of my life, all are dependent on the categories of the others in my community. My very character, then, is a gift from the community and requires that I trust the community.[95] It is through making the story of God our own as it is embodied in the narrative of the community that we gain peace with ourselves.[96]

At the center of the Christian narrative of God's way with the world is the story of Jesus. In Jesus's story we see "God's way with Israel." God does not impose the divine will on Israel but calls her again and again. This "way" is perfected in the cross, where we "see decisively the one who, being all-powerful, becomes vulnerable even to being a victim of our refusal to accept his Lordship."[97]

This does not entail a stoic acceptance of tragedy or evil, for Christians have hope in the God who has "already determined the end of history in the cross and resurrection of Jesus Christ."[98] That hope, that present existence in the peaceable kingdom, is the difference between a stoic resignation and Christian patience. Christians do not abandon the way of God for the world's ways of coercion even for manifestly good ends.

By deliberately existing in the peaceable kingdom, a form of non-coercive resistance is manifested and evil structures and practices are challenged by the truth.[99] Because belief in God grounds our confidence, we can resist the temptation to take up violence to "secure relative goods." To engage in violent means is to misunderstand our calling, for "our task is not to bring God's kingdom, but rather to witness to it by being the earnest of his kingdom of peace. We are confident . . . his kingdom will prevail."[100] We live in the peaceable kingdom, says Hauerwas, "not because it is effective, but simply because it is true."[101]

95. Hauerwas, *Peaceable Kingdom*, 45.

96. Hauerwas, *Peaceable Kingdom*, 39.

97. Hauerwas, *Peaceable Kingdom*, 81.

98. Hauerwas, *Peaceable Kingdom*, 145.

99. Hauerwas, *Peaceable Kingdom*, 145.

100. Hauerwas, *Truthfulness and Tragedy*, 12.

101. Hauerwas, *Peaceable Kingdom*, 151.

Modernist Misgivings: The "Sectarian" Critique

Hauerwas admits with some frustration that he has not been able to avoid being characterized as "fideistic and/or sectarian."[102] Such characterizations, Hauerwas complains, "presuppose the epistemological and social positions I am challenging . . ."[103]

Hauerwas's point is that "sectarian" and "fideist" have been defined according to a modern epistemology. To be sectarian was to refuse to acknowledge public criteria of rationality as authoritative. Modern thinkers demanded that Christians start with a public prolegomenon. However, the modern appeal to public reason has proven abortive. Hauerwas contends that there is no neutral ground, for rationality has a narrative form. Everyone inescapably participates in particular narratives that structure their intentions, understanding, and rationality. The modern categories "fideist" and "sectarian," therefore, become incoherent in a postmodern epistemology.

For Christians to appeal to the Scriptures as their canonical set of stories is simply for them honestly to acknowledge the formative nexus of stories that conditions their narrative. That acknowledgment, and a refusal to substitute the formative nexus of a different narrative, does not make them either fideistic or sectarian. To the contrary, "one is tempted to wonder whether everyone does not accept a set of stories as canonical."[104] Those who critique Hauerwas should perhaps ponder whether identifying those stories that are canonical for them might be a basic aspect of discovering "the shape one's basic convictions take."[105] Since this would be fundamental to self-understanding, one might argue that to be "unable to do so would either mark a factual incapacity or an utterly fragmented self."[106]

Hauerwas calls on Christians to acknowledge the particularity of their narrative and to accept the postmodern ethical reflection that such an acknowledgement entails. Christians must accept that there "is no point outside our history where we can secure a place to anchor our moral convictions."[107] Christian ethics, therefore, begins without apology within the narrative of the "community that carries the story of the God who wills us to participate in a kingdom established in and through Jesus of Nazareth."[108]

102. Hauerwas, *After Christendom?* 16.
103. Hauerwas, *After Christendom?* 16.
104. Hauerwas, *Truthfulness and Tragedy*, 39.
105. Hauerwas, *Truthfulness and Tragedy*, 39.
106. Hauerwas, *Truthfulness and Tragedy*, 39.
107. Hauerwas, *Peaceable Kingdom*, 62.
108. Hauerwas, *Peaceable Kingdom*, 62.

CRITIQUE: SOME TROUBLING TENDENCIES

On Jeffrey Stout: The Adequacy of the Pluralistic Tradition

Stout contends that the invaluable accomplishment of modernity was to end the civil strife of the seventeenth century by teaching us to settle for a provisional *telos*. He comforts us by focusing on our society's vast body of platitudes. We are invited to abandon the standard picture of modernity as a centuries-long, bankrupt quest for certainty and to revision it as the centuries-long emergence of a pluralistic tradition.

Stout urges us to admit that we have always been moral *bricoleurs*, addressing the practical needs of the moment and using diverse resources to patch together a provisional *telos*. Consequently, when we ask, "who are the adherents of the pluralistic tradition?" Stout answers that, however unwittingly, we all are. We all tacitly share the provisional *telos* of our Western society. Stout has stepped beyond troubling theories that divide and dares even to unite Bellah, MacIntyre, Rorty, and West.[109] He offers a new unity and comfort in moral consensus.

Stout protects the integrity of the moral consensus that constitutes our provisional *telos* with his strong distinction between the epistemic relativity of justification and the absoluteness of truth. While this split aids him in directing our attention to the truth and away from rival justificatory schema, it puts Stout's tradition at risk of attaining only verbal agreement.[110]

For example, argue Hauerwas and Kenneson, even southern slave owners, abiding by Stout's definition, could have agreed that "slavery is evil." They could have argued that they did not practice slavery because "their workers were not human beings but possessions."[111] While Stout may gain agreement to the proposition "slavery is evil," it is at this level an "empty notion of agreement."

Stout masks the superficiality of his moral consensus by using Davidson's argument to justify not "pushing agreement too far down." But as Hauerwas argues, while Davidson's argument may be used to show "that there can be no *meaningful* disagreement that is at the same time *complete* disagreement," it "remains unclear why such a recognition should stand as a vindication of Stout's entire project."[112] By basing his argument so significantly on its assertion concerning the impossibility of total disagreement, Stout fails to explicate adequately what would constitute *meaningful agreement*.

109. Stout, *Ethics after Babel*, 276–78.

110. Hauerwas and Kenneson, "A Review Essay," 691, 694.

111. Hauerwas and Kenneson, "A Review Essay," 694.

112. Hauerwas and Kenneson, "A Review Essay," 696.

Stout should consider deep disagreements concerning questions like, "what is the *telos* of our being?" or "who is human?" These disagreements remain invisible when one focuses on societal platitudes, but how are ethical quandaries addressed or abominations evolved without appeal to these deeper questions as fundamental? Even apparently significant agreements like "slavery is evil" or "human life is invaluable" remain shallowly verbal until the narrative depths justifying and explaining the positions are explicated.[113] It is only when these depths are plumbed that we establish meaningful agreement. Stout's "consensus," consequently, neglects the narrative traditions that give the moral positions within his *bricolage* their validity and depth.[114]

Stout's position is inadequate to the degree that the distance that allows him to celebrate the conversation itself (i.e., the distance between justification and truth) is the distance between his account and real-life practices. We do not hold to our moral convictions *because* they are part of a societal consensus; we hold them because of our participation in the depths of a distinct narrative tradition. Individuals do not adhere to a provisional *telos*, they adhere to one of a myriad of distinct narratives.

Contrary to Stout's depiction, people do not split truth from its justification. When asked why they take a certain moral stance, people strive to articulate a coherent and elegant and deep account of their moral convictions. Our moral convictions and truth-talk need not depend on a foundationalist appeal; we do not work our way back to incorrigible first principles. However, neither do we appeal to societal consensus. Complex explanations support our moral convictions. Stout's use of the language of truth trades on these deep, narrative-specific structures of explanation, for the power of truth-talk is derived from the justificatory schema that warrants attributing "it is true" to a given assertion, not from our recognition of societal consensus.

Settling for a provisional public *telos* may be a practical compromise of multiple mainstream narrative traditions, but people's deepest commitments are masked when this pluralism is lifted up as itself the fundamental tradition of Western society. The pluralistic tradition, for example, does not provide definitive guidance on ethical issues such as active or passive euthanasia, genetic engineering, or abortion (i.e., where there is no consensus). Pluralists can only urge us to invest in and trust the conversation; they voice no distinct position *qua* pluralists. At these junctures the pluralistic tradition is most blatantly parasitic upon traditions that take moral positions and debate these issues.

113. Hauerwas and Kenneson, "A Review Essay," 694–95.
114. Hauerwas and Kenneson, "A Review Essay," 691.

The question of the adequacy of Stout's pluralistic tradition has direct bearing on Stout's call to theologians. Noting that recently theologians have tended to say "nothing atheists don't already know," Stout calls on theologians to re-enter the conversation with a distinctly theological voice.[115] This appears to be an open-minded invitation, but (as Hauerwas rightly recognizes) Stout's call entails making the Christian narrative subservient to the narrative of Stout's pluralistic tradition.

The distinctive mark of the pluralistic tradition is to celebrate a conversation between distinct voices and to trust in the wisdom of its evolving consensus. Stout's invitation, therefore, is not innocent, for our primary allegiance would be transferred from the distinctive narrative of the Christian tradition to the conversation itself. Once again, the split between justificatory structures and truth underlies the problem.

An atheist friend and I (a Christian) may both "know" that sexism is wrong, and on the basis of this consensus we should certainly work together to eliminate sexism globally. The question is *how*, by virtue of what explanatory structures, do my friend or I "know" that sexism is wrong? How does this knowledge relate to our moral judgments on other issues? How will each of us argue for our position when we encounter other cultures which do not "know" this? We both participate in the public discourse of our time, but neither of us is truly understood if we are merely grouped commonly into the pluralistic tradition. An exclusive emphasis on our common participation in the provisional *telos* of our society is actually a denial of diversity. As Hauerwas avers, Stout's pluralistic tradition finally functions as "a meta-tradition that tends to level the distinctions among other identifiable traditions and make their coexistence a good in itself."[116]

Stout's misdiagnosis of the nature of our participation in the "pluralistic tradition" results in a failure to discern the true nature of the "peacefulness" of our society. An invaluable accomplishment of the Enlightenment in the wake of the religious wars of the seventeenth century was indeed the development of religious tolerance, but this achievement cannot be generalized into a positing of a pluralistic tradition whose defining moment is its willingness to settle for a provisional *telos*.

What Stout has helpfully identified is the post-seventeenth-century marginalization of religion as the nexus of power from which and concerning which conflicts spring. What he has failed to identify is the new centering of this nexus of power around cultural allegiances and a specific set of

---

115. Stout, *Ethics after Babel,* 163–65. Christians may wish to respond that the moral truths atheists "know" seem to be little more than Judeo-Christian platitudes split from the narrative contexts that originally lent them their profundity.

116. Hauerwas and Kenneson, "A Review Essay," 690.

political and economic ideas and interests. This shift has allowed dominant groups in the West to unite sufficiently to marginalize internal dissenters and focus their power on external opportunities and threats in their quest for security and prosperity. Neocolonial relationships between the "West" and the "Third World" are sustained through an imbalance of power, not through any consensually derived provisional *telos*. Even within the United States scores of right- and left-wing groups do not willingly compromise on a provisional telos but are kept in check by a lack of power. In a similar manner, many women and minorities recognize the systemic violence perpetuated against them but have little power of appeal outside mainstream processes.

Our situation, therefore, may be far less benign than Stout suspects. A shallow focus on a consensual truth split from justificatory structures is problematic, for "public consensus" is largely a function of the particular interests of dominant groups in society. The conversation is not "open," and all are not equally represented in it. Thus, a focus on public consensus accompanied by a neglect of justificatory structures may mask illicit ideological supports that perpetuate the very sorts of injustices about which Stout himself is so clearly concerned.[117]

On Stanley Hauerwas: Still Sectarian?

Hauerwas is not sectarian in the modern sense. Since rationality has the form of narrative, there is no universal public reason from which to isolate oneself. Neither, however, are there any isolated narratives. Unfortunately, Hauerwas fails to develop the implications of this latter insight.

Christian doctrine and exposition of Scripture has shaped and been shaped by potent cultural forces. Constantine's conversion, Augustine's Platonism, Aquinas's Aristotelianism, the encounter with Islam, Enlightenment rationality, the rise of the nation-state and of capitalism and socialism—these and many other developments, and the narratives within which they are embedded, are inextricably intertwined with Christianity.

117. This is the particular danger that attends Stout's delineation of our dependence on conversation and consensus. Reacting to this danger by urging the opposite extreme—that is, by insisting that everyone be given an equal opportunity to propagate extremist views without any public censure—risks engendering what Herbert Marcuse termed "repressive tolerance." The difficulty in avoiding both of these extremes is presently emerging on university campuses: officials utilizing a rhetoric of inclusivity to urge the inclusion of disempowered voices are finding it difficult to justify the "repression" of sexist or racist speech.

A helpful metaphor with recent currency is that of a "web." This metaphor helps us picture the innumerable connections that subtly link us all. Growing awareness of our cultural and historical facticity has resulted in the recognition that the self is better pictured as a particular and creative focal point in a nexus of connections than as a discrete unit. Likewise, a distinct tradition (e.g., Christianity, Humanism) is not a discrete entity but a distinct, enduring nexus of connections. Recognition of our fundamental interwovenness does not entail the disappearance of Christianity any more than it entails the disappearance of the self. It does, however, contradict any claims to absolutely *discrete* personhood or narrative tradition. We may be *distinctly* Christian, but we are not *exclusively* Christian. In our global village the existence of a discrete narrative tradition is impossible.

Hauerwas fails to appreciate the degree to which distinct narratives interact. Just as he argues that the individual within the community is heavily dependent on other individuals of the community, so Christians must understand that the existence of their own narrative is significantly dependent upon that of other narratives.

Two main consequences follow from a realization that no narrative is discrete. First, Hauerwas's call for Christians to "witness" must be modified. Since the Christian narrative is interwoven with other narratives, it should interact with other narratives not only from the superior stance of "witness" but also as a careful listener. The witness of the Scriptures, the church, and the confessions will remain primary for Christians, but acknowledgment of the integrity of other traditions and of their centuries-old interaction with the Christian tradition implies that they may provide insights into how Christians should understand themselves. Within these parameters Christians should, as Stout urges, be open to correction when conversing with those from other narratives.[118]

Christians such as Hauerwas, therefore, need to enter the public conversation Stout identifies. They need to put their distinctive voice into play, to put their positions at risk, to enter into open dialogue and not only to "witness." Hauerwas could remain distinctively Christian and yet acknowledge the integrity and value of other traditions. He could engage in a moral *bricolage* that utilizes all resources available, not only those issuing from the Christian narrative. In such a fashion, Christians can benefit from and contribute to public conversation without shifting their primary commitment to that conversation itself.

The recognition of Christianity's fundamental interwovenness with other traditions has, secondly, serious implications for Hauerwas's pacifism.

118. Stout, *Ethics after Babel*, 164–65.

This pacifism is predicated upon the supposition that Christians can witness to the world as a community that does not participate in the world's coercive means. To admit that we are inextricably intertwined with the narratives and institutions of the world, however, is to deny the possibility of being a kingdom set apart.

As James Cone argued, "no one can be nonviolent in an unjust society."[119] For example, insofar as international corporations depend on the stability and balance of power maintained by military forces around the globe, any patron of multinational products or investor in multinational corporations is inextricably bound up with the wielding and threat of force. Or again, it would be self-deception for a WASP male like myself to deny complicity in racism and sexism at a structural level. Christians are inextricably bound up in these other narratives, inextricably bound up with patterns of coercion and violence. Christians cannot be a peaceable community set apart.

Hauerwas's analysis of coercion, therefore, is inadequate. As J. Philip Wogaman has argued (in response to Yoder), pacifist analysis does not adequately perceive and develop the implications of its dependence on the "order maintaining (and justice securing) functions of the state."[120] Since the Christian narrative is not discrete, we must confess that we are caught within the coercive and often unjust structures of our world.

I cannot develop this tangential point at length, but I would argue that this recognition eliminates pacifism as an option for Christians. Since we begin complicit in the world's coercive structures, even those who would hold pacifism as the ideal cannot rightly choose to be pacifists. The option is between better and worse coercive acts. On rare occasions the fitting response may even be violent. To refuse to act coercively on an individual or communal level when one is inescapably complicit in coercion on a structural level is an irresponsible flight from moral responsibility.

SUGGESTIVE INSIGHTS: LEARNING FROM STOUT AND HAUERWAS

Our study of Stout and Hauerwas allows us to articulate the threat of postmodernism precisely. The sense of chaos that haunts us stems from the fear that without an appeal to objective reason we will slide helplessly into nihilism and relativism. This is commonly mistaken as the threat postmodernism

---

119. Cone, *God of the Oppressed*, 219; cf. Wogaman, *Christian Perspectives on Politics*, 63.

120. Wogaman, *Christian Perspectives on Politics*, 46.

poses. As we have seen, however, the Cartesian expectations that stimulate this Cartesian anxiety can be neutralized.

Stout helps us identify the true threat of postmodernism. The sectarian chaos of the seventeenth century was overcome through the evolution of the very clear modernist distinction between the public and the private. The flight from tradition and revelation was the flight to universal reason. Ethical criteria were to be grounded in reason alone. Appeal to revelation and tradition was tolerated in private, but in the public realm the only appeal was to the natural light of reason.

The ethical dream of modernity was never realized, but the belief in the power of reason was alone sufficient to sustain the parameters of the public realm. As MacIntyre's *After Virtue* made painfully clear, however, postmodernism shatters that modern belief and reveals the fragmentation of the philosophical underpinnings of public ethics. This is the true threat postmodern discourse uncovers: the public realm that saved us from the sectarian strife of the seventeenth century is now sustained only on the dying momentum of a spent epistemology.

MacIntyre, lamenting these "new dark ages," sees no other option than Nietzsche or Aristotle and takes refuge with the peripatetics (i.e., the Aristotelians). Stout, fearing that this retreat may lead to a renewal of sectarian chaos, chooses a pragmatic focus on our society's significant moral consensus. Stout's revisionist "provisional *telos*" is precisely that set of public ethical standards believed to have been grounded upon reason alone. His fundamental point is that, while modernist foundations were never established, the appeal to public consensus *worked*.

With the failure of modernism, neither the "public realm" nor "public ethics" can be sustained with an appeal to the natural light of reason. Stout, therefore, uses Davidson to carve out a "public" that is the realm of conversation and utilizes a "modest" pragmatic split between justification and truth to establish a "provisional *telos*" that is grounded in consensus. Stout's astute diagnosis is tremendously useful in helping us understand how to sustain the peaceable evolution of our pluralistic society, but it has a troubling potential to lend support to the *status quo* and to settle for superficial understandings of moral beliefs.

Hauerwas, in contrast to MacIntyre, chooses Christianity over Nietzsche or Aristotle. Unlike Stout, however, Hauerwas reestablishes no public realm. As a consequence, he feels fully justified in answering only to his own narrative; there is no responsibility to develop a paradigm for public conversation *between* narratives because such an approach necessarily trades on a further *meta*-narrative. Hauerwas's conceptions of narrative, community, and character provide a powerful vocabulary for rich and deep moral understanding and capture the nature of persons' moral commitments far more profoundly than Stout's. His understanding of narratives as discrete, however, is untenable. Consequently, his understanding provides inadequate guidance for conducting public interaction in a pluralistic society, tempts one to deny complicity in society's coercive (and often oppressive) structures, and without warrant confines ethical actions within pacifist parameters.

ON A CHRISTIAN MORAL *BRICOLAGE*

With Stout, I think that moral *bricoleurs* must accept their contingency and utilize every available resource to meet the needs of the moment. With Hauerwas, I think Christian moral *bricoleurs* must reflect, judge, and understand first and foremost according to the Christian narrative to which they give their "assent of faith."

The term *bricolage* acknowledges the fundamental interwovenness of all our narratives and hence readies us for mutually enriching conversation within our pluralistic society. The qualifier "Christian" identifies a narrative depth from which a *bricoleur* might work. Some qualifier must attach to any *bricoleur*. Christians, therefore, need not apologize for their qualified *bricolage*.

Christians who have been tempted to imitate their modernist contemporaries may be troubled by the lack of certainty entailed by an acceptance of *bricolage*. However, it is entirely consistent with the Christian understanding that "yet we see through a glass darkly." Humility is fitting in our epistemology.

Precisely such a sense of ambiguity (and a correlating humility) should be fostered within *every* qualified ethic. In the final analysis, even Stout offers too much comfort with his appeal to moral platitudes. The shedding of our Cartesian anxieties frees us to hold our moral beliefs with conviction and warrant them with deep, non-foundationalist, narrative-specific justifications that appeal to coherence, elegance, and reasonableness. The postmodern sense of ambiguity is important to foster, however, for precisely this will mitigate against the sectarian chaos Stout rightly fears. Internalization of this sense of ambiguity should temper dogmatism and foster tolerance and openness to correction. That is to say, we recognize the contingency of our understanding and our inherent interconnectedness, therefore we hold our convictions openly and tolerate diversity. There is a core to any system of beliefs, however, over which there will be no compromise. Which is to say, Christians retain the wherewithal to sign Barmen or to plot with Bonhoeffer.

Christians are called to plumb the depths of our narrative tradition, to acknowledge and listen to other traditions, to articulate moral convictions with humility, depth, and elegance, and to engage in fitting action. The contemporary Christian *bricoleur* should, like an Augustine or an Aquinas, utilize all materials at hand while remaining faithful to and enriching the Christian narrative.

Chapter 8

Irreducible Tensions

Private Convictions in Public Space

My respondents' thoughtful critiques reveal several critical aporias in my essay on Christian moral *bricolage*: 1) an inadequate clarification of the argument's philosophical context; 2) an inadequate specification of the nature of "tradition" (or, "narrative") and 3) the need to defend my appeal to narrative traditions from deconstructionist critique.[1]

The argument's philosophical context is the so-called liberal/communitarian debate. This context is somewhat masked since Stout, my representative of liberalism, deliberately develops his modest pragmatism with the intention of transcending liberalism and communitarianism. I will begin, therefore, by considering the recent work of liberal John Rawls, for problems subtly felt in Stout are more easily discerned in Rawls.[2]

---

1. The Spring 1994 issue of *Koinonia* focused upon the essay which constitutes the prior chapter, "Christian Ethics in a Postmodern World?" Six authors wrote essays in conversation with this, my centerpiece article. This chapter constituted my response to those articles and was published concurrently. My respondents were: Lois Malcom, "The Divine Name"; J. Francis Watson, "An Ecclesiological Approach"; Morag Logan, "Christian Moral Bricolage"; Willette A. Burgie-Gipson, "On Christian Pluralism"; Gavin Ferriby, "Christian Ethics"; and Stanley Hauerwas, "To be or not to be a *BRICOLEUR*."

2. The late Professor Lewis S. Mudge, serving for a year as a Fellow at the *Center of Theological Inquiry* in Princeton, reached out in response to a public reading of a late draft of my *Koinonia* essay and directed my attention to Rawls's notion of "overlap." In this essay, I am also indebted to his insights, conversation, and convivial spirit.

JOHN RAWLS: FROM *A THEORY OF JUSTICE* (1973) TO *POLITICAL LIBERALISM* (1993)

In *Political Liberalism*, John Rawls addresses the same critical question that worries Jeffrey Stout, namely, "how is it possible that there may exist over time a stable and just society of free and equal citizens profoundly divided by *reasonable though incompatible* religious, philosophical, and moral doctrines?"[3] Rawls's solution is to acknowledge frankly the irreducible plurality of comprehensive doctrines but to distinguish religious or philosophical doctrines from the "political conception of a constitutional regime."[4] "Political liberalism" is then developed not as a competing *comprehensive* doctrine but as a politic constructed within that sphere of "overlap" shared by reasonable but incompatible comprehensive doctrines. This sphere of overlap, the sphere of the "reasonable," constitutes the domain of "public reason."[5]

To carve out this domain of public reason Rawls distinguishes between the "reasonable" and the "rational." To discern the need to distinguish the reasonable from the rational one must acknowledge the "burdens of judgment."[6] These burdens include conflicting and complex evidence, disagreements about how evidence should be weighed, the existence of paradigmatic "hard cases," and that interpretive dimension of our judgments which is conditioned by our "total experience."[7] Because these burdens of judgment condition our ratiocination, we may anticipate that *reasonable* people in a democracy will have to deal with enduring *rational* disagreement. The "unrealistic idea" of *A Theory of Justice* (1971), Rawls concludes, lies in its thinking that all citizens would endorse justice as fairness on the

---

3. Rawls, *Political Liberalism*, xviii (emphasis mine).

4. Rawls, *Political Liberalism*, xviii.

5. Rawls, *Political Liberalism*, 212–54.

6. Rawls, *Political Liberalism*, 54–58.

7. Rawls, *Political Liberalism*, 56–57. One "quick" but misguided way of dismissing this entire line of argument is to assert that the position is self-referentially inconsistent. Alasdair MacIntyre deals with this critique neatly: "even if Aristotle was successful, and I believe that he was, in showing that no one who understands the laws of logic can remain rational while rejecting them, observance of the laws of logic is only a necessary and not a sufficient condition for rationality, whether theoretical or practical. It is on what has to be added to observance of the laws of logic to justify ascriptions of rationality . . . that disagreement arises concerning the fundamental nature of rationality and extends into disagreement over how it is rationally appropriate to proceed in the face of these disagreements." MacIntyre, *Whose Justice? Which Rationality?* 4, cf. 346; and Rawls, *Political Liberalism*, 52–54.

basis of a rational, comprehensive doctrine.[8] Thus his shift from a *theory* of justice to *political* liberalism.

The public domain is the sphere of the reasonable. "Reasonable persons," explains Rawls, "are not moved by the general good as such but desire for its own sake a social world in which they, as free and equal, can cooperate with others on terms all can accept."[9] The "rational," by contrast, has to do with a person's ability to act effectively in accord with her own ends; as such the "rational" is not concerned with the pluralism of the public world.[10] In a reasonable society all retain their own rational ends, but "all stand ready to propose fair terms . . . so that all may benefit and improve on what everyone can do on their own."[11] Thus Rawls presupposes that anyone with a reasonable comprehensive doctrine will accede to the demand that one act politically only on the basis of public reasons.[12]

Christians or others with competing religious or philosophical doctrines, however, might wonder if acceding to this demand will make their convictions "morally secondary."[13] Rawls himself asks the critical question:

> How can it be either reasonable or rational, when basic matters are at stake, for citizens to appeal only to a public conception of justice and not to the whole truth as they see it? Surely the most fundamental questions should be settled by appealing to the most important truths, yet these may far transcend public reason![14]

Rawls replies that it is not reasonable to coerce others on the basis of beliefs that cannot be justified in light of their own comprehensive doctrines, that is, without appeal to public reasons.[15] Rawls, however, admits that some hold "unreasonable" comprehensive doctrines that must be "contained."[16]

The "root difficulty," as Bruce Brower argues, "is that political liberalism is not merely the acceptance of a political *modus vivendi* between competing theories of the good; it is itself a moral theory, even if not a comprehensive doctrine."[17] If we appeal to our own vision of the good to reject political val-

8. Rawls, *Political Liberalism*, xvi.

9. Rawls, *Political Liberalism*, 50.

10. Rawls, *Political Liberalism*, 53–54.

11. Rawls, *Political Liberalism*, 54.

12. Rawls, *Political Liberalism*, xvi.

13. Hauerwas, *The Peaceable Kingdom*, 11.

14. Rawls, *Political Liberalism*, 216.

15. Rawls, *Political Liberalism*, 60–63, cf. 217.

16. Rawls, *Political Liberalism*, xvi–xvii.

17. Brower, "The Limits of Public Reason," 13.

ues, Rawls objects that we are "unreasonable" and thereby justifies coercive measures. But to be "unreasonable" has simply been defined as the refusal to order the desire for public reasons above the desire to pursue one's own comprehensive religious or philosophical doctrine. That does indeed make these doctrines' values "morally secondary" to Rawls's paramount value, for the call to prioritize public reasons is "one more value, to be weighed against other values."[18] Political liberalism, therefore, constitutes a rival doctrine at least insofar as it requires one to compromise one's own (rational) vision of the good whenever that vision conflicts with the public (reasonable) vision of the good.[19]

In this regard Stout's language of compromise—his provisional *telos* and modest pragmatism—is superior to Rawls's political liberalism. Public space is that area within which diverse philosophies, moralities, and religions encounter one another. However, with the collapse of appeals to the "natural light" or universal reason the logical space for public reasons disappears—reasons, justifications, all are tradition-specific. Rawls's attempt to situate public reasons (i.e., the reasonable) in public space is, therefore, futile, a surreptitious privileging of the liberal vision of the good. Stout recognizes this problem but still wants to make a modest claim from public space, so he appeals not to public *reasons* but to public *consensus*. The locus of sheer consensus, split from justificatory structures, is indeed public space. Stout, however, reveals his proclivity for liberalism when he asserts that acceding to society's provisional *telos* is morally superior to remaining faithful to one's own detailed vision of the good. Identifying a level of consensus is one matter, *recommending* the consensus, however, unveils tradition-specific normative commitments.

Liberalism, then, is ultimately a species of communitarianism (one which is highly inclusive and attractive). Its strength lies in its ability to begin to explain enduring peaceable relations in our pluralistic society. But its failure to theorize itself as a tradition truncates its explanatory potential (as I, utilizing a contrast between an atheist friend's and my own belief that men and women are equal, argued [in the last chapter] in "Christian Ethics in a Postmodern World?").[20] Thus Stout fails to capture the nature of one's assent to society's provisional *telos*. He is unable to explain when and why

18. Brower, "Limits of Public Reason," 5.

19. Cf., MacIntyre, *Whose Justice? Which Rationality?* 345.

20. Consider also how Charles Taylor relates the moral ideals of affirming "ordinary life," of universal benevolence, and of freedom to particular political structures; note especially his explication of the complex historical processes that led to the articulation of each of these ideals (*Sources of the Self,* esp. 393–418). See further MacIntyre, *Whose Justice? Which Rationality?* 326–48.

one might *not* be willing to compromise, for it is only when the ordering of one's values is made explicit that such comprehensive understanding is realized. Full acknowledgment and explication of one's tradition is required. Such a requirement is satisfied, I argued, when one attends to Hauerwas's description of rationality as narrative in form (i.e., tradition dependent). Burgie-Gipson and Watson, however, have raised significant questions about my understanding of tradition. I will attempt to clarify my position by appropriating some insights from Alasdair MacIntyre.

ALASDAIR MACINTYRE: TRADITION AND TRADITIONS

Alasdair MacIntyre's *Whose Justice? Which Rationality?* (1988) demonstrates the existence of distinct, irreducible traditions (including liberalism) with equally distinct practical rationalities and coordinate conceptions of justice. MacIntyre defines a tradition as an historical argument whose core is defined relative to two types of conflict: 1) with critics external to the tradition; that is, those who reject key aspects of the tradition's core and, 2) with critics internal to the tradition, through whose debates "the meaning and rationale of the fundamental agreements [the core] come to be expressed and by whose progress a tradition is constituted."[21] Thus Arius and Athanasius, Calvin and Sadoleto, Schleiermacher and Barth are all part of the Christian tradition (narrative), while Plato and Mohammed and Nietzsche are external. The boundaries are blurred by a web of relationships, but still we can distinguish strands within a tradition (e.g., Antiochene from Alexandrian christology) and between traditions (e.g., Islam from Christianity).

Since there is no non-traditioned grounding for our inescapable activity as moral agents, self-understanding requires explicit awareness of the nature of one's own embeddedness within a tradition.[22] Such self-understanding, however, does not signal a cloistered end. As MacIntyre argues, once we affirm, "this is true," of a particular tradition, recognition of the plurality of traditions and of the contingency of our own traditioning makes it incumbent upon us both to engage ongoing arguments within the tradition and to engage rival traditions.

There are, however, limitations intrinsic to our embeddedness within a tradition. One cannot be a member of two traditions simultaneously since "genuinely to adopt the standpoint of a tradition thereby commits one to its view of what is true and false and, in so committing one, prohibits one

21. MacIntyre, *Whose Justice? Which Rationality?* 12.

22. Hauerwas, *Truthfulness and Tragedy*, 39.

from adopting any rival standpoint."[23] This is the deep significance of the Hauerwasian recognition that rationality itself is narrative in form. The task of engaging rival traditions, therefore, involves adopting a "second first language," the placing of oneself "imaginatively within the scheme of belief" of the rival tradition.[24]

Communitarians typically come under critique for retreating into isolated intellectual enclaves. I acknowledged this "troubling tendency" in Hauerwas but argue that we "must reflect, judge, and understand first and foremost according to the Christian narrative."[25] Clearly, consideration of concepts such as first and second languages demands more complex analysis than is here possible; hopefully, however, the preceding sketch will allow us to appreciate one highly nuanced paragraph in which MacIntyre expresses well the paradoxical attitude I hoped to advocate for Christians:

> The only rational way for the adherents of any tradition to approach intellectually, culturally, and linguistically alien rivals is one that allows for the possibility that in one or more areas the other may be rationally superior to it in respect precisely of that in the alien tradition which it cannot as yet comprehend. The claim made within each tradition that the presently established beliefs shared by the adherents of that tradition are true entails a denial that this is in fact going to happen in respect of those beliefs, but it is the possibility of this nonetheless happening which . . . gives point to the assertion of truth and provides assertions of truth and falsity with a content which makes them other than even idealized versions of assertions of warranted assertibility.[26]

I have now clarified my critique of liberalism and my qualification of communitarianism. I hope the depth of my sympathy for Malcolm's project, insofar as it develops understandings critical to the "public of the church," is evident. It remains for me to address Ferriby and Logan's important deconstructionist challenges to the very idea of identifying a tradition. I have argued that it is possible to discern between traditions, but this is admittedly a forced and inexact activity. I will attempt to explain why I nevertheless think it essential.

---

23. MacIntyre, *Whose Justice? Which Rationality?* 367.

24. MacIntyre, *Whose Justice? Which Rationality?* 394.

25. Greenway, "Christian Ethics in a Postmodern World?" 27.

26. MacIntyre, *Whose Justice? Which Rationality?* 388.

DAVID HARVEY: UNIVERSAL MARGINALIZATION, OPPRESSION, AND POWER

The liberationist impulse in deconstruction manifests itself in the belief that if *everyone* is marginalized then no one can be an oppressor. While such a scenario may be theoretically possible, it is so distant from extant distortions of power that those offering it seriously in the present context risk abetting global oppression. Deconstructionists delight us with their playfulness; my fear is that this insouciance is a luxury available in the relatively secure context of Western academe but absent in third world seminaries or base communities.

A case for resisting the deconstructive play of postmodernity is powerfully developed in David Harvey's *The Condition of Postmodernity: An Enquiry into the Origins of Cultural Change* (1989). In a neo-Marxist structural critique, Harvey portrays postmodernity as a dangerous subterfuge which cloaks and thereby protects a powerful, global, "late-stage" form of capitalism. With regard to the ethical implications of deconstruction, Harvey issues only dire warnings.

"Obsessed with deconstructing," Harvey warns, deconstructionists "can end only in condemning their own validity claims to the point where nothing remains of any basis for reasoned action."[27] Of course, this objection manifests a certain Cartesian anxiety, a longing for irretrievable comforts of bygone days. But this does not vitiate what Harvey notes as an insidious consequence of a complete fall into the sheer multiplying of narratives:

> Worst of all, while it [deconstruction] opens up a radical prospect by acknowledging the authenticity of other voices, postmodernist thinking immediately shuts off those other voices from access to more universal sources of power by ghettoizing them within an opaque otherness, the specificity of this or that language game. It thereby disempowers those voices (of women, ethnic and racial minorities, colonized peoples) in a world of lop-sided power relations.[28]

Unfortunately, lament is as far as Harvey advances in countering the postmodern deconstruction of appeals to universal reason. Describing invidious consequences of a position, however, is inadequate argument against it, and Harvey introduces no constructive alternative to the portrait of postmodernity he paints so starkly.

27. Harvey, *The Condition of Postmodernity*, 116.
28. Harvey, *The Condition of Postmodernity*, 117.

On the one hand, then, with the collapse of modernist epistemology we recognize that there is no "access to more universal sources of power" through reason alone. On the other hand, our need to take ethical stands *for* "women, ethnic and racial minorities, colonized peoples" and *against* fundamentalist chauvinists, neo-Nazis, and the "cabal of international bankers" who are Harvey's villains, requires we who are moved by the plight of affected peoples to take actions based on *universalistic* claims. In the face of centuries-old, oppressive master-narratives deconstruction may be a necessary step, but insofar as deconstruction has in and of itself no constructive content, it is necessarily transitory, inherently unstable, and forever unable to generate a politic. I will explicate my own constructive response to the deconstructionist challenge by moving through the work of liberation theologian Mark L. Taylor.

MARK L. TAYLOR: THE POSTMODERN TRILEMMA

Mark Taylor addresses the nexus of problems that spring from the attempt to relate ethics and postmodernism in *Remembering Esperanza: A Cultural-Political Theology for North American Praxis* (1990). Taylor argues that the communitarian tendency to retreat into discrete narrative traditions corrects classic liberal tendencies towards individualism and neglect of tradition. But communitarian projects too often engender a "postmodernism of reaction" that can muster only a facile analysis of the plurality of narratives that inform the understanding and politics of diverse communities today.[29]

This "postmodernism of reaction" is helpfully and convincingly deconstructed by pluralists, argues Taylor, but the constructive resources of pluralists such as Mark C. Taylor or John Caputo are dangerously limited. "Celebration of difference does seem to be a posture of critique," Taylor concedes, but "whether it can move beyond that critical posture to real strategies or sustained discursive and extradiscursive practices of resistance is another question."[30] The deconstructionist critique is necessary but insufficient for development of a "postmodernism of resistance." Citing Langdon Gilkey's conclusion that pluralism "is toothless if one faces oppression," Taylor argues that "persistent identification and resistance to the destruction of life we already see and the global destruction that threatens" is required "to check sheer celebration of the flux."[31]

---

29. Taylor, *Remembering Esperanza*, 32–34.
30. Taylor, *Remembering Esperanza*, 39
31. Taylor, *Remembering Esperanza*, 40.

Taylor proposes we theorize our situation as a "postmodern trilemma." The three traits of the trilemma are acknowledgment of tradition, celebration of plurality, and resistance to domination.[32] Taylor does not dissolve the tensions between the three traits of his trilemma, but in a subtle analysis insists that all three, never any one or any two, must be continually kept in play if we are to theorize and act constructively in our postmodern *milieu*.

As we did with Rawls and Stout, however, we must ask from *where* is this analysis advanced? Why "celebrate" plurality? Why is "resistance to domination" the third trait? These two aspects of Taylor's trilemma reveal a host of commitments not entailed by the widespread recognition that our thought is conditioned by tradition and the sister recognition that there are a plurality of traditions. Clearly Taylor's exposition functions one level beyond his most fundamental commitments. Taylor freely concedes this point, noting that each trait of his postmodern trilemma correlates with a major theme of his re-membering of the most significant formative aspects of his own narrative history. He offers no foundationalist justification for his position but ends self-consciously "hoping to invoke some sense these are indeed traits of a situation that is more than my own set of thematic interests."[33]

Through description, Taylor hopes to spark from within a recognition of "truth." This recognition springs not from any essentialist *anamnesis* but from the contingencies of one's own tradition, from the depths of one's personal heritage, from the memory of one's contact with those who are other. While Taylor seeks conversation and intersubjective agreement, therefore, he must grant that one's own narrative and tradition constitute an inescapable, contingent, and formative starting point for one's reflection and judgment. For instance, his third trait, resistance to domination, is a function of his own participation in a particular tradition to a degree that recognition of plurality is not, for many who acknowledge tradition and recognize plurality neither "celebrate" plurality nor see "resistance to domination" as a third trait. Thus a question remains: when rational but incompatible doctrines are in play (i.e., when conversation will not yield inter-subjective agreement), how are we to relate to those with whom we differ profoundly? For example, what is Taylor's relation to those who see the just distribution of rewards in a market economy where he may see unjust consequences of power distortions, or his relation to those who see legitimate role assignments based on intrinsic differences between male and female where he sees oppressive hierarchies? Full recognition of plurality demands acknowledgment of these

32. Taylor, *Remembering Esperanza*, 31–43.
33. Taylor, *Remembering Esperanza*, 45.

rival perspectives as candidates for truth. They are not necessarily incoherent; they may be part of comprehensive and consistent doctrines. Taylor's delineation of our postmodern trilemma is very important, but his analysis points beyond itself to even deeper tensions.

IRREDUCIBLE TENSIONS: PRIVATE CONVICTIONS IN PUBLIC SPACE

After exposing the Enlightenment's "prejudice against prejudice" Hans-Georg Gadamer rehabilitates "tradition" and "authority."[34] Since we have no non-prejudiced ground upon which to judge other horizons of understanding, Gadamer presses the virtue of conversation and suggests that we adopt as our mode of being in the world the open structure of a question.[35] Conversants who adopt this open structure of a question, however, are almost as "toothless" in the face of oppression as sheer deconstructionists. Indeed, in daily life we regularly confront moral "forced live options" (James) when we must act and where any action reflects a decisive ordering of values which renders any attempt at adopting the stance of the question impossible. "Conviction" best describes our "forced" orientation toward our vision of the good in such instances.

When "tradition," "authority," and "conviction" are put into play history haunts us with visions of the Crusades, the Inquisition, and the Thirty Years War. But, as I have argued, we cannot escape this foreboding trinity through appeals to the natural light of reason, public reasons, or consensus. The tensions between rival private convictions, convictions conditioned by rival traditions, are irreducible. I suggest we reintroduce the category of "mystery." Theologically, "mystery" is rooted biblically in the holiness of God and philosophically in the otherness of God. For our purposes, however, "mystery" need reference only the comparatively thin recognition of our inescapable embeddedness in one of a plurality of traditions, the acknowledgment of the impossibility of ever knowing "Truth."

Taken in tandem, "mystery" and "conviction" help us name the contradictory tendencies wrought by the irreducible tensions elicited by holding private convictions in public space. "Conviction" names well our felt experience as moral agents that racism, for instance, is absolutely wrong. "Mystery," by referencing truth as a regulative ideal forever beyond our grasp, names well our recognition that our convictions (and attendant justificatory schemes) may be mistaken. "Conviction" empowers our moral agency

34. Gadamer, *Truth and Method*, 245–53.
35. Gadamer, *Truth and Method*, 325–33.

where decisive action is forced but moral consensus is lacking. "Mystery" tempers our actions and opens us to the possibility that those with different convictions may teach us.

Furthermore, by putting "conviction" and "mystery" into play we gain greater clarity and real-to-life precision in describing our situation as moral agents. *Conviction* signals *why* we would have participated in the Underground Railroad, why we applaud Bonhoeffer's "treason," why we sanction coercive measures to check the activities of white supremacists or neo-Nazis; "conviction" also signals *how* we are empowered to act when facing forced live options regarding which there is no societal consensus or how we determine to resist oppression legitimated by the provisional *telos* itself (e.g., remember the history of the struggle for women's rights).

Mystery signals *why* we are willing to settle for a provisional *telos*, why we do not immediately resort to violence to enforce our vision of the good, why we listen to others for words of correction. A sense of mystery should absolutely minimize any recourse to coercion, for it renders us continually conscious that there are no universal criteria or certain foundations by which to justify coercion. For instance, even where public reasons justify state coercion (e.g., IRS action against those who take a principled stand against paying taxes) we must concede that such actions are not fully supported by the demands of rationality.[36]

Within this context I hope it is clear that my rejection of pacifism is aimed not at warranting violence but at refusing to sanction denials of complicity in structures of coercion. In particular, we must remember that the interests of Western elites are cloaked in currents of coercion that run deep close to home but often crash violently on distant shores. That is why pacifism is an ideal, almost invariably supportive of the *status quo*, not often helpful in the West.

CONCLUSION

I have argued that *de facto* more elemental than the public question, "how are we to preserve the peaceable evolution of our pluralistic society" is the private question, "at what points and to what degree does my vision of the good require me to withdraw my provisional assent to society's provisional *telos*?" Peaceableness within our pluralistic society is exceedingly valuable, but one must *decide* how this value should be ordered relative to other values. It is impossible to speak ethically *from* public space. We speak and act ethically according to our participation in a particular tradition. The tension

36. Brower, "The Limits of Public Reason," 26.

between rival doctrines in public space, therefore, is irreducible. Given this irreducible tension, putting "mystery" and "conviction" into conceptual play enhances our ability to articulate ethical and political realities at an existential level. The precision and depth of such real-to-life descriptions betters our ability to comprehend, for instance, the dynamics underlying our uneasy tolerance of increasingly vitriolic anti-Semitic, racist, and sexist speech, the self-understanding that empowers the violent fanatical fringe of the anti-abortion movement, the debate embroiling efforts to harvest organs from anencephalic infants, or the existential intricacies of the debate over the vices or virtues of ethnocentrism (e.g., consider recent cross-cultural discussion of female circumcision/genital mutilation).

In contemporary global public space appeals to tolerance and conversation alone appear increasingly inadequate. A more complex and fluid understanding, one which traffics heavily in such historically troublesome categories as "tradition," "authority," "the good," and "conviction" while retaining a constant awareness of "contingency" and "mystery," might be essential if we hope to evolve into a peaceable and just global community. For the Christian, such an understanding initiates Christian moral *bricolage.*[37]

---

37. For a mature statement of my views see not only the following chapter on two later works by Stout (chapter 9, "Jeffery Stout, Original Sin, and Christian Faith"), but also Greenway, *Agape Ethics.*

Chapter 9

Jeffrey Stout, Original Sin, and the Significance of Christian Faith

"Above all . . . the idea of original sin is blight on the human spirit."
—Jeffrey Stout, *Democracy and Tradition*[1]

"'That is my place in the sun.' That is how the usurpation of the whole world began."
—Pascal, *Pensees*, 112[2]

Despite valiant efforts to the contrary, the "more militant atheist" in Sabina Lovibond cannot help but suggest that, "Christian belief *per se* is symptomatic of a 'rationality deficit.'"[3] This worry results in wary affirmation of Jeffrey Stout's *Democracy and Tradition* (2004), for Stout, an atheist, refuses to declare theism irrational. Stout is sympathetic with Lovibond. In his very first book, Stout recalls, he too argued at length that, "social and intellectual developments since Hume's day have brought it about that no one in the

---

1. Stout, *Democracy and Tradition*, 20.

2. As cited in Levinas, *Otherwise Than Being*, vii.

3. Lovibond, "Religion and Modernity," 627–30, with general reference to the critical theorist Seyla Benhabib.

modern period is rationally entitled to hold religious beliefs."[4] However, Stout continues firmly, since then "much has changed in the philosophy of religion," and he has now "come to think that I can no longer responsibly impugn the rationality of modern theists en masse."[5]

Accordingly, in *Democracy and Tradition* Stout refuses "to rule out a class of claims simply because they refer to something *beyond* or *above* the ontological framework assumed in the natural sciences."[6] This refusal lies at the heart of what Stout sincerely intends to be a generous engagement with Christianity. Stout's open spirit of engagement is critical to his defense of secular democracy, for his project is politically viable only to the degree he convinces Christians they can embrace secular democracy without facing prejudice and without abandoning their beliefs at the gate to the public square. Stout's generous spirit of engagement led Stanley Hauerwas to declare *Democracy and Tradition* "a gift to . . . to all Christians" because "Jeff Stout thinks theology matters."[7]

Stout's generous spirit, however, is severely compromised by metaphysical convictions he continues to share with Lovibond (and a powerful segment of intellectual elites). For Stout's reflections are decisively conditioned by an inherently atheistic metaphysical naturalism (henceforth designated "physicalism"). As a direct result, Christians across the theological spectrum have shied from Stout.[8] Even Hauerwas, in his promotional blurb on *Democracy's* back cover, continues to contrast "advocates of democracy" with "those who hold substantive Christian convictions." Stout's affirmation of people, faith, and churches in his more recent *Blessed Are the Organized*—"if one subtracted churches from . . . organizing networks, then grassroots democracy in the United States would come to very little"—while appreciative, remains equally equivocal.[9]

I argue that Stout's physicalism prevents him from discerning a vital axiological challenge that sets the context within which Christianity's significance is manifest. Stout's moral spirit is redolent of Jesus and the prophets, but Stout's physicalism renders him *incapable* of thinking theology really matters (other than in a *de facto* political sense). On Stout's account,

---

4. Stout, "Comments on Six Responses," 713, in reference to Stout, *The Flight from Authority*.

5. "Comments on Six Responses," 713.

6. Stout, *Democracy and Tradition*, 256.

7. Hauerwas, *Performing the Faith*, 217.

8. Gaston, "Augustine or Emerson?" 25. See the similar conclusions of Meilander, "Talking Democracy," 27–30; Lovin, "Christian and Citizen," 34; and Long, "Jeffrey Stout," 172–74.

9. Stout, *Blessed Are the Organized*, 4–5.

Christian faith may not be demonstrably irrational, but Christianity has no valid, non-instrumental (i.e., *vis-à-vis* politics) significance. I argue that the moral spirit Stout shares with Jesus and the prophets should lead him not merely to withholding of judgment, but to affirmation of the reality and character of a spiritual reality that is congruent with a realist Christian affirmation that God is love.

AFFIRMATION: STOUT'S PROMISING POLITICAL PROPOSAL

Jeffrey Stout is concerned about the future of secular democracies. Though not himself a person of faith, Stout frankly acknowledges that modern political theory and non-religious cultural elites have demanded believers leave religious reasons behind if they want to enter public debate. He realizes this is a condition faithful Christians (or faithful Hindus, Muslims, Jews, and so forth) cannot accept—indeed, this condition makes democracy and people of faith implacable antagonists. Given the number and influence of Christians (especially in the United States), Stout sees this as a serious problem for secular democracies.

Fortunately, Stout argues in *Democracy*, the source of the problem is a relatively recent "secularist" account of the secular. Stout reminds us that modern secular democracies had their origins in societies that were overwhelmingly Christian. Historically, Stout points out, the secular is the product not of rejection or marginalization of theism, but of diversity *among* theists. Secular democracy resulted from attempts in early modern Europe to minimize sectarian violence by tailoring "institutions and vocabularies to accommodate diverse reasonable perspectives on theology and the good."[10] "Secular," Stout suggests, should be understood accordingly. "Secular" should mean not a-religious but multi-religious. It should mean only "that participants in a given discursive practice are not in a position to take for granted that their interlocutors are making the same religious assumptions they are."[11]

In addition to this historical argument, Stout articulates an internal theological/idealist reason for the faithful of any one tradition to affirm a wider pluralism: epistemological humility. Stout argues for a recovery of classic Christian understanding of Understanding that transcends (finite, Fallen) understanding. The Cartesian pretension to Knowledge led to an idolatrous equation of truth and Truth. Forgetting that the equation truth/

10. Stout, *Democracy and Tradition*, 127.
11. Stout, *Democracy and Tradition*, 97.

Truth is itself Cartesian, many mistakenly conclude that the demolition of Descartes's pretension entails the demolition of the idea of Truth. But it entails only the demolition of the idolatrous equation. With the fall of Cartesian epistemology, Stout realizes, realist Truth and Christian Truth endure as reasonable but super-human possibilities, and all human truth claims are accordingly humbled.

Along these lines, Stout makes clear he means to recommend a pragmatic epistemology that can be affirmed by atheist and Christian, by nominalist, naturalist, idealist, moral and theological realist alike. He explicitly affirms the reasonableness of belief in Truth in moral realist/idealist terms. With regard to moral truth, Stout affirms for believers God's own moral understanding as Truth, and for classically realist philosophers an "imaginative projection," the exhaustive and completely coherent "*Concise Encyclopedia of Moral Truth.*"[12]

The idealist/religious idea of absolute Truth, Stout points out, precisely because it is always beyond the grasp of finite beings, plays a cautionary role, keeping us humble and relatively open-minded by preventing us from ever identifying our finite understanding with ultimate Understanding.[13] Notably, this means that *even if Christianity is true, Christians do not gain any specific epistemic privilege when adjudicating ethical quandaries.* To the contrary, belief in God's perfect Understanding entails relative humility regarding one's own understanding.

For parallel reasons regarding human finitude, the *Concise Encyclopedia* should humble all idealist philosophical claims to Truth. In short, both the theist and the philosopher may believe that their understandings imperfectly but faithfully approach God's understanding or Ultimate Truth, and they may indeed be correct, but neither has a position of epistemic privilege over the naturalistic nominalist, for given our finite (plus, for traditional Christians, fallen) understanding, neither has the ability to appropriate either the *Encyclopedia* or God's understanding in order to establish or justify their positions. Any attempt to do so Stout rightly rejects as "metaphysics in the pejorative sense."

For Stout, then, epistemological humility entails ontological openness and both philosophical idealism and theological realism entail epistemological humility. Stout does not believe that there are eternal truths in the realist/idealist Augustinian or Platonic sense. Humbled epistemologically, however, Stout explicitly rejects the idea that those who do believe in Platonic Truth or God are necessarily less than rational. He also asserts explicitly

12. Stout, *Democracy and Tradition*, 245.
13. Stout, *Democracy and Tradition*, 243.

that pragmatism, "understood strictly as a critique of metaphysics in the pejorative sense," does not quarrel "with the God of Amos and Dorothy Day, or even with the God of Barthian theology, but with the God of Descartes, and with the God of analytic metaphysics."[14]

Stout's public square subsists not by virtue of theoretical appeal to objective Reason or any single metaphysic, and not by excluding the moral wisdom of religious traditions, but by virtue of practices pivoting about epistemic humility and the desire to cultivate virtues and institutions that maximize possibilities for a peaceable coexistence wherein all flourish. His public square is neither naked nor uniform, but full of folks dressed in various metaphysical garb whose epistemic humility and virtuousness gives each reason, on internal grounds, to participate in and mutually sustain a democratic public sphere that blends sufficient consensus (think of the "overlapping consensus" of Rawls's *Political Liberalism*) with significant ethical, metaphysical, and religious pluralism.[15]

Stout's political proposal is promising. The success of his proposal, however, turns upon the ability of atheists like himself truly to understand and respect the significance of Christianity. Stout's physicalism precludes that possibility. I will argue that it is reasonable for anyone with Stout's moral passion to leave physicalism behind.

STOUT, ORIGINAL SIN, AND THE SIGNIFICANCE OF CHRISTIAN FAITH

Stout's Physicalist Blinkers

Despite sincere intentions to the contrary, Stout remains firmly in the grip of the metaphysical naturalism (i.e., physicalism) that quietly anchors Western intellectual elites' disdain for faith in God. Nancy Frankenberry, a professor of religion at Dartmouth, illustrates the contemptuous attitude physicalism authorizes towards believers even among scholars of religion:

> To many investigators, the phenomenon of religion resembles a petri dish brimming with exotic specimens and puzzling data. Viewed under the microscope, it teems with strange cultures. Even to a trained eye, the study of religion—its structure, persistence, and meaning—poses acute interpretative challenges .... *Radical Interpretation in Religion* consists of original chapters by ten prominent authors in these fields who propose a

14. Stout, *Democracy and Tradition*, 268.
15. See Rawls, *Political Liberalism*.

> variety of new ways of interpreting believers . . . they stand in a
> critical tradition that explains religion in entirely naturalist [i.e.,
> physicalist] terms, rather than on supernatural or faith-based
> premises.[16]

Frankenberry's portrayal of herself in the role of a natural scientist is not innocent. It surreptitiously asserts that there are no truths beyond the physicalist parameters of modern science. By contrast, Stout's epistemological humility and claimed openness to truths "*beyond* or *above* the ontological framework assumed in the natural sciences" stands in sharp relief.

Then again, Stout, a contributor to Frankenberry's volume, may find her words not untrue but unhelpful. In his contribution, Stout interprets religion within the wholly physicalist framework of Robert Brandom's *Making It Explicit*.[17] Brandom's physicalist horizon precludes ontological truths beyond the metaphysical arc of modern science. It leaves no conceptual space for any religious "more." In Brandom the idea is not even refuted. The requisite ontological space is thought not to exist, so no question of any "more" can even arise. Stout calls Brandom "ideal" for interpreting religion because he affirms no ontological truths beyond modern scientific ontological parameters. So it is little surprise that, despite his claimed ontological openness, Stout's "public philosophy" in *Democracy* and in *Blessed* remains within the bounds of physicalism.

Consider, for instance, Stout's imposition of physicalist boundaries when he argues for "a *social* theory of moral objectivity."[18] Stout dismisses the classically realist/idealist question with a rhetorical wave of the hand: "But what about the question of whether the individuals really have the right we have attributed to them? This question gets us on the wrong track if we take it as an invitation to do an inventory of everything there *really* is."[19] "For practical purposes," Stout says, we can replace this question by asking more concrete questions. For instance:

> Do we (really) have sufficiently good reason, all things consid-
> ered, to attribute the right not to be smashed on the head with
> a sledge-hammer?" This question is analogous to the question,
> "Do we have sufficiently good reason to remain committed to
> the rule against tackling from behind in soccer?" Both of these
> questions have the merit of directing our attention explicitly
> to reasons, to rational considerations that would count for or

---

16. Frankenberry, "Preface," xiii–xiv.

17. Brandom, *Making It Explicit*.

18. Stout, *Democracy and Tradition*, 275.

19. Stout, *Democracy and Tradition*, 275.

against the rule being discussed. The answers to both of these questions happen to be clear, for we have every reason to remain committed to our conception of these particular properties.[20]

Stout sees no essential difference with controversial cases, where, similarly, "what we are actually faced with is a conflict or balance of rational considerations, not an absence of such considerations."[21] In every case, it is such "rational considerations" that form the basis for debate.

It is critical to affirm that, insofar as rejection of metaphysics in the pejorative sense is concerned, there is no problem with Stout's argument. Theists, idealists, and moral realists enjoy no epistemological edge when it comes to adjudicating ethical quandary cases. Problems arise, however, when Stout conflates the epistemological and the metaphysical by leveling norms in ethics with ideals in (American) soccer.

Stout says the only critical distinctions he sees between ethical norms and the ideals of soccer are that "ethical norms are much more important in most contexts, and much harder to assess critically, than the properties and ideals of soccer are."[22] That claim depends upon a metaphysical, not an epistemological, premise. Classic moral realists, for instance, would be aghast at a failure to draw a *metaphysical* distinction between prohibitions against murder and tackling from behind in soccer. They would also be baffled at Stout's blanket contention that ethical norms are "harder to assess critically" than the ideals of soccer—does Stout really think this *vis-à-vis* killing for profit, torture for personal pleasure, pedophilia, rape, genocide, and a multitude of other horrors?

"Why," the classic realist asks, "is murder more important?" Because, the realist answers, "murder is a violation of what is Good; tackling from behind in soccer violates *only* a social construction" (murder is *also* a social construction, but for moral realists it is not *only* a social construction). "An innocent person should not be smashed with a sledge-hammer" is not a "right" we "attribute" but a moral truth by which any sane person is seized (here we work with a defining trait for sanity). The question here is not about epistemological certainty in the unattainable Cartesian sense, not about adjudication of quandary cases, and not about the admitted strength and essential role of socio-cultural formation.

The question is whether or not the fullness and depth of our moral convictions are adequately and most reasonably expressed when we equate their ontological status to that of the rules of soccer. Why, for instance, does

20. Stout, *Democracy and Tradition*, 275.

21. Stout, *Democracy and Tradition*, 276.

22. Stout, *Democracy and Tradition*, 275.

Stout feel the need to use language of "moral *objectivity*" (emphasis mine) in relation to socially contingent standards, language that sounds bizarre if applied analogously to the rules of soccer (i.e., who would claim that the rules of soccer are objective in such a strong sense?). Why, with regard to some moral offenses, does Stout feel the need to speak of the "horrendous," of "evils," of our "deepest concerns and passions," of violation of the "sacred," and of "reverence"? Why does Stout *not* think he is discerning some ontological reality?[23]

Absent some strong reason to affirm the contrary, it is wholly reasonable to conclude that ethical convictions by which we are seized and over which we have no real doubt are *misrepresented* and *weakened* insofar as they are understood to be epiphenomenal, wholly contingent, socio-cultural products. We are speaking here not of quandary cases, where ethical judgments are by definition unclear and contestable. We are speaking of ethical convictions over which there is no real debate. We are speaking of the evil of the torture of children, of pedophilia, rape, genocide, sex trafficking, on the one hand (the list of horrors is long and painful), and we are speaking, on the other hand, of the good of aiding those who are wounded, visiting those unjustly imprisoned, defending and/or meeting the needs of those who are hungry, naked, and exploited. And with reference to such evil and good it is wholly reasonable to affirm moral realism, for it is wholly reasonable to conclude that, as Charles Taylor says, our "deepest moral instincts, our ineradicable sense that human life is to be respected" is "our mode of access to the world in which ontological claims are discernible and can be rationally argued about and sifted."[24]

We will always face ethical quandaries in our complicated world. But that ineradicable epistemological challenge does not entail rejection of a realist moral ontology, most especially with regard to that host of ethical ideals over which we have no real doubt and over which there is historically deep and wide cross-cultural consensus. The question is, why, given the clear depth and certitude of Stout's central moral convictions, and given that he says it is not unreasonable to affirm truths beyond the ontological boundaries of modern science, why does Stout not make the next, wholly reasonable step and affirm that moral convictions over which we have no real doubt provide access to "the world in which ontological claims are discernible" (Taylor)?

My hunch, again, is that Stout is in the grip of a powerful ideology prominent among modern Western cultural elites, namely physicalism (or,

23. Stout, *Blessed Are the Organized*, 211–12.

24. Taylor, *Sources of the Self*, 8.

"naturalism"). But why does Stout remain committed to physicalism? If I am correct, the real answer to that question *must remain hidden in order to remain effective*, because the real answer is that physicalism *allows people to shield themselves from moral condemnation by dismissing moral realism*. Accordingly, Stout subverts the question of moral realism by arguing that the realist distinction is empty and by claiming to avoid metaphysics altogether.

In fact, however, Stout works within the metaphysical parameters of physicalism. Stout is not deliberately deceptive. He is in the grip of an ideology that is especially powerful among modern Western cultural elites, an ideology that is both unwarranted and that subverts (Stout's own) concerns over social justice. Stout is sincere when he explicitly portrays his pragmatism as metaphysically innocent. He is sincere when he subtly and unwittingly elides the metaphysical question and identifies metaphysics with theology:

> Pragmatism comes into conflict with theology in ethical theory mainly at those points where someone asserts that the truth-claiming function of ethics depends, for its *objectivity*, on positing a transcendent and perfect being. Metaphysics asserts the need and then posits the divine explainer to satisfy it. Pragmatism questions the need and then doubts the coherence of the explanation.[25]

On the basis of this illicit identification of theology and metaphysics, Stout advertises "ethics without metaphysics."[26] But what he actually delivers is ethics within the boundaries of a physicalist metaphysic.

In the above quote, moreover, Stout misrepresents the "need" of classic Christian theology, which does not posit the divine in order to secure the objectivity of its ethical truth claims. Certainly, some Christians construe God as a posit necessary for human certainty (e.g., those duped into attempting to meet Cartesian criteria for rationality). But this betrays mainstream Christian theology, for which God is neither an explanation nor a needed posit. Theological talk of the God who is righteous, just, gracious, steadfast, love, and so forth, is how theists name and unfold experiences of moral reality, evil, good, horror, joy, reverence, love, forgiveness, and grace with a complexity and sophistication that far surpasses Stout. By reducing "God," Cartesian-style, to a "divine explainer" or "human justifier" (the conclusion, posit, or linchpin of some human system or logical

---

25. Stout, *Democracy and Tradition*, 268.

26. "Ethics Without Metaphysics" is the title of chapter 11 of Stout, *Democracy and Tradition*.

contention), Stout caricatures Christian faith, making it easy to group and dispatch Christianity's metaphysical claims as a species of "metaphysics in the pejorative sense."

Once metaphysics in the pejorative sense is dispatched, Stout simply cannot see anything significant at stake in theistic faith. Stout's respect for Christians feels genuine. In accord with his physicalism, however, he cannot but render realist Truth- or God-talk essentially decorative. Thus, in reference to the *Concise Encyclopedia of Moral Truth* Stout stresses without qualification that there is "no harm in granting that there is a set of truths like this, provided that we rigorously avoid treating it as something we could conceivably know and apply."[27]

Stout applies the same rationale to God. Christianity's "controversial" and "questionable" ontological claims are allowable because they are harmless additions to important ethical affirmations.[28] They are harmless because belief either in God's Truth or the *Concise Encyclopedia* has been accepted only to the degree that even believers "rigorously avoid treating it as something [they] could conceivably know and apply."[29] On Stout's account, God has no more significance or power than an imaginative projection, which is why an imaginative projection (i.e., the *Concise Encyclopedia*) can do equally well for atheists what God does for Christians. Aside from concern over "metaphysics in the pejorative sense," Stout treats God as a difference who makes no difference. Faith in God amounts to flowery embellishment of ethical convictions that can stand as solidly on their own.

Stout's naturalistic bracketing of God's significance is patent when he consistently casts the stakes of the metaphysical question in exclusively epistemological terms. "My complaint about realism," he says, "is that I do not see any explanatory value in the notion of correspondence that realists lay over it."[30] Once pejorative metaphysics is neutralized, Stout simply cannot discern anything in the demise of moral realism that constitutes an appropriate "focal point for large-scale cultural angst."[31] For Stout, realism amounts to nothing more than an empty distinction, as if the moral realist is simply insisting "murder is not just really wrong, it is Really Wrong." Even when Stout makes passing reference to human despair, his epistemological focus upon pejorative metaphysics stunts his moral and spiritual reflection:

27. Stout, *Democracy and Tradition*, 240.

28. Stout, *Democracy and Tradition*, 259–60.

29. Stout, *Democracy and Tradition*, 240.

30. Stout, *Democracy and Tradition*, 249.

31. Stout, *Democracy and Tradition*, 252.

> Especially for those on the verge of despair, it might well be a
> saving comfort to believe that our highest ideals are instantiated
> in an actual being—not only a perfect paradigm of goodness but
> a power capable of seeing to it that everything will eventually
> turn out well. I do not gainsay people of good will and common
> decency who accept faith in such a God. Who am I to judge
> them? Yet I do question the wisdom of treating the objectivity
> of ethics as if it depended, in effect, upon a faith shared by only
> some of the people.[32]

Here, Stout both caricatures Christian hope and misses the significance of
his own words. The caricature of Christian hope may be understandable, for
even many pastors turn Christianity into a crude, self-centered game whose
raison d'etre is life after death in heaven (and, even worse, material success
in the here and now). Such caricature in a scholarly study purportedly committed to serious consideration of theology, however, is not innocent. Indeed, as will become clear, Stout's seemingly sympathetic move here is part
and parcel of an unwitting but significant misunderstanding of faith.

Stout is right to focus upon despair. But he is wrong to think the Christian response to despair depends upon affirmation of a "power capable of
seeing to it that everything will eventually turn out well." Given the character of life, it would be mean-spirited not at least to hope in such a power. But
even if there is some sort of literal heaven, it is not clear how that addresses
the religious/moral issue of despair. The abuser giving his wife expensive
presents tomorrow does not undo the violation of yesterday—and in the
only life we know it is always "yesterday."

Stout should be afflicted by the same aching despair. The critical question is not about faith being essential for affirmation of ethical objectivity.
This misunderstands the genesis and meaningfulness of faith. Stout is right
to forbid Christians metaphysics in the pejorative sense, faith in God yields
no epistemological advantage. But Stout's paradigmatically modern fixation
upon epistemology and God as an Archimedean point or as the means to
a literal heaven forecloses upon the possibility that he might recognize the
devastating challenge that the pervasive suffering and injustice suffusing
reality poses to our ability to affirm existence and ourselves. That is, Stout
masks the existential challenge posed by evil. As a result, a critical dimension of the origins and meaningfulness of faith is elided. Stout is the victim
of an unconscious protective strategy, a powerful, unconscious, modern
Western ideology that elides the existential challenge and encourages people to shield themselves from moral censure by dismissing moral realism.

32. Stout, *Democracy and Tradition*, 268.

The Moral/Religious Significance of Evil: The Challenge of Affirmation

Stout's too-easy reference to those "on the verge of despair" should provoke a more searching interrogation of the precise character of religious and/or moral despair. What sort of person, perceiving the overwhelming suffering and injustice permeating reality, would not taste bitterness, would not despair? Who, aware that their own existence is inextricably tied up with all who exist, aware that their being has been purchased at a price which includes all the suffering suffusing reality, would not confess bitterly that, as Pascal put it, "the I (*mon*) is hateful"?[33] Who would not resonate with the apparent ethical sensitivity of Dostoyevsky's Ivan Karamazov, who needs not multitudes, but for the tears of one child would give back his ticket to this world?[34]

As Emmanuel Levinas put it, "One comes not into the world but into question."[35] *Ab initio*, one finds oneself *already* complicit in all the evils of the world. This, continues Levinas, is a "guiltless responsibility, whereby I am none the less open to an accusation of which no alibi, spatial or temporal, could clear me."[36] The question, then, is, "the question of my right to be which is already my responsibility for the death of the Other, interrupting the carefree spontaneity of my naïve perseverance."[37] For Levinas, consciousness of this question, ethical consciousness, marks the truly human:

> The human is the return to the interiority of non-intentional consciousness, to *mauvaise conscience*, to its capacity to fear injustice more than death, to prefer to suffer than to commit injustice, and to prefer that which justifies being over that which assures it.[38]

The properly self-regarding "why me?" remains, but as a species of a prior and overwhelming, "why evil?" Levinas's philosophical genre can cloak the enveloping angst of the question. One does not grasp this question. It is not out there, a puzzle. One is seized, shaken. The issue is not accepting death but accepting life. Not "ask not for whom the bell tolls" but, "*I* hurt them, *I* torture them, *I* kill them." Indictment of existence and of our own selves screams out from and at us, a desperate, pained cry in an enveloping abyss.

33. Pascal, *Pensees*, as cited in Levinas, *The Levinas Reader*, 82.
34. See Dostoyevsky, *The Brothers Karamazov*, close of Book V, Section 4, "Rebellion."
35. Levinas, *The Levinas Reader*, 81.
36. Levinas, *The Levinas Reader*, 83.
37. Levinas, *The Levinas Reader*, 86.
38. Levinas, *The Levinas Reader*, 85.

Why, God damn it all, why? How now joy, affirmation, yes? Not amorality or moral relativism but supremely convicted moral sensitivity to all the suffering and injustice that immediately delivers damnation. That is the abyss. That is where every human *qua* fully awakened moral being, beyond any protestation of personal innocence, lives.

Charles Taylor acutely depicts this existential plight as a "dilemma of mutilation": we either acknowledge our deepest moral intuitions and, given our complicity in this damnable cosmos, instantly damn ourselves, or we manage *yes* by denying our deepest moral intuitions, and so mutilate ourselves spiritually.[39] Is there any escape? As Levinas warns, all-embracing physicalism appears to offer one avenue of escape, for the challenge itself turns upon a "responsibility for my neighbour, for the other man, for the stranger or sojourner, to which nothing in the rigorously ontological order binds me—nothing in the order of the thing, of the something, of number or causality."[40] As Taylor knows, Nietzsche, grandson and son of Lutheran pastors, possessed of the moral conviction of Ivan, knew the question, knew the abyss, and thought it would be negated if the challenge could be elided. Nietzsche had no illusions about the ontological order of modern science, the ontological order of the thing:

> the acting man is caught in his illusion of volition . . . his assumption that free will exists, is also part of the calculable mechanism. . . . Man's complete lack of responsibility, for his behavior and for his nature, is the bitterest drop which the man of knowledge must swallow . . .[41]

But Nietzsche, having discounted the possibility of divine grace, saw in this bitter pill our only hope for salvation. For in the "ontological . . . order of the thing" the moral accusation that accompanies life in this vale of tears is elided. Nietzsche urged us to swallow the pill, to affirm the ontological order of the thing, to elide the human *qua* moral being, to effect the self-overcoming that empowers a post-moral *yes* to "becoming who you are" and to all that is.

At the turn of the twenty-first century, neo-Nietzschean Bernard Williams also confessed the truth entailed by modern scientific reasoning to be "bitter." It obliterates, he says, an ideal presented in "most moving" fashion by Kant: "the ideal that human existence can be ultimately just," for the truth (of physicalism) reveals there is no hope of "a voluntariness that will . . .

---

39. Taylor, *Sources of the Self*, 518–21.
40. Levinas, *The Levinas Reader*, 84.
41. Nietzsche, *Human All Too Human*, 74 (sections 106–7).

cut through determination, and allocate blame and responsibility on the ultimately fair basis of the agent's own contribution."[42] The truth, modern knowledge has discovered, is that morality in this sense is illusory.

Williams realizes the illusion is built into socially sustained frameworks of meaning. Individuals (e.g., Nietzsche) cannot singly escape. But from a physicalist perspective, frameworks, wholly socio-cultural products, are plastic. Over time, perhaps, the frameworks can be shifted. Accordingly, in his final work, *Truth and Truthfulness*, Williams embraces hope in a post-moral future in which salvation from the dilemma of mutilation, now dimly glimpsed, might be realized. Williams was unsure if society could ever transparently be aware of such bitter truth, but he hopes we can avoid ongoing mystification. Williams closes *Truth* urging us to develop the institutions and vocabularies necessary to effect the needed transvaluation of the foundations of our values (unlike Nietzsche, Williams prizes liberal democratic values) so that some future people might be enabled to live contentedly without belief in voluntariness and in accord with a post-moral ethic—as Williams says, might be enabled "to see the [physicalist] truth and not be broken by it."[43]

Since the vital challenge of affirmation of the world and our own selves is moral, it is illusory on Williams's account. Nonetheless, insofar as even for Williams the challenge currently does in fact arise as certainly as do equally mistaken beliefs about free will and morality, it is significant that Williams's summary of Kant subtly elides the challenge of affirmation in the face of Taylor's dilemma of mutilation. Williams's framing makes it seem as if Kant's ideal of just existence is devastated by loss of free will and moral responsibility in and of themselves. This elides moral realism and, here again, protects modern thinkers from the challenge of affirmation, which is axiological (i.e., he perpetuates physicalist ideology). It also profoundly misrepresents Kant.

First, free will and morality immediately deliver not fairness and justice, but the challenge of affirmation from within the abyss. Second, Kant realized this, which is why he postulated God, afterlife, and ultimate realization of perfect justice with precisely the same conviction with which he postulated free will. Of course, insofar as Williams successfully encourages readers to elide the challenge, he cultivates advance toward the post-moral society of which he and Nietzsche can—confined yet within inescapably moral frameworks of meaning and, if we are right, striving, *per impossibile*, to deny the essential, moral dimension of reality—can only dream.

42. Williams, *Ethics and the Limits of Philosophy*, 195.
43. Williams, *Truth and Truthfulness*, 268–69.

In stark contrast to Williams and Nietzsche, in the face of the dilemma Taylor gestures towards, "a hope that I see implicit in Judaeo-Christian theism . . . and in its central promise of a divine affirmation of the human, more total than humans can ever attain unaided."[44] Taylor does not develop this gesture, but correlations are easily sketched. In classic Christian theology, "God" names a finite but opening extant experience of "yes," the experience of being seized by a surpassing grace even as one lives in the abyss. The abyss is named "fallenness." Our complicity *ab initio* is one aspect of "original sin." Far from being threatened by Ivan's indictment, classic Christianity (if not modern theodicy) accentuates and embraces it, plumbing our cosmic embeddedness even more fully. Ivan's stance presumes the paradigmatically modern and deluded assertion of a primordial personal innocence (e.g., implicit in Descartes's *cogito* and Locke's *tabula rasa*). Pascal's "the 'I' is hateful," also critical for Levinas, plumbs the depths of our cosmic embeddedness more acutely because it rightly acknowledges that the self, wholly the child of this fallen world, first becomes conscious of itself already complicit and full of selfish, destructive desires.

Christianity (along with all theistic faiths) joins Levinas and Taylor in affirming our most profound ethical and spiritual intuitions as intimations of the Real (i.e., *not* plastic, *not* to be elided), rejects the belief that modern scientific metaphysics is exhaustive, and embraces the transcending, extant reality of a "yes" that seizes us within the abyss and frees us to live and work in assurance of the lived experience of divine grace.

For Christianity, unflinching confession of complicity and depravity only extends the reach and profundity of the enduring divine "yes," for the dynamic existential experience of the two moments of the experience of oneself as simultaneously justified and sinful (*simul iustus et peccator*) is directly proportional. Lighten one's hatred of the "I" apart from God, and one compromises the joyful release of 'yes' and affirmation of "I" in God. For classic Christianity, the mortal mistake is, *per impossibile*, denial of complicity, proclamation of innocence, any attempt at an autonomous "yes."

From a Christian perspective, then, Stout's pivotal mistake is signaled by his lack of despair. Stout is rightly offended when realists contest his ethical sensitivity. For Stout, like Ivan, Levinas, and Taylor, fully affirms the classic, essentially Jewish, Christian, and Platonic ethical intuitions of mainstream Western civilization. However, Stout, like Ivan, Nietzsche, and Williams, also rejects any hope in God. So, shy of some significant mitigating appeal, Stout should be asking "is it righteous to be?" and hearing only a devastating "No!" There is no significant mitigating appeal and no despair.

44. Taylor, *Sources of the Self*, 521.

Instead, Stout frames his argument within physicalist parameters and casts the ethical stakes in exclusively epistemological terms, thereby eliding the axiological challenge of affirmation, the dilemma of mutilation, conscious confrontation with the abyss—the entire context within which the question of God and theological talk of the fall, original sin, grace, and salvation are of signal moment apart from any metaphysics in the pejorative sense or belief in a literal heaven.

As Taylor discerned with his "dilemma of mutilation," apart from hope in God the predominant extant Western options are precisely the excruciating indictment of Ivan or annihilation of our deepest moral and spiritual aspirations (à la Nietzsche and Williams). So an evidently unconscious incoherence like Stout's—which simultaneously affirms classic moral intuitions, denies God, *and* remains blissfully oblivious to the abyss—arguably reflects the influence of a highly motivated, if unconscious, interest in eliding the axiological challenge of affirmation.

It is the eliding of the axiological challenge, not profound insight or argument, which protects Stout from wrenching, give-back-my-ticket cosmic and self-condemnation. Notably, Dostoyevsky makes clear the futility of denial and the reality of life lived on in honest but enduring self-enclosure from grace. At the close of *The Brothers Karamazov*, Ivan, having been confronted by circumstances that bring home his complicity, lives on in a coma. At this conceptual juncture, Stout's Emersonian perfectionism needs enriching. This correlates to a point where Stout offers a classic sign of unconscious denial: the bare assertion and uncharacteristic name-calling he offers as argument in defense of his Emersonian piety in chapter 1 of *Democracy and Tradition*.

Confession, Grace, and Affirmation: How Faith Matters

Stout begins chapter 1 of *Democracy* in a friendly tone. He notes that Emersonians and Augustinians, in contrast to mainstream twentieth-century political theorists, agree that piety, a spiritual virtue in the sense of "a morally excellent aspect of character," is critical to the health of a democracy.[45] But, he asks on behalf of Augustinian critics, do not Whitman and Emerson famously advocate a self-reliance that is incompatible with piety? No, responds Stout. To the contrary, they affirm profound "gratitude" as virtuous insofar as it is a "fitting or just response to the sources of our existence and progress through life."[46] But, Stout continues, was not just this form of piety

45. Stout, *Democracy and Tradition*, 20.
46. Stout, *Democracy and Tradition*, 37.

rejected by Nietzsche, since it imposed a crushing existential burden insofar as "we owe more to the sources of our existence . . . than we could ever repay"?[47] Yes. But Nietzsche was confused, for:

> No genuine virtue requires more of a human being than a human being could conceivably do. It is not an expression of justice but a mark of sadomasochistic pathology to demand perfect reciprocation where only imperfect reciprocation is possible.[48]

Sadomasochistic pathology is debilitating, which is why, "Above all . . . the idea of original sin is blight on the human spirit."[49] By contrast, Emerson's genius lies:

> in the grateful but life-affirming spirit in which he was able to receive—and acknowledge dependence upon—gifts that could not be fully reciprocated. He knows full well that he is indebted, beyond all capacity to repay, to the sources of his existence and progress through life, but his is a piety cleansed of sadomasochistic tendencies by democratic self-respect. . . . He is saying that what he really does deserve to be praised for, whether it be his genius or his character, is itself conditioned. His merit does not go all the way down. It is rather part of the receiving, part of the gift.[50]

Stout notes, quite rightly, that "it would be foolish to expect Augustinians to read such a remark in context and not detect in it a trace of pride," for Dewey's "self-respect" and Emerson's "self-reliance" are "the fruit of a perfectionist spiritual practice that self-consciously refuses to be disciplined by Augustinian warnings."[51]

It is hard to imagine a more profound rejection of Christianity. The correlate ideas of original sin and humanity's final dependence upon divine grace for salvation (i.e., for affirmation, for "yes"), which Stout bluntly declares a "sadomasochistic pathology," lie at the heart of Christian faith. Astoundingly, given the severity of the attack, Stout's argument turns upon sheer assertion: "No genuine virtue requires more of a human being than a human being could conceivably do." Not only is this not self-evident, but as Pascal, Dostoyevsky, Nietzsche, Levinas, Taylor, and

---

47. Stout, *Democracy and Tradition*, 38.
48. Stout, *Democracy and Tradition*, 39.
49. Stout, *Democracy and Tradition*, 20.
50. Stout, *Democracy and Tradition*, 39.
51. Stout, *Democracy and Tradition*, 39–40.

Williams all agree, our most profound moral intuitions strip us of any such pretension to innocence.[52]

Stout, however, needs to elide the question so that Emersonian "grace" might suffice. Note how Stout subtly neuters the axiological dimension of Nietzsche's struggle. Stout speaks of us "owing more than we can pay," but the nature or currency of this "indebtedness" is never delineated. As a result, talk of our "debt" to the "sources of our existence" quietly strips our reflection of the concrete Levinasian moral dimension that relates us to our neighbors. Having dimmed the crushing axiological dimension of the question, Stout offers Emersonian grace. Emerson achieves a "life-affirming spirit" despite his recognition of impossible indebtedness, Stout claims, because his piety has been "cleansed" by "democratic self-respect." Unfortunately, "democratic self-respect," which here emerges as the pivot of Stout's entire case for existential affirmation, is never further explained or even mentioned. It can appear to suffice not because of its profundity, but because the axiological challenge to self and world affirmation has been elided.

Meanwhile, the resonance of Stout's talk of Emerson being "grateful" for "the gift" is parasitic upon the theism he rejects. Gratitude is not something one extends to inanimate objects or evolutionary process. I may say I am "grateful" that it did not rain. But if you later discovered me outside sincerely thanking the clouds for not raining that afternoon, then you would most likely think that while I was right to be glad, I was confused in my gratitude. Far from attempting to articulate an alternative understanding of "gratitude" with adequate subtlety and power, Stout continues in the vein that aligns Christian gratitude with sadomasochistic pathology and so immediately qualifies "grateful" with "but life-affirming." For "grateful" alone suggests dependency, and above all Emersonian self-reliance requires rejection of any such dependence (e.g., upon divine grace).

Consider the paragraph with which Stout closes chapter 1:

> What is it about a human being that freedom of conscience honors? For that matter, what is it about a human being that the prohibition of murder honors, or the prohibition of cruel and unusual punishment? Christians answer these questions by telling a story about souls created in the image of God. Emerson and Whitman also often talk about souls and about something divine and wondrous that can be discerned in a human being. They are self-consciously waxing poetic at those moments. They think of the Christian story as ossified poetry, and are striving for fresh images of their own. Their intent is not to take dogma

52. My objection here also applies to the commonly asserted but equally indefensible "ought implies can."

and argue with it on its own terms. Their intent is simply to express faithfully something they have experienced and to enliven a similar capacity for awe and love in their readers.[53]

First one notes Stout's uncharacteristic lack of generosity. From the Psalmists to Augustine to Schleiermacher to Bonheoffer, the great theologians have been precisely about "striving for fresh images" so that they might "express faithfully something they have experienced" in the hope of opening their readers to like experiences of "awe and love."

Far more significant, Emerson and Whitman's experiences are such that they too talk of "souls" and "the divine." It is hard to see "self-consciously waxing poetic" as anything but a dampening of the clear intuitive power of their originating experiences in response to Stout's competing interest, namely, to his physicalist conviction that precludes affirmation of realities—for instance, souls (i.e., trans-empirical selves, what Levinas calls "faces"), transcending love, the divine—beyond the ontological boundaries of modern science (here again, one wonders what to make of Stout's appeals to "horrendous" violations of "the sacred"). Such denial of moral reality *may not* be unreasonable, but it is far from being obviously true. Neither, as Stout explicitly acknowledged, is it unreasonable to trust one's sense that the reality of animal being, let alone of the divine, is not confined within the bounds of the ontological order of the thing.

Christians believe that both their moral apprehensions and their experiences of transcending benevolence, of "yes" are real, if fleeting. They cannot reject the logical possibility they are misled, but they see no reason to conclude that they are waxing poetic. They quite reasonably embrace their hope, affirmation, confession of complicity, and sense of responsibility. Of course, even after the physicalist ontological exclusion is set aside there remains Stout's objection that Christian faith is hostile to life (i.e., because a core doctrine is blight on the human spirit). This objection turns, *contra* Levinas, upon preferring that which assures being over that which justifies it or, as is the case apart from grace, that which renders it unjustifiable.

Christians, in the spirit of the Talmudic scholar (i.e., Levinas), refuse to abandon their most profound moral convictions. Thus, they not only judge the world fallen but also confess original sin. From a Christian perspective, *contra* Nietzsche or Emerson, this cultivates and sustains not sickness, but moral honesty. The honesty is painful, for it immediately turns in our hands and condemns us. Is it righteous to be? No, for the world is fallen and as a result I appear from the first already complicit with all the suffering and evil (original sin). However, at the same time Christians proclaim *iustus*,

53. Stout, *Democracy and Tradition*, 41.

they testify to their experience of the ultimacy of a divine "yes," of having been seized by a benevolence that transcends every economy, that ever overcomes the enduring *peccator*.

It is the *iustus* side of Luther's *simul* that Emerson and Nietzsche, like Ivan, evidently did not or would not experience. As Ivan illustrates, the immediate yield of retaining only the *peccator* (i.e., no *iustus*) is world and self-condemnation. One might admire a love so offended by suffering that it cannot but become hostile to real life taken whole (mirroring what Nietzsche considered the pathological intolerance for suffering that distinguished the *evangel*).[54] Without mitigation, such love makes it impossible to embrace those portions of life, however slight and unjustly distributed, which are good and joyful. Taken on their own terms, closed off from grace, Nietzsche and Emerson were quite right to attack the *peccator*, to attack the Western mainstream's most profound moral intuitions, to attack *mauvaise conscience*. But it is not the case that, taken on Christian terms, such love entails Ivan's excruciating stance (as Nietzsche also noticed but failed to understand, the *evangel* wanted to share his extant experience of glad tidings, that is, his extant experience of a transcending "yes").

In sum, Christian faith in God, faith even that our most profound ethical convictions reflect God's own convictions, is not anything we can "use or apply" in order to resolve specific ethical quandaries. So, Stout rightly attacks metaphysics in the pejorative sense. Nor is faith in God affirmation of the proposition "God exists," let alone the product of some theistic proof. So, Stout also rightly attacks the God of analytic metaphysics. Faith in God is life lived in the light of Luther's *simul*, it is living the despair trumped by joy of *simul peccator et iustus*. It is the *mauvre conscience* that nonetheless experiences itself redeemed. Faith is utter surety that despite my sinfulness I am embraced by a transcending benevolence (Calvin).[55] Whatever else "God" may signify, then, it signifies the experienced reality of a redemptive "yes" that is enabled without denial of evil or Nietzschean transvaluation—and if this is the case then God is most reasonably understood to be something more than an "imaginary projection."

Contrary to a widespread supposition that Christianity quite automatically tends toward an escapism that directs attention away from evil (e.g., Marx's "opiate,"), the opposite is the case. The profundity of Christianity turns precisely upon unmitigated naming and confession of evil, including evils done "in the name of faith." On the other hand, for those striving for

---

54. Nietzsche, *The Anti-Christ*, remarks 29, 30, and 35–37; Nietzsche uses "*evangel*" to reference Jesus.

55. See Calvin, *Institutes*, III, ii, 7.

self-reliance, the need to escape Ivan's fate quite automatically tends toward a need to deny evil and complicity. At this juncture, then, a legitimate moral realist dimension of Christian faith, though nothing that grants epistemic privilege *vis-à-vis* one's position on ethical quandaries, comes into view.

Consider that insofar as Westerners are in fact existentially constituted by a classically Jewish and Christian moral orientation but now find themselves incredulous over classic theistic hope in divine grace that allowed affirmation in the face of the abyss . . . well, here is Stout's ample "focal point for widespread cultural angst." This angst is sustained by classic moral sympathies, so the angst would subside to the degree we achieved Nietzschean transvaluation and self-overcoming (i.e., eliminated all moral conviction).

However, and here the concrete consequences of the question over moral realism become evident, if moral reality is not wholly a function of socio-cultural conditioning, if reality itself has an ineradicable moral dimension, then successful self-overcoming of all moral sensitivities would amount to self-mutilation of our inherently moral being. It would require continual denial of reality. It would require firm reinforcement of the fantasy that one is not guilty of original sin, not part and parcel of this fallen world, that one somehow stands alone and innocent. Relative success in eliminating all of one's moral compunction would mark massive, immoral denial of the fundamentally moral character of reality.

Notably and to the contrary, Stout's moral sympathies throughout *Democracy* and *Blessed* are far more redolent of the prophets and Jesus than of the spiritual isolation he reads and recommends in Emerson.[56] It is hard to see how lessening or eliminating classic moral sympathies cannot but make realization of Stout's ethical ideals more difficult. For if all sense for profound responsibility to and love for neighbor is overcome, from whence motivation for preferring that which justifies life to that which assures it, for preferring not only justice but grace and kindness, for a desire to work and even to sacrifice for the good of others?

To the contrary, does not secular rationality run the risk of being not merely amoral but immoral insofar as it equates rational action with self-interested action? Is not the idea that everyone's self-interests, sufficiently enlightened, will urge us to an adequate vision of moral reality and the common good: is that not utter fantasy? Do not a multitude of justifications for illicit actions of nations or multinational corporations end with appeal to survival or profit (self-interest), period? Do not all the complaints about religion as the root cause of all wars (which wars, precisely?) distract us from the political and economic oppression and/or greed and drive for

56. Emerson, "Self-Reliance," 144–45.

power that actually foments most wars and terror attacks? Are not attacks upon religion (upon "sermonizing" or "moralizing") actually attacks upon the idea that we may be called by and be subservient to moral reality? Does Stout really want to follow Alinsky and place "self-interest" and "anger" at the motivational heart of the struggle for justice, when the overwhelming majority of activists we meet in *Blessed* explain themselves in terms of faith, heed Augustinian warnings, and center themselves upon love of God and neighbor?

Does Stout not, despite his prophetic impulses, remain caught within the grasp of a metaphysic that reinforces a greedy, immoral worldview that runs exactly contrary to his passions and concerns? Does not denial of original sin actually amount to assertion of Pascal's "my place in the sun"? Have not many transnational elites, in the devastating, socio-economic sense of the Deuteronomist and the prophets, forgotten God? Is it surprising that elites with no sense for grace readily express disdain for all faiths and moral realism? Does not Taylor's dilemma of mutilation explain why, once grace is discounted, the denial of moral realism is attractive to those who want to shield themselves from an ontological reality that brings condemnation?

Stout realizes (in theory, at any rate) that physicalism remains provisional. He is inarticulate regarding moral sources and reality. His blending of morally realist *mauvre conscience* (with its need for grace) and Emersonian self-reliance (which has no room for grace) is unstable. But he is nonetheless seized by the moral convictions of Jesus and the prophets. In *Blessed*, Stout literally walks with the oppressed and writes on behalf of their struggle. But physicalism blinkers his understanding. So I close with a call to overt awakening.

When Stout sees the oppressed and exploited, he has no real doubt that moral reality has been violated. He is also fully aware that biology and history tell overwhelming tales of suffering and exploitation, that we all find ourselves thrown into being already complicit. In other words, Stout realizes the essential truth of the Christian doctrines of fall and original sin. A critical question: when Stout considers those who do evil, is he overcome with love for them? Would he (and would we) love to see them freed from their bondage to oppressing?

If so, then we know the reality of a transcending love that is alpha and omega, we know the reality of a love that condemns evil but still loves the enemy, the enemy we struggle against as enemy, the enemy that we too are. If so, then we abide in love, in a gracious, transcending love that both provokes and transcends awareness of fallenness and sinfulness. Insofar as to live by faith is to live in the light of this love divine, sure of divine benevolence towards myself and all, then I can quite reasonably and without any real doubt confess that we live by faith in God. In sum—and analogous faith may be found in other faith traditions—given Stout's professed ontological openness, it would be most consistent and reasonable for Stout to affirm that the central Christian confessions I have discussed are *reasonable* (violate no established metaphysical boundaries and are in accord with personally passionate, historically deep, and cross-culturally wide moral affirmations), and *prophetic* (provoke struggle against oppression), and *saving* (alleviate despair by allowing for affirmation).

Chapter 10

On Paul's Philosophical Spirituality

*Is it true that "what can be known
of God is plain"? Yes.*

> For I am not ashamed of the gospel; it is the power of God for
> salvation to everyone who has faith, to the Jew first and also
> to the Greek. For in it the righteousness of God is revealed
> through faith to faith; as it is written, "The one who is righteous
> will live by faith." For the wrath of God is revealed from heaven
> against all ungodliness and wickedness of those who by their
> wickedness suppress the truth. For what can be known of God
> is plain to them, because God has shown it to them. Ever since
> the creation of the world [God's] eternal power and divine na-
> ture, invisible though they are, have been understood and seen
> through the things [God] has made. So they are without excuse;
> for though they knew God, they did not honor God or give God
> thanks, but they became futile in their thinking, and their sense-
> less minds were [clouded]. Claiming to be wise, they became
> fools. (Rom 1:16–22)

What is wisdom? Love of wisdom is, of course, what philosophy *should* be—
if it is to be true to its name (*philo/sophia*, "love of wisdom"). But what is
wisdom? One classic answer about the beginning of wisdom is: "fear of the
Lord." But what is "fear of the Lord"? If the essence of the Law is summarized

in two commands, the first of which is to love the Lord your God with all your heart, soul, strength, and mind, would not "fear of the Lord" somehow be to love God with all your heart, soul, strength, and mind?

But, how does one love God with all one's heart, soul, strength, and mind? And, *why* fear the Lord? *Why* love God? Because the Bible says so? But why should we believe the Bible? Because it's a smart wager with a potentially massive payoff? Because that is what we and ours have always said we should do and believe, thank you very much? Those are poor reasons. Why should we believe the Bible? Why love God? For that matter, what precisely does the word *God* signify in these sentences? What do we name when we say "God"? Why even believe "God" signifies anything real? Do we have some argument for God that is itself wise, smart, reasonable, compelling? Indeed, considering all the pain, random suffering, violence, and injustice that fill the world, would we not have to be naïve or perhaps willfully ignorant to say it is wise to fear and love anything that remotely deserves the honorific title "God"?

These are philosophical questions. Reasonable questions. If there is wisdom in faith then philosophy, that is, the love of wisdom, must respond to these questions. What does wisdom have to say? Well, today the general conclusion, even among people of faith, about what wisdom has to say in answer to all of these questions is this: *nothing convincing.* As a result, even among people of faith, wisdom is considered incapable of grounding, founding, establishing, or awakening wholly reasonable faith. Indeed, for many "faith" means by definition a leap beyond the evidence, beyond what is warranted, beyond what is generally considered to be reasonable and good. Pretty much no one thinks a path to faith that modern reason would consider wholly good and reasonable can be found in wisdom (or any other) texts, and few people think of Paul's letters as wisdom literature.

Paul, however, is all about wisdom. Remember that Paul is a near contemporary of Jesus, and that his letters are the earliest of all the writings that will eventually (centuries after Paul) be canonized as the "New Testament." Paul has no New Testament to appeal to, and his central appeal from the only Scriptures he knows is to Abraham, his exemplar of faith, who himself had no Law or Scriptures to turn to, but who responded directly to God—that is, Abraham, like Paul, is reliant upon general revelation, wisdom. Or, perhaps, if I can say this with a smile, Paul, like Abraham, engages in philosophical spirituality, engages in theology that remains wholly within the bounds of reason, wholly within the bounds of what is by overwhelming consensus regarded as reasonable and good.

Paul claims that "what can be known about God is plain . . . because God has shown it," that, "Ever since the creation of the world [God's] eternal power and divine nature, invisible though they are, have been understood and seen through the things God has made" (Rom 1:19–20). Paul places this claim right at the front of his letter. This claim about the knowledge of the nature of God pertains to those who have hardened their hearts and made themselves fools, so how much more clear and plain must Paul think the nature of God is to people of faith? These verses are not an unfortunate digression. And this is not a claim that can be bypassed in Romans, for this knowledge of God, which Paul takes to be *obvious*, which Paul presumes God-fearing readers will agree is *obvious*, is the ground and foundation of every claim he makes in the balance of the letter.

In Romans, Paul asserts his apostleship, but he does not appeal to his apostolic status in order to ground his argument. Paul does not engage in appeals to authority or in special pleading. Paul grounds his argument in general revelation, love of wisdom, in what can obviously be known of God.

Insofar as we do not realize how this knowledge of God is obvious to us—and let me be clear that I think this knowledge actually is obvious to our hearts, but at the moment, due to the influence of modern Western rationality, we do not enjoy the comfort of knowing it with our minds—insofar as we do not realize how this knowledge of God is obvious to us, we have been swept away by the wisdom of our age, by the rationality of those who, claiming to be wise, become foolish, tragically futile in their thinking, their purportedly enlightened minds clouded.

But here we are. What "can be known about God" and God's "divine nature and power" most certainly does not seem obvious to us. Where can we turn? Clearly, whatever Paul is thinking is related to the Law in some positive sense, and related to Jesus in some positive sense, and near the end of Romans, Paul, in one of his only references to a saying of Jesus, says that all commandments, all the Law, can be "summed up in this word: 'Love your neighbor as yourself'" (Rom 13:9).

Now, believe it or not, over the last couple of decades a host of the most avant-garde philosophers in Europe and the States, most all of them atheists, Enlightenment thinkers to the core, have been writing commentaries on Paul.[1] And they seize upon this saying, "love your neighbor as yourself," as a sign of Paul's *radical break from Jesus*, as a sign Paul is deliberately starting a faith different from Jesus's faith, for, according to them, Paul has deliberately, tellingly, dropped Jesus's famous first summary statement of the Law: "love your God with all your heart, soul, strength and mind" (Matt 22:37–40; Luke 10:25–28). They contend that Paul quite deliberately

---

1. See, for instance, Agamben, *The Time That Remains*; Badiou, *Saint Paul*; Taubes, *The Political Theology of Paul*; and Žižek , *The Puppet and the Dwarf.*

is breaking decisively from Jesus when he says *only* "love your neighbor as yourself." In other contexts, one imagines these same philosophers would balk at drawing so massively significant a conclusion from silence. But they like this conclusion, for then they can argue that, *essentially*, Paul, like them, has no need to posit God in any sense—and they *know* (the secular "wisdom" of the modern age) actually positing God would be senseless.

It gets worse. For, without God, these "enlightened" philosophers proceed to read "love your neighbor as yourself" backwards and upside down. Since the only love modern Western thought knows is *eros*, desire, perhaps good I desire for others, but nonetheless at root my desire to desire something for others, since desire as *eros*, desire for self, is the only sort of love they can make sense of, they have to read "love your neighbor as yourself" backwards. That is, they have to begin with the ending, "as yourself." They think it is simply obvious that one has to begin with love for self, for there is no more basic and powerful love than this. Then, they contend, and this is the move they love in Paul, you need to universalize this love, you have to love everyone else as much as you love yourself, and the conviction that you must do this, the "militant" demand that everyone must do this, is faith, which is now rooted in you, in your decision, in your conviction over the necessity of universalizing love of self to love for every neighbor.

So, backwards, because it starts with love of self, and upside down, because faith, the decision/conviction we should love everyone as much as we love ourselves, is now rooted in us, not in God.

At this point, their understanding becomes inane. For, given the absolute priority of my love for myself, they cannot begin to explain *why* I would decide to love everyone as much as I love myself. Even if you can provide a personal reason for why you would prefer such a thing, on what basis would you impose this universal demand upon anyone else? No answers to these questions are forthcoming—notably, this is essentially a return to nineteenth-century utilitarian theory, and to Henry Sidgwick's 1906, still unresolved, dualism of practical reason.

Not only is their position inane, it is patently absurd in the light of our daily experiences.

It is significant that when Jesus unfolds the meaning of "love your neighbor as yourself," he tells a story, the story of the Good Samaritan. Notably, insofar as that story depends upon listeners discerning the general revelation of an obvious truth, Jesus too is depending upon a philosophical appeal, an appeal to what is generally considered reasonable and good. So, the parable of the Good Samaritan is another piece of (love of) wisdom literature (i.e., philosophy), and the plain truth unveiled by the parable of the Good Samaritan is utterly contrary to the backwards, upside down, confused "wisdom" of mainstream modern Western rationality, for the answer to the question "who proved neighbor" absolutely does not begin with love of self.

There is nothing about anything the Samaritan does that is self-interested, and no part of what inspires us about the Samaritan involves us thinking of how he acted in self-interest. To the contrary, the story portrays the Good Samaritan taking considerable risk and time as he cares for the wounded man. The essential dynamics of the parable are unfolded with extraordinary precision by an iconoclastic twentieth-century Western philosopher, another Jew (like Jesus, like Paul) who thinks the law can be summed up in "love your neighbor as yourself," namely, Emmanuel Levinas, who unfolds the dynamic of love of neighbor in terms of our being taken hostage to care and concern for the Faces of others. What we recognize in the Samaritan is someone who has been seized by love for the Face of another. Insofar as we do not harden our hearts, this is the love by which we too are seized in both wondrous and horrific circumstances. We see the survivors of the shooting, or the tsunami, or the floods, fearful, silenced immigrants laboring at dangerous jobs, we see desperate families crowding boats to cross the Mediterranean, elderly Greeks lined up in front of bank machines, and we are seized by care and concern, by love for those Faces. In such awful circumstances our having been seized by love is immediately manifest in our grief and protest.

Or perhaps the circumstances are joyous. We see a little girl laughing joyfully at her birthday party, or the smiling newlyweds descending the church steps hand in hand, and we are likewise seized by love for those Faces, now manifest in our joy for them.

Whether we are seized by love for Faces in contexts of horror or of joy, our response, insofar as we do not harden our hearts, is not a product of our decision, our reason, our initiative, or our obedience to some biblical passage, to the Law, or to some philosophical ideal. No, it is not a product of any of these. For insofar as we do not harden our hearts we are directly seized by love for the Faces of others. Let me be very clear, for there is a widespread tendency to confuse others with the Other: we are not seized directly by the Faces of others, we are seized directly *by love for* the Faces of others, we are seized by love, which is to say, insofar as God *is* love, *we are seized by God (the Other) for others.*

This is why Jesus says that when I have not hardened my heart, when I have surrendered to having been seized by the Faces of others and I've comforted them, or clothed them, or visited them in prison, or fed them, I have comforted, clothed, visited and fed God (Matt 25:31–45). It is not because I have done these things for God, or in obedience to some idea of God or to some sacred text, but because I have surrendered in obedience to the direct manifestation of God, of agape. This, says Levinas, is how God comes to the human mind, invisible yet eternally powerful: as love for the Faces of all others. This is how you love God with all your heart, soul, strength, and mind: by surrendering to God, who *is* love/agape. You surrender to God with all your heart, soul, strength, and mind by surrendering to love for every concrete Face with all your heart, soul, strength, and mind—and acting in your particular context as passionately, decisively, powerfully, and intelligently as possible.

This is why Paul cites only "love your neighbor as yourself." Not because he is rejecting Jesus', "love your God with all your heart, soul, strength, and mind," but because, following Jesus, consistent not only with Jesus's teachings but with the faith of Jesus, Paul recognizes the spiritual unity of the two commands: the concrete way one loves God in this world is precisely by surrendering directly to God, surrendering to love, for neighbor.

This is the faith of Jesus, the faith visible and proven to the nth degree when Jesus arrives at the proverbial "moment of truth," death, even death on a cross. The cross, the symbol of Roman imperial terror. A form of execution designed to terrify subjugated, colonized people into hardening their hearts, to terrify people into valuing nothing more than their personal survival—keep quiet, keep your heads down! Through the faith of Jesus, that is, through Jesus's unwavering surrender to agape for every other even unto death on a cross, through the faith of Jesus the symbol of imperial terror becomes the symbol of new life, of the life of those who have died with Jesus and who are already raised to new life in this world, to life beyond the terror of the cross, to life lived in surrender to having been seized in and by love, to life lived in surrender to having been seized in and by God, already raised up to life that in fidelity to love for all speaks and acts against exploitation and oppression.

Insofar as people—not all, for some harden their hearts, but multitudes of people, including all of every faith who are celebrated as saints—insofar as people since the creation of the world have not hardened their hearts and have been seized by love, seized by agape, seized by God for the Faces of every creature of every kind, insofar as they have lived faith, lived surrender to love for every other, lived surrender to God for every other, lived having been seized in and by love for every other—in times of wonder and times of horror—insofar as people since the creation of the world have not hardened their hearts but have lived surrender to having been seized in and by love for every creature of every kind, God's eternal power and divine nature, invisible though they are, have indeed been understood and seen through all God has made.

This is all perfectly reasonable, even obvious.

There is more. In the moment when we are seized wholly in and by love for the Faces of others, *we* are seized by love, we ourselves, *we too* are seized by love, by God, by the God who is love, we *receive* the love of the "as yourself," that transcending love for self that is in no way a selfish love, in no way our own love for ourselves, but love for ourselves to which we surrender, love for ourselves which we receive as a gift, the very same love to which we surrender for others.

Consider that even in popular conversation, when people recite the most meaningful, treasured, and profound moments of their lives, they typically do not recite occasions of momentous selfish success, they name times when they have been wholly seized in and by love for others.

There is more. Remember that on that Damascus road we are talking not about Paul, we are talking about Saul. In other words, we are not talking about Levinas the innocent Jewish victim. When we speak of Saul we are talking about Heidegger, the Nazi, the one who remembers holding the cloaks while Stephen is stoned to death, Saul the militant, the killer (Acts 7:1–53; 22:1–29).

Most of us can think of ourselves as pretty good. Saul had no such illusion. So, in the moment when Saul surrendered to having been seized by love for every Face he recognized two asymmetrical realities simultaneously. In that moment when he surrendered wholly to having been seized in and by love for the Faces of others he realized the essential, horrible, awesome reality of his violation of the Face of Stephen and so many others, so in the utterly clear light of surrender to love he experienced "fear of the Lord," full awareness of his awful violation. Simultaneously, in that self-forgetful moment of wholesale surrender to love for others, surrender to God for others, in that moment of faith he experienced no condemnation—indeed, he received the "as thyself," the surrender to having been seized in and by love for neighbor wherein one is oneself simultaneously seized by that very same love. On that Damascus road Paul found himself seized by love, knew himself to be beloved.

I think this is why Paul talks neither about the justice of God (which would suggest that justice is the final word), nor about the grace of God (which may suggest that justice is wholly lost), but about the *righteousness* of God, wherein one surrenders to the awesome fullness of having been seized by infinite love for each and every Face, wherein the awfulness of one's violation of Faces resounds ("fear of the Lord," *peccator*), while simultaneously (*simul*), the final word is not judgment but transcending love (*iustis*), the love which both brings the basis for judgment but simultaneously instills conviction over God's transcending benevolence, alpha and omega, toward us.

In other words, surrender to having been seized in and by love brings the free gift of "yes," of life wherein we are reckoned righteous. This is not essentially a matter of biological life and death, but of spiritual life and death, the ability to live with joy, to glory in new lives in the spirit, in surrender to having been seized in and by love, recipients of love for others and for ourselves, to glory in this love for others and ourselves *after helping to stone Stephen, after leaving our neighbors hungry, lonely, oppressed.* The righteousness of God names transcending love that convicts us about evil even as, alpha and omega, it allows us to affirm ourselves as reckoned righteous (forgiven) in the free gift of that same transcending love, *simul iustus et peccator.*

Is not all of this wholly reasonable and good? Are we not speaking of what after all can be known of God? Should we not rejoice over a faith that puts the radically transposed symbol of the cross at its center and baptizes its members to new life in the spirit through participation in the death of Jesus Christ? Should we not conclude this faith is wise about the realities of this world and about the eternal power and divine nature of God? Is this not a wisdom we see in the saints and at the heart of all the world's great faith traditions?

Is this not a wisdom that even the self-proclaimed atheist philosophers who are confusedly trying to appropriate Paul, and who are doing so in large part out of a concern for the widow, the poor, and the oppressed—for reasons they cannot make any sense of—is this not a wisdom they could recognize? Are they not unwitting sheep, have they not surrendered to having been seized in and by love for the Faces even as, their minds clouded by worldly wisdom, they are cut off from true understanding and an untrammeled ability to glory in the joy of the Lord?

Paul is right. We have no need to be ashamed of the gospel. It is the power of God for salvation for all who have faith, that is, for all who surrender to having been seized in and by God, by agape, by love for every other and for ourselves, for all thereby and therein receive the free gift of grace.

A caution before I close. Obvious, but worth saying. It is not wise to celebrate or focus upon wisdom. The sooner these sorts of arguments are unnecessary and can be left behind the better. What is really wise is to seek ever more fully to live surrender to God, that is, to strive ever more fully to live fidelity to having been seized in and by love for every concrete Face before us, to imitate with all of our heart, soul, strength, and mind the faith of Jesus Christ. This is how we love God with all our heart, soul, strength, and mind. This love is not from us but to us from God. It is the gift of God, the power of God for salvation for everyone who surrenders to having been seized in and by love.

So, remaining wholly within the limits of reason, this is a lesson of real wisdom, of true philosophy: clothe yourselves with the saving faith of Jesus Christ, that is, live surrender to having been seized in and by love for all the Faces that surround you, surrender to love for every flower of the field, every sparrow, for everyone glorying in a new day, surrender too to love for you yourself, and surrender to love for all who are hungry, naked, scared, exploited, forgotten. Thank God and glory in this faith. Glory in the wholly reasonable, plain, firm, and certain knowledge—knowledge as plain, reasonable, and certain as any knowledge we have—that neither death, nor life, nor angels, rulers, things present, things to come, nor powers, height, depth, nor anything else in all creation can separate us from the love of God (Rom 8:38–39).

Chapter 11

A Time for Prophets?

Non-Sectarian Affirmation of Particularities and Universal Morality

Epipens are life-saving devices that allow anyone to give a shot and save themselves or someone else from an allergic reaction to something like a bee sting. I carried "epis" on the Outward Bound-styled "Adventure in Wilderness and Spirituality" trips I led into the Colorado Rockies for thirteen years. The medicine expires after a year, so every year I paid around $10 to $12 for a new epi. Of course, parents of kids with allergies buy them annually, and now schools are legally required to have them. Recently the cost of epipens has risen dramatically. The cost increase is due *only* to desire for more profit. Epis are now sold in two-packs, and while the active ingredient costs less than one dollar per dose, this year the cost for a two-pack was $600. The pharmaceutical company's CEO, Heather Bresch, received around $18 million dollars in compensation this past year. Testifying before Congress, she defended herself by pointing out that our economic system incentivized precisely the moves she made. However, unless she has spent her personal resources fighting this incentivizing (a legitimate if rarely exercised option for people in her position), she still bears significant personal responsibility.[1]

---

1. Popken, "Mylan CEO's Pay Rose Over 600 Percent as EpiPen Price Rose 400 Percent."

Whatever Bresch's personal character and culpability, she is right that the real story is a system that incentivizes profit above all else, a system that holds captive, tempts, and bullies not only executives, lawyers, and doctors, but people from all walks of life, coercing them to adopt its sacrifice of basic moral values or to suffer the consequences. It is a system within which those with the least scruples are best adapted to flourish, and it is a completely legal and increasingly state-transcending, globalized system.

Lamenting the legalization of morally indefensible global profiteering, a host of secular scholars have been attacking the spiritual poverty of modern Western rationality. This began in the 1990s, in the wake of the so-called "postmodern turn" in mainstream Western philosophy, a turn of the '60s and '70s that undercut the modern West's own signature appeal to objective, universal reason, modernity's signature appeal to a purportedly objective rationality that, in fact, largely reflected the perspectives and opinions of dominant peoples. The postmodern chastening of reason opened intellectual/cultural space for long-marginalized populations like the poor, women, African-Americans, and indigenous peoples, and facilitated the emergence of liberation, Black, feminist, womanist, mujerista, queer, and a host of other theologies since the 1970s.

As scholars like David Harvey warned in the 1980s, however, wholesale rejection of all meta-narratives and unqualified stress on particularities and the diversity of discrete communities cuts us off from access to the, "kind of meta-theory which can grasp the political-economic processes (money flows, international divisions of labour, financial markets, and the like) that are becoming ever more universalizing in their depth, intensity, reach and power over daily life."[2]

In other words, as all theory becomes local, all ethics becomes local, so ethical claims have come to be widely understood to be relative to their respective communities, relativizing the power of all ethical claims. So, the postmodern stress on the discrete identities of diverse communities has been resulting in a sectarian fragmentation that leaves all these discrete communities enfeebled in the face of global economic forces. From this ethically relativist perspective, Western postmodernity's wholesale celebration of diversity is a real-world ethical disaster, because all the truly wonderful diversity—and it is truly wonderful, we do not want to forget that—is a real-world ethical disaster, because it surreptitiously masks and thereby protects actual global systems of power (not diversified, not fragmented) and simultaneously undercuts global ethical appeals by rendering ethics relative to culture.

2. Harvey, *The Condition of Postmodernity*, 117.

Widespread recognition of an urgent need for universal, ethical appeals spurred Western secular philosophy's surprising, post-postmodern turn to religion in the 1990s, and motivated a bevy of writings by secular philosophers on Saint Paul. For instance, in the late '90s a leading French philosopher, Alain Badiou, published a post-postmodern book, *Saint Paul: The Foundation of Universalism*. Badiou appeals to Paul for the foundations of a post-postmodern universalism in response to two predominant global developments.

First, he says, there is an "extension of the automisms of capitalism" wherein the world is being "*configured* as a market," thereby rendering all communities subject to the global "rule of an abstract homogenization."[3] The problem is that the god of capital markets is growth/productivity for the sake of profit measured in monetary terms, and so all resources, including human resources, are ultimately valued solely insofar as they maximize profit. Let me stress that this is not a matter of being for or against capitalism: it is a matter of recognizing the conceptual limits of capitalism, recognizing its inability to discern and give substantive, political/legal weight to ethical ideals. One can affirm capitalism and still recognize how naïve it is to imagine that unfettered transnational market regimes will somehow create better societies unless the god of growth/productivity/profit is substantively/legally subservient to basic ethical ideals.

Second, Badiou says, there is the problem of the very diversity of human communities, the postmodern "process of fragmentation into closed identities, and the culturalist and relativist ideology that accompanies this fragmentation."[4]

These two developments mutually reinforce one another, for under the stress of homogenization and economic need people turn for protection and power to narrowly defined, people-like-me identity groups, and the sectarian, more or less militant, closed dynamics of identity groups and their "identitarian protests" aid and abet the "abstract homogenization of capital" because they leave abstract, homogenizing market forces as the only truly transcending political forces mediating relations among diverse groups.

Confronted with an either/or between the automisms of capital and a balkanized world fragmented into a multitude of cultural identities, Badiou calls for the post-postmodern universal foundationalism I mentioned a moment ago. He calls for a return to what he sees as Paul's God, the "universal singularity" before whom there is "neither Jew nor Gentile, neither slave

3. Badiou, *Saint Paul*, 9–10.
4. Badiou, *Saint Paul*, 10.

nor free . . . male nor female" (Gal 3:28), to a God that is not the product or preserve of market dynamics nor any particular identity group.[5]

Typical of post-postmodern Western philosophy's turn to religion, however, Badiou wants Paul's God only as an abstract principle, and he wants nothing to do with any of the world's historic faith communities. More troubling with regard to Badiou, and hopes for a peaceable world, he draws and idealizes Paul as the figure of the *militant* subject—which may explain why in Badiou Paul wholly displaces Jesus.

I can now state the real question of this essay, not the obvious question of whether or not this is an age for prophets—*it is an age for prophets*—but the question of whether or not prophetic calls to societal justice can succeed without God, not just the idea of God of philosophers who want nothing to do with religion, but whether or not prophetic calls can succeed apart from the reality of the living God and vital communities of faith.

Jeffrey Stout, a Professor of Religion at Princeton University, is an American atheist philosopher profoundly concerned about creating a just and good world. Stout argues that in fact the disdain of mainstream cultural elites for faith in God and for faith communities—Christian, Jewish, Islamic—is disastrous for social justice. Speaking within a US context, Stout observes that faith communities played essential roles in the three most significant prophetic movements in US history—the nineteenth-century abolitionist movement, the early twentieth-century suffrage movement, and the 1960s civil rights movement. Moreover, after extensive research at the beginning of the twenty-first century into grassroots movements actually making a difference in public policy, Stout, an atheist, concludes much to his surprise that in fact *without faith communities—churches, temples, mosques—there would be no grassroots social justice movements in the US.*[6]

Stout's concern, however, is wholly practical, and in recent decades, numerous predominantly secular social justice movements have emerged. Among many others, there are the most visible streams of the environmental, animal rights, and LGBTQ movements, and most recently the Occupy Wall Street and Black Lives Matter movements. Is Stout right to doubt these movements can finally make progress without fully incorporating faith communities? I suspect so, and moving beyond Stout, I want to begin to pursue the far more radical conclusion that such movements, and for that matter communities of any sort, from local interest groups to international communities of communities, cannot succeed in being good and just without out faith in the living God.

---

5. Badiou, *Saint Paul*, 13–15.

6. Stout, *Blessed Are the Organized*, 4–5.

Obviously, this is just a gesture, but let me make a start in conversation with the wisdom of the ancient Israelites, in particular the call of Abram, the Deuteronomic history, the prophets' calls to remember God, and the eschatological vision of a new heavens and a new earth. I interpret these texts as a philosophical theologian greatly dependent upon modern biblical studies, which means I read these Scriptures as the conglomerated, highly redacted product of contending parties' *ex post facto* attempts to narrate the identity of Israel.

The call of Abram is placed in the immediate wake of the Tower of Babel narrative (Gen 11:1–12:3). The Tower narrative describes a people who have forgotten God and who are trying to secure themselves through material might. In stark contrast to the tower builders, who along this narrative trajectory were scattered into all the discrete peoples of the world—including, among many others, the Caananites, and also Abraham's native people, the Chaldeans in Ur—in stark contrast to the Tower builders with their dreams of establishing themselves with a mighty city, in the call of Abram we hear this:

> Now the LORD said to Abram, "Go from your country and
> your kindred and your father's house and to the land that I will
> show you. I will make of you a great nation, and I will bless
> you, and make your name great, so that you will be a blessing.
> I will bless those who bless you, and the one who curses you,
> I will curse; and in you all the families of the earth shall be
> blessed." (Gen 12:1–3)

If we read the tower of Babel builders' quest for security through material power as the figure of a homogenized global market wherein the motivating dynamics are material power and security, and if we read the diversity of the scattered city builders into diverse peoples who do not understand one another's language as the figure of postmodernity's relativistic, discrete cultural identity groups, we can read the call of Abram as a biblical answer to the question of how to move beyond both the universal homogenizing of economic forces and cultural relativism.

First, even as the call narrates the creation of a discrete people, namely, the Israelites, note how Abram is called to settle among foreign people in a distant land. This reinforces the Tower narrative's image of all peoples as migrants. Today we know we live upon a biological and social history of strife, blood, and migration stretching back far behind even Homo sapiens' triumph over the Neanderthals. *By portraying everyone as migrants, the Hebrew Scriptures mitigate against sectarian origin stories.* Father Abraham of Israel is an immigrant from Haran and Ur of the Chaldeans, an immigrant in Canaan. Other Scriptures build upon this motif, appealing to the memory of Abraham as they celebrate the ideal of hospitality towards strangers.

Obviously, there is an affirmation of discrete peoples: the peoples of Haran, the Chaldeans of Ur, the Canaanites, and the children of Israel. At the same time, not only is the hospitality of all these peoples implicitly celebrated, but there is no conquest motif in the call of Abraham, no indication that Abraham's relation to the Canaanites will be hostile. Of course, we know this call story develops into the promised land motif, and the promised land motif is frequently used to justify precisely the sort of violent, sectarian ends that sectarian origin stories are all too often used to justify. At its worst, this motif can be used to propagate manic intolerance of difference and insistence upon purity, and this is just what happens in the portrayal of the conquest of Canaan, above all in the awful destruction of Jericho, where Joshua—exceeding (note well) what the narrative itself says God commanded (Josh 6:2–5)—instructs the people to retrieve all the silver, gold, bronze, and iron, but to destroy every living creature in the city:

> so the people charged straight into [Jericho] and captured it.
> Then they devoted to destruction by the edge of the sword all
> in [Jericho], both men and women, young and old, oxen, sheep,
> and donkeys. (Josh 6:20–21)

The call of Abram opposes such awful appropriation of the promised land motif, for it says God will bless Abram so he can be a blessing, so that through Abram all families on earth will be blessed. The call of Abram distinguishes the Israelites as a distinct people, but this is not sectarian particularity because God does not set the Israelites apart only for the sake of the Israelites, but also for the sake of "all families on earth."

At the heart of the origin story of Israel, then, one finds a *non-sectarian affirmation of particularity*. One can be pro-Israelite, fully affirm and celebrate the distinctive traditions, language, religion, and culture of Israel, but only insofar as this affirmation and celebration is ultimately consistent with Israel being a nation through which God's blessings are extended to all other peoples. When the promised land motif is affirmed while the framing of the call narrative is forgotten, the Israelites cease to be a blessing, they forget the God who called Abram, the migrant from Ur of the Chaldeans, they forget hospitality, perpetuate horror.

In addition to the call of Abram framing Israel as a distinct people even as it inscribes ideals of universal hospitality and blessing, the Deuteronomist relates the fortunes of the nation to the Israelites remembering or forgetting God. It is too easy and too common to dismiss the Deuteronomist's account as magical thinking, too easy to think the Deuteronomist is saying that God magically acts to make just societies flourish and oppressive and exploitative societies fail. Once one understands "remember God" concretely in prophetic terms, that is, in terms of doing justice and loving kindness, one can understand the Deuteronomist to be drawing conclusions from long-term empirical observations, identifying inexorable socio-cultural dynamics that flow through wealthy, powerful, and seemingly robust societies, and discerning the complex ways those dynamics hollow those societies out from within, right beneath the noses of uncomprehending elites, leaving those societies and those elites vulnerable to external attacks and internal collapse.

If the Deuteronomist accurately describes a socio-cultural logic true for all societies, then it is more critical than ever for us to heed the prophets, for it is not clear how well our nuclear, globalized civilization can survive widespread political collapse—to cite just one example of our heightened vulnerability, consider Japan's Fukushima nuclear reactor disaster, a near global catastrophe that unfolded as a result of only a few days of lost power in one of the most advanced societies on earth, and consider that there are 444 nuclear power plants in operation around the world.[7]

It is vital to be precise about what it means to "remember God." For one thing, remembering God is not the same as affirming orthodox beliefs or observing religious rituals. Micah is typical when he proclaims that God has had enough of empty ceremonies and burnt offerings; this, proclaims Micah, is what the Lord wants:

> O mortal, what is good? And what does the Lord require of you?
> But to do justice, and to love kindness, and walk humbly with
> your God? (Mic 6:8)

To remember God is precisely to feed the hungry, comfort the mourning, clothe the naked, free the oppressed. To remember God is to risk getting off your ride and helping a wounded stranger in the ditch.

Affirmation of this basic reality—love for every creature of every kind, of a fidelity to God or what is righteous in terms of basic care for the needy, opposition to exploitation, desire to see all flourish as fully as possible—is found in every major religious and ethical tradition in the world. We should celebrate all the cultural, racial, ethnic, and religious diversity, but what keeps that celebration from becoming sectarian is the shared moral call signaled in our traditions by "remember God."

Consider Princeton Seminary Professor Peter Paris's celebrated book *The Spirituality of African Peoples: The Search for a Common Moral*

---

7. For a sobering account of the Fukushima disaster, see Lochbaum et al., *Fukushima*.

Discourse.[8] Paris distinguishes the distinctive cultural traditions and religious practices of diverse Africans and African Americans. He names and celebrates diversity. But amidst the diversity, in the shared affirmation of basic moral values, he sees a transcending, common spirituality which equates to the prophets' "remembering God."

I read Paris from the perspective of a second-generation Italian, Irish-English American. I celebrate and learn from diverse African and African American social traditions, music, literature, and art even as I affirm and appreciate diverse European and European American social traditions, music, literature, and art. And in what Paris describes as the transcending, unifying spirit of diversely realized African and African American spiritualities, I recognize the same transcending unifying spirit of diversely realized European and European American spiritualities, that same spirit to which we have all been called by the prophets of Israel millennia ago.

I am not talking about all the famous quandary issues in ethics. There are no shortcuts there. But *ethical quandaries must not distract us from what is not really questionable.* Ethical quandaries must not distract us from "remembering God" in relation to access to adequate food and shelter, basic education and medical care, and space for expression of basic physical, emotional, and intellectual gifts—all issues over which there is no real ethical debate among the world's diverse religious and ethical traditions.

For instance, to mention one of a thousand examples, there would be no real ethical debate among any of the world's diverse religious traditions over the conclusion that a society that incentivizes health care so that $2 epipens cost $600 has *obviously* forgotten God. A society that remembers God will restructure the incentives, will harness market forces in order to create as just and peaceable a society and world as is possible.

The prophets are realistic. Not only do they own and condemn their own Jerichos—and we all have our Jerichos, and we should all confess them frankly—because their visions of a new heavens and earth is always eschatological. We will never create a perfectly good and just world, but *insofar as we "remember God" our realism does not undercut our idealism.* We do not act out of guilt or because we can finally succeed. We are motivated by concrete love for others and we measure success in terms of making things better than they are or would otherwise be.

Finally, consistent with this celebration of diverse communities who in different ways remember God, let us explicitly note that self-proclaimed atheists like Jeffrey Stout, who are themselves, above all, struggling to be a blessing to all people, let us say explicitly that they too truly remember God,

8. Paris, *The Spirituality of African Peoples.*

are themselves people of true faith, surprised sheep (Matt 25:31–46). Across diverse faith, cultural, racial, ethnic, advocacy, and national communities, people who share the prophetic heart of true faith are, with regard to a host of basic and vital ethical issues, spiritually united.

We should maintain and celebrate the sensitivities and wonders diversity yields, and the diverse, multivalent, nested identities they gift to all and each of us. But even as we identify, affirm, and celebrate diverse communities, we must also heed the prophetic, transcending, singular call, a call with diverse names in diverse communities, a call realized in one particularity in the call to Abram, a call realized in another particularity in the call to follow one who faithfully spoke prophetic truth to empire all the way to death on a cross. We should join in following the prophetic call to be a distinct community through whom all communities are blessed, to remember God, not the God of one religion or nation over and against another, but the God who *is* love, the God who is the concrete reality that seizes us in concern for every creature and all peoples.

We should remember God where remembering is immediately striving to feed the hungry, comfort the afflicted, clothe the naked, free the oppressed, where remembering God is immediately striving to formulate municipal, national, and international laws to create regimes which are not only great and powerful but good, and to harness and incentivize global market forces so that they do as much good as possible. Now is a time for prophets, and a time for harkening unto the prophetic call concretely to remember the living God who is love.

> "Lord, when was it that we saw you hungry or thirsty or a stranger or naked or sick or in prison, and did not take care of you?" Then he will answer them, "truly I tell you, just as you did not do it to one of the least of these, you did not do it to me." (Matt 25:44–45)

> O mortal, what is good; and what does the LORD require of you; but to do justice, and to love kindness, and to walk humbly with your God? (Mic 6:8)

Bibliography

Agamben, Giorgio. *The Time That Remains: A Commentary on the Letter to the Romans.* Translated by Patricia Dailey. Stanford, CA: Stanford University Press, 2005.

Allen, Barry. "Another New Nietzsche." *History and Theory* 42 (October 2003) 375.

Augustine. *Confessions.* Translated by R. S. Pine-Coffin. New York: Penguin, 1961.

Badiou, Alain. *Saint Paul: The Foundation of Universalism.* Translated by Ray Brassier. Stanford, CA: Stanford University Press, 2003.

Benson, Bruce Ellis, and Norman Wirzba, eds. *Words of Life: New Theological Turns in French Phenomenology.* New York: Fordham University Press, 2010.

Burgie-Gipson, Willette A. "On Christian Pluralism and Christian Pacificism: A Response to 'Christian Ethics in a Postmodern World.'" *Koinonia* VI (1994) 69–78.

Bernstein, Richard. *Beyond Objectivism and Relativism: Science, Hermeneutics, and Praxis.* Philadelphia: University of Pennsylvania Press, 1983.

Brandom, Robert. *Making It Explicit: Reasoning, Representing, and Discursive Commitment.* Cambridge, MA: Harvard University Press, 1994.

Braybrooke, David. "Inward and Outward with the Modern Self." *Dialogue* 33 (1994) 101–8.

Brower, Bruce W. "The Limits of Public Reason." *The Journal of Philosophy* XCI (1994) 5–26.

Calvin, John. *Institutes of the Christian Religion.* Edited by John T. McNeill. Translated by Ford Lewis Battles. Philadelphia: Westminster, 1977.

Cone, James. *God of the Oppressed.* San Francisco: Harper & Row, 1975.

Critchley, Simon. *The Faith of the Faithless: Experiments in Political Theology.* New York: Verso, 2012.

Davidson, Donald. *Essays on Actions and Events.* Oxford: Clarendon, 1973.

———. *Inquiries into Truth and Interpretation.* New York: Oxford University Press, 2001.

Dawkins, Richard. *The God Delusion.* New York: Houghton Mifflin Harcourt, 2006.

Dennett, Daniel. *Breaking the Spell: Religion as a Natural Phenomenon.* New York: Viking Penguin, 2006.

———. *Darwin's Dangerous Idea: Evolutions and the Meaning of Life.* New York: Touchstone, 1995.

————. *Freedom Evolves*. New York: Penguin, 2003.

Descartes, Rene. *The Philosophical Writings of Descartes: Volume II*. Edited by J. Cottingham and R. Stoothoff. Translated by D. Murdoch. Cambridge: Cambridge University Press, 1984.

Descombes, Vincent. "Is There an Objective Spirit?" In *Philosophy in an Age of Pluralism: The Philosophy of Charles Taylor in Question*, edited by James Tully, 96–118. Cambridge: Cambridge University Press, 1994.

Dilthey, Wilhelm. "The Types of World-view and Their Development in the Metaphysical Systems." In *Dilthey: Selected Writings*, edited by H. P. Rickman, 133–154. Cambridge: Cambridge University Press, 1979.

————. *Wilhelm Dilthey, Selected Works, Volume I, Introduction to the Human Sciences*. Edited by R. A. Makkreel and F. Rodi, 55–72. Princeton, NJ: Princeton University Press, 1989.

de Vries, Hent. *Philosophy and the Turn to Religion*. New York: Fordham University Press, 1999.

————, ed. *Religion: Beyond a Concept, the Future of the Religious Past*. New York: Fordham University Press, 2008.

Dostoyevsky, Fyodor. *The Brothers Karamazov*. Translated by Constance Garnett. New York: Signet Classic, 1999.

Dworkin, Ronald. *Religion without God*. Cambridge: Harvard University Press, 2013.

Emerson, Ralph Waldo. "Self-Reliance." In *The Essential Writings of Ralph Waldo Emerson*, edited by Brooks Atkinson, 132–53. New York: Modern Library, 2000.

Ferriby, Gavin. "Christian Ethics in a Postmodern World: A Historian's Response." *Koinonia* VI (1994) 79–87.

Fleischacker, Samuel. "Review of *Truth and Truthfulness* by Bernard Williams." *Ethics* 114 (January 2004) 381.

Frankenberry, Nancy. "Preface." In *Radical Interpretation in Religion*, edited by Nancy Frankenberry, xiii–xv. Cambridge: Cambridge University Press, 2002.

Gadamer, Hans-George. *Truth and Method*. Edited by John Cumming and Garret Barden. New York: Crossroad, 1988.

Gaston, William. "Augustine or Emerson?" *Commonweal* (January 30, 2004) 25.

Greenway, William. *Agape Ethics: Moral Realism and Love for All Life*. Eugene, OR: Cascade, 2016.

————. "Chalcedonian Reason and the Demon of Closure." *Scottish Journal of Theology* 57 (Winter 2004) 56–79.

————. *The Challenge of Evil: Grace and the Problem of Suffering*. Louisville: Westminster John Knox, 2016.

————. "Charles Taylor on Affirmation, Mutilation, and Theism: A Retrospective Reading of *Sources of the Self*." *Journal of Religion* 80 (January 2000) 23–40.

————. "Christian Ethics in a Postmodern World? Hauerwas, Stout, and Christian Moral *Bricolage*." *Koinonia* 6 (1994) 1–31.

————. "Cosmodicy." *Insights* 121 (Spring 2006) 36–40.

————. "Irreducible Tensions: Private Convictions in Public Space." *Koinonia* VI (1994) 89–104.

————. "Jeffrey Stout, Original Sin, and the Significance of Christian Faith." In *Always Being Reformed: Challenge and Prospects for Reformed Theology*, edited by David H. Jensen, 187–210. Eugene, OR: Wipf & Stock, 2016.

————. "Modern Metaphysics, Dangerous Truth, Post-Moral Ethics: The Revealing Vision of Bernard Williams." *Philosophy Today* 51 (Summer 2007) 140–54.

————. *A Reasonable Belief: Why God and Faith Make Sense.* Louisville: Westminster John Knox, 2015.

————. Review of *Actual Consciousness* by Ted Honderich. *Scottish Journal of Theology* 70 (February 2017) 119–21. Oxford: Oxford University Press, 2014.

————. "Review of *Faith and Reason: A Kierkegaardian Account* by C. Stephen Evans." *Christian Century* (September 12, 2000) 922–24.

Hacking, Ian. "Language, Truth and Reason." In *Rationality and Relativism*, edited by Martin Hollis and Stephen Lukes, 48–66. Cambridge: MIT Press, 1982.

Harris, Sam. *The End of Faith: Religion, Terror, and the Future of Reason.* New York: Norton, 2004.

————. *Waking Up: A Guide to Spirituality without Religion.* New York: Simon & Schuster, 2014.

Harvey, David. *The Condition of Postmodernity: An Enquiry into the Origins of Cultural Change.* Oxford: Blackwell, 1989.

Hauerwas, Stanley. *After Christendom? How the Church Is to Behave If Freedom, Justice, and a Christian Nation Are Bad Ideas.* Nashville: Abingdon, 1991.

————. *The Peaceable Kingdom: A Primer in Christian Ethics.* Notre Dame, IN: University of Notre Dame Press, 1983.

————. *Performing the Faith: Bonhoeffer and the Practice of Nonviolence.* Grand Rapids: Brazos, 2004.

————. "To be or not to be a *BRICOLEUR.*" *Koinonia* VI (1994) 105–9.

————. *Truthfulness and Tragedy: Further Investigations into Christian Ethics.* Notre Dame, IN: University of Notre Dame Press, 1977.

Hauerwas, Stanley, and Philip D. Kenneson. "A Review Essay: Flight from Foundationalism, Or, Things Aren't As Bad As They Seem." *Soundings: An Interdisciplinary Journal* 71 (1988) 683–99.

Hitchens, Christopher. *God is not Great: How Religion Poisons Everything.* New York: Twelve Books, 2007.

Hobbes, Thomas. *The English Works of Thomas Hobbes.* Vol. 5. Edited by W. Molesworth. London: Scientia Aalen, 1962.

Honderich, Ted. *Actual Consciousness.* Oxford: Oxford University Press, 2014.

————. *How Free Are You? The Determinism Problem.* Oxford: Oxford University Press, 2003.

————. "Radical Externalism." *Journal of Consciousness Studies* 13 (2006) 3–13.

Huemer, Michael. Review of *The Oxford Handbook of Free Will*, edited by Robert Kane. *The Philosophical Review* 113 (2004) 279–83.

Hunsinger, George. *How to Read Karl Barth: The Shape of His Theology.* New York: Oxford University Press, 1991.

James, William. *The Varieties of Religious Experience: A Study in Human Nature.* New York: Penguin, 1982.

Janicaud, Dominique. *Phenomenology and the Theological Turn: The French Debate.* New York: Fordham University Press, 2001.

Kane, Robert. "Responsibility, Luck, and Chance: Reflections on Free Will and Indeterminism." *The Journal of Philosophy* 96 (May 1999) 21–240.

————. *The Significance of Free Will.* New York: Oxford University Press, 1998.

Kelly, J. N. D. *Early Christian Doctrines.* New York: Harper & Row, 1978.

Kerlin, Michael J. "Review of *Truth and Truthfulness*." *Theological Studies* 65 (2004) 221.

Lane, Melissa. "God or Orienteering? A Critical Study of Taylor's *Sources of the Self*." *Ratio* (New Series) V (June 1992) 46–56.

Laplace, Pierre-Simon. *A Philosophical Essay on Probabilities.* Translated by F. W. Truscott and F. L. Emory. New York: Dover, 1951.

Levinas, Emmanuel. *The Levinas Reader.* Edited by Sean Hand. Oxford: Blackwell, 1989.

———. *Otherwise Than Being or Beyond Essence.* Translated by Alphonso Lingis. Pittsburgh, PA: Duquesne University Press, 1981.

———. *The Theory of Intuition in Husserl's Phenomenology.* 2nd ed. Evanston, IL: Northwestern University Press, 1995.

Lochbaum, David, et al. *Fukushima: The Story of a Nuclear Disaster.* New York: New Press, 2014.

Logan, Morag. "Christian Moral *Bricolage*: Defining the Conversation." *Koinonia* VI (1994) 61–67.

Long, D. Stephen. "Jeffrey Stout: Democracy and Tradition." *Contemporary Pragmatism* 1 (April 2004) 171–74.

Lovibond, Sabrina. "Religion and Modernity: Living in the Hypercontext." *Journal of Religious Ethics* 33 (2005) 617–31.

Lovin, Robin. "Christian and Citizen." *Christian Century* 121 (May 4, 2004) 31–34.

Low-Beer, Martin. "Living a Life and the Problem of Existential Impossibility." *Inquiry: An Interdisciplinary Journal of Philosophy* 34 (June 1991) 217–36.

MacIntyre, Alasdair. *After Virtue: A Study in Moral Theory.* Notre Dame, IN: University of Notre Dame Press, 1984.

———. *Whose Justice? Which Rationality?* Notre Dame, IN: University of Notre Dame Press, 1988.

Malcom, Lois. "The Divine Name and the Task of Christian Moral *Bricolage*." *Koinonia* VI (1994) 33–47.

Meilander, Gilbert. "Talking Democracy." *First Things* (April 2004) 25–30.

Migliore, Daniel. *Faith Seeking Understanding.* Grand Rapids: Eerdmans, 1991.

Nagel, Thomas. "Honesty and History." *The New Republic*, October 21, 2002, 26–28.

———. *Mind and Cosmos: Why the Materialist Neo-Darwinian Conception of Nature is Almost Certainly False.* Oxford: Oxford University Press, 2012.

Nietzsche, Friedrich. *The Anti-Christ, Ecce Homo, Twilight of the Idols and Other Writings.* Edited by Aaron Ridley and Judith Norman. Cambridge Texts in the History of Philosophy. Cambridge: Cambridge University Press, 2005.

———. *Human All Too Human: A Book for Free Spirits.* Translated by M. Faber and S. Lehmann. Lincoln, NE: University of Nebraska Press, 1984.

Paris, Peter. *The Spirituality of African Peoples: The Search for a Common Moral Discourse.* Minneapolis: Augsburg Fortress, 1995.

Peirce, Charles S. "Some Consequences of Four Incapacities." In *Charles S Peirce: Selected Writings (Values in the Universe of Chance)*, edited by Philip P. Weiner, 39–72. New York: Dover, 1958.

Pope Francis. *Laudato Si: On Care for our Common Home.* Vatican City: Libreria Editrice Vaticana, 2015.

Popken, Ben. "Mylan CEO's Pay Rose Over 600 Percent as EpiPen Price Rose 400 Percent." *NBC News*, August 23, 2016. https://www.nbcnews.com/business/consumer/mylan-execs-gave-themselves-raises-they-hiked-epipen-prices-n636591.

Proudfoot, Wayne. "Religious Belief and Naturalism." In *Radical Interpretation in Religion*, edited by Nancy Frankenberry, 78–92. Cambridge: Cambridge University Press, 2002.

Rawls, John. *A Theory of Justice*. New York: Belknap, 1971.

———. *Political Liberalism*. New York: Columbia University Press, 1993.

Ricoeur, Paul. "Hermeneutics and the Critique of Ideology." In *Hermeneutics and the Human Sciences: Essays on Language, Action and Interpretation*, edited and translated by John Thompson, 63–100. Cambridge: Cambridge University Press, 1988.

Rivera, Mayra. *Poetics of the Flesh*. Durham, NC: Duke University Press, 2015.

———. *The Touch of Transcendence: A Postcolonial Theology of God*. Louisville: Westminster John Knox, 2007.

Rorty, Richard. *Achieving Our Country*. Cambridge: Harvard University Press, 1998.

———. *The Consequences of Pragmatism*. Minneapolis: University of Minnesota Press, 1982.

———. *Contingency, Irony, and Solidarity*. Cambridge: Cambridge University Press, 1989.

———. "'Cranes and Skyhooks,' review of *Darwin's Dangerous Idea: evolution and the meanings of life* by Daniel Dennett." *Lingua Franca* (August 1995) 62–66.

———. "Cultural Politics and the Question of the Existence of God." In *Radical Interpretation in Religion*, edited by Nancy Frankenberry, 53–77. Cambridge: Cambridge University Press, 2002.

———. *Objectivity, Relativism, and Truth*. Cambridge: Cambridge University Press, 1991.

———. *Philosophy and Social Hope*. New York: Penguin, 1999.

———. *Philosophy and the Mirror of Nature*. Princeton, NJ: Princeton University Press, 1989.

———. "Religion as Conversation Stopper." *Common Knowledge* 3 (1994) 1–6.

———. "'To the Sunlit Uplands,' review of *Truth and Truthfulness* by Bernard Williams." *London Review of Books* 24 (October 31, 2002) 13–15.

Rosen, Michael. "Must We Return to Moral Realism?" *Inquiry: An Interdisciplinary Journal of Philosophy* 34 (June 1991) 183–94.

Sartre, Jean-Paul. "Existentialism is a Humanism." In *Existentialism from Dostoyevsky to Sartre*, edited by Walter Kaufmann, 345–69. Translated by Philip Moiret. New York: New American Library, 1975.

Skinner, Quentin. "Modernity and Disenchantment: Some Historical Reflections." In *Philosophy in an Age of Pluralism: The Philosophy of Charles Taylor in Question*, edited by James Tully, 37–48. Cambridge: Cambridge University Press, 1994.

———. "Who Are 'We'? Ambiguities of the Modern Self." *Inquiry: An Interdisciplinary Journal of Philosophy* 34 (1991) 133–53.

Smilansky, Saul. *Free Will and Illusion*. Oxford: Oxford University Press, 2000.

———. "Why Not Libertarian Free Will." www.ucl.ac.uk/~uctytho/dfwVariousSmilansky.htm.

Spivak, Gayatri Chakravorty. "A Moral Dilemma." In *What Happens to History: The Renewal of Ethics in Contemporary Thought*, edited by Howard Marchitello, 215–36. New York: Routledge, 2001.

Stout, Jeffrey. *Blessed Are the Organized: Grassroots Democracy in America*. Princeton, NJ: Princeton University Press, 2010.

———. "Comments on Six Responses to *Democracy and Tradition*." *Journal of Religious Ethics* 33 (2005) 709–744.

———. *Democracy and Tradition*. Princeton, NJ: Princeton University Press, 2004.

———. *Ethics after Babel: The Languages of Morals and Their Discontents*. Boston: Beacon, 1988.

———. *The Flight from Authority: Religion, Morality, And the Quest for Autonomy*. Notre Dame, IN: University of Notre Dame Press, 1981.

Taubes, Jacob. *The Political Theology of Paul*. Translated by Dana Hollander. Stanford, CA: Stanford University Press, 2003.

Taylor, Charles. "Comments and Replies." *Inquiry: An Interdisciplinary Journal of Philosophy* 34 (1991) 237–54.

———. *Hegel and Modern Society*. Cambridge: Cambridge University Press, 1979.

———. *Human Agency and Language: Philosophical Papers 1*. Cambridge: Cambridge University Press, 1985.

———. *Philosophical Arguments*. Cambridge, MA: Harvard University Press, 1995.

———. "Reply and Re-articulation: Interpreting Modernity (Quentin Skinner)." In *Philosophy in an Age of Pluralism: The Philosophy of Charles Taylor in Question*, edited by James Tully, 213–57. Cambridge: Cambridge University Press, 1994.

———. "Reply to Braybrooke and de Sousa." *Dialogue* 33 (1994) 125–31.

———. "Reply to Commentators." *Philosophy and Phenomenological Research* 54 (March 1994) 203–13.

———. *Sources of the Self: The Making of the Modern Identity*. Cambridge, MA: Harvard University Press, 1989.

Taylor, Mark L. *Remembering Esperanza: A Cultural-Political Theology for North American Praxis*. Maryknoll, NY: Orbis, 1990.

Ward, Keith. *The Christian Idea of God: A Philosophical Foundation for Faith*. Cambridge: Cambridge University Press, 2017.

Watson, J. Francis. "An Ecclesiological Approach to Christian Ethics." *Koinonia* VI (1994) 49–59.

Wennberg, Robert. "Animal Suffering and the Problem of Evil." *Christian Scholars Review* 21 (1991) 120–40.

Williams, Bernard. *Descartes: The Project of Pure Enquiry*. London: Penguin, 1978.

———. *Ethics and the Limits of Philosophy*. Cambridge: Cambridge University Press, 1981.

———. "Getting it Right." *London Review of Books* 11/22 (November 23, 1989) 3–5.

———. *Making Sense of Humanity*. Cambridge: Cambridge University Press, 1995.

———. *Moral Luck: Philosophical Papers: 1973–1980*. Cambridge: Cambridge University Press, 1981.

———. *Shame and Necessity*. Berkeley, CA: University of California Press, 1993.

———. *World, Mind, and Ethics: Essays on the Ethical Philosophy of Bernard Williams*. Edited by J. E. J. Altham and Ross Harrison. Cambridge: Cambridge University Press, 1995.

———. *Truth and Truthfulness*. Princeton, NJ: Princeton University Press, 2002.

Wogaman, J. Philip. *Christian Perspectives on Politics*. Philadelphia: Fortress, 1988.

Žižek, Slavoj. *The Puppet and the Dwarf: The Perverse Core of Christianity*. Cambridge, MA: MIT Press, 2003.

Index of Names

www.ingramcontent.com/pod-product-compliance
Lightning Source LLC
Chambersburg PA
CBHW030305100426
42812CB00002B/565